Introduction to
COMPUTER CONCEPTS
Hardware
and
Software

LARRY W. DICKEY

Bell Telephone Laboratories

Prentice-Hall, Inc., *Englewood Cliffs, New Jersey*

Library of Congress Cataloging in Publication Data

DICKEY, LARRY W
  Introduction to computer concepts.

    1. Electronic digital computers. 2. COBOL
(Computer program language)   3. FORTRAN (Computer
program language)   I. Title.
QA76.5.D46   001.6'4   73-16452
ISBN   0-13-480004-4

Printed in the United States of America

10   9   8   7   6   5   4   3   2   1

Prentice-Hall International, Inc., *London*
Prentice-Hall of Australia, Pty. Ltd., *Sydney*
Prentice-Hall of Canada, Ltd., *Toronto*
Prentice-Hall of India Private Limited, *New Delhi*
Prentice-Hall of Japan, Inc., *Tokyo*

**IN MEMORY OF
OUR SON ALAN
1967–1973**

The exuberance of this boy has left us with a message, which Rev. Dr. Atkinson has paraphrased, "The life of our years is more precious than the years of our life."

Contents

Preface

As a result of teaching computer technology courses for Bell Telephone Laboratories' employees, I became aware that careful consideration is needed in presenting complex information. My pursuance of these aims has led to this introductory textbook, specifically written for community college students studying data processing or technical aspects of computers. The textbook is applicable to a wide range of other courses, including enrichment courses for programmers studying in universities or working in government or industry. My objective is a book that is logically organized and clearly presented for an audience that is believed to be interested in an up-to-date and accurate coverage of this timely subject.

Computers have become part of our lives and we should understand them. They are used to process customer billings, bank records, payrolls, and even college enrollments. We generally appreciate the labor savings offered by computers. We are amazed at their speed and flexibility and want to understand them. To take advantage of the capabilities of computers, we need to understand them.

Computers are based on simple concepts. I have tried to approach them as machines being supplied with electrical pulses in the particular sequence that represents the problem to be solved. The logic circuits in the computer function to produce the solution as another pulse sequence.

The course level does not require prior knowledge of computers, circuits, or mathematics beyond high school algebra. I have tried to keep prerequisites at a minimum and to include all important aspects of an introductory course. In dealing with those topics that are normally complex but important, I use a straightforward approach and rely on logical organization to achieve simplicity. Further, example problems are used to illustrate the simplicity of mathematical manipulations. To avoid confusion in the figures showing circuits, I use the same format in all circuit drawings in hopes that the new item being illustrated will be evident.

To motivate student interest and learning inclination, I have included questions and problems. Computer hardware courses are a natural source for homework. For example, the problems for Chapter 5 on Karnaugh maps are as entertaining as crossword puzzles. Students studying logic design tend to come to class with circuits for timing household appliances, lighting fixtures, etc.

The ten basic chapters are intended to provide an understanding of digital computer designs. In Chapter 10, computer units from the preceding chapters are organized into a control system to execute the programmer's instructions.

In using this book as a data processing text, the instructor may concentrate on the software in Chapters 11 through 17 more than the hardware in Chapters 2 through 10. It is my opinion that most instructors prefer to cover hardware concepts in introducing data processing. Several sections in Chapters 2 through 10 are marked with a star, signifying that the material is of lesser importance to data processing students. These sections are, by no means, beyond the student's grasp; however, they can be skipped without loss of continuity.

The textbook is organized to provide flexibility to the data processing instructor. The old argument persists of whether the chicken or the egg came first. Another argument, almost as unresolvable, is whether the student's first exposure should be to computer hardware or software. Instructors can be their own judge in this matter because the material is purposefully written to accommodate either option. After covering Chapter 1 (and perhaps Chapter 2), the class may proceed with programimng in Chapters 11 through 17 and then return to hardware in Chapters 2 (or 3) through 10.

In introductory computer science courses, the instructor will probably follow an outline quite close to the order of presentation in the text. The starred sections should be of interest to the student; however, Chapters 13 and 14 may be skipped.

I want to express my appreciation to three people who helped prepare this book. Nancy, my wife, typed the manuscript; John J. Duerr prepared the illustrations; and Maureen Wilson of Prentice-Hall did a superb job of production editing. My contribution was a stack of papers with handwritten scribble and messy sketches, which these talented people composed into a textbook for your enjoyment.

LARRY W. DICKEY
Bell Telephone Laboratories

1 Introduction

1.1 HISTORICAL DEVELOPMENTS

The electronic digital computer first appeared on the scene in 1946. Then it was a specialized tool of scientists. Today, they are used for many things by many people. As a result, the term "computer" is a word that is familiar to almost everyone. Computers are used by institutions and businesses for a variety of purposes, including accounting, inventory records, and payroll processing. They also perform calculations in finding solutions to complex scientific problems. The first electronic computer was specially built to calculate the trajectory of rounds fired from artillery weapons. The trajectory could be expected to be shortened or shifted by unfavorable winds. The scientists computed data for trajectory charts by calculating the effects of wind velocity. These charts were used by the artillery men to correct their aim and improve the weapon's effectiveness.

Computers are electronic devices that are capable of manipulating pulses that represent digits of numbers. The history of computers is normally approached by discussing *earlier machines* for performing numerical calculations. We will also pursue this approach; however, it is also important that we discuss *earlier electronic devices,* mainly the radio. *Vacuum tubes* were used in the amplifier circuits of radios in the 1946 period when the first electronic computer called the ENIAC (Electronic Numerical Integrator and Calculator) was built for the U.S. Army. This machine, developed at the Moore School of Electrical Engineering, University of Pennsylvania, contained 18,000 vacuum tubes. As time progressed, *transistors* were used in radios and then later in computers. Thus, the early computers were built of existing devices from radio circuits; however, the present immense size of the computer market is certainly sufficient to warrant special devices. Efforts to develop smaller, faster, and less expensive

1

devices for making computer circuits may lead to a vestpocket-sized computer with capabilities equal to the 25-ton ENIAC.

By the term "digital computer" we imply the use of digits or numbers. It is usually assumed that man developed the concept of numbers and counting before he developed an effective written language. His first countings were with sticks, pebbles, or whatever.

The Abacus—500 B.C.

The abacus was the first counting tool. It has been used for the last 2000 years and is still used in parts of Asia.

Ex. 1–1

How is the number 827 represented on an abacus?

The abacus is a rectangular frame with several parallel wires. Each wire is threaded with seven beads, two above the horizontal bar and five below. Numbers are represented by pushing the free-sliding beads against the bar. Each bead above the bar is worth 5 and the beads below are 1; *thus, 827 is represented* as shown in Fig. 1–1. The existing tally in Fig.

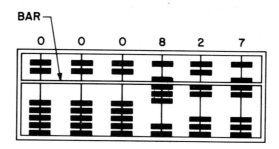

FIG. 1–1   Abacus Registering 827.

1–1 can be increased. For example, to add *521,* we start with the right group of beads and push *one* more unit's bead toward the bar. We push *two* beads in the next column. In the third column we want to add *five* to the existing 8, which means a carry to the next column.

$$
\begin{array}{r}
827 \\
+521 \\
\hline
1348
\end{array}
$$

The final answer is illustrated in Fig. 1-2.

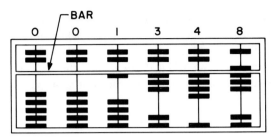

FIG. 1–2   Abacus Registering 1348, the Sum of 827 and 521.

A skillful abacus operator can add, subtract, multiply, and divide with amazing speed. In contests the *abacus has been shown to be faster* than modern calculating machines.

Figures 1–1 and 1–2 represent the Chinese abacus. The Japanese abacus has one bead above the bar and four below.

Pascal Arithmetic Machine—1643

Pascal at the age of 19 devised the *first mechanism for calculations.* The principles of this machine are still used today in automobile odometers and pocket-sized calculators. It was operated by dialing a series of wheels bearing the numbers 0 to 9 around their circumference. Figure 1–3 shows

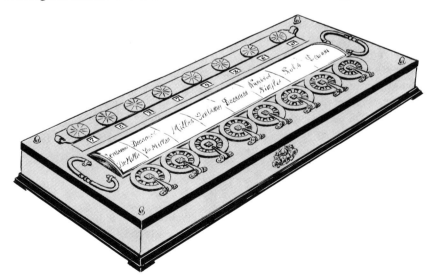

FIG. 1–3   French Mathematician Blaise Pascal's Arithmetic Machine. (Courtesy of Elias M. Awad, *Automatic Data Processing: Principles and Procedures,* 2nd Ed., © 1970, Prentice-Hall, Inc.)

the top face. The wheel on the right represents the value of the least significant digit, which would be units place for whole numbers. To "carry" a number to the next column after 9 was reached, the next wheel was geared to advance one digit when the wheel to the right made a complete revolution. Answers appeared on the face above the dials.

Leibniz Calculating Machine—1694

The principles of Pascal's machine were used by Leibniz, who developed the first machine to multiply and divide directly. Addition and substraction were accomplished exactly as in Pascal's machine. Gears were added to enable multiplication and division. Leibniz believed that scientists should be free from laboring with manual calculations and hoped that his machine would help in this respect. Throughout the years, mechanical calculator designs continued to exhibit most of the principles of the original Leibniz calculator.

Babbage Analytic Engine—1834

Leibniz's design is still used after nearly 300 years, but Charles Babbage's contribution to the computer is even more remarkable. Babbage was 100 years ahead of his time with his ideas for a really powerful tool to handle any sort of mathematical computation automatically. He planned an *analytic engine* that had all the major features of a modern computer. It would process instructions from a program on punched cards. It would include a memory and output devices for printing results. However, the components just weren't available to build the analytic engine. The inventor was determined to see his design work, and petitioned officials in his native England for funds to build the machine using steam power and all mechanical parts. His plan became known as Babbage's Folly and was never completed. There was no technological base for his ideas. In fact, Babbage's forerunner to the computer was forgotten until Howard Aiken of Harvard University rediscovered his writings in 1937.

Hollerith Punched Cards—1890

Although Babbage had already conceived of punched cards, Herman Hollerith used electromechanical devices developed after Babbage to assemble a practical punched-card reader. Holes in the cards represented numbers and letters of the alphabet. Figure 1–4 shows the code used for the *80-column Hollerith card*—the universal standard of today. The card reader consisted of a series of metal pins with a wire attached to one end. The pin could descend and touch mercury in a pan below if there happened

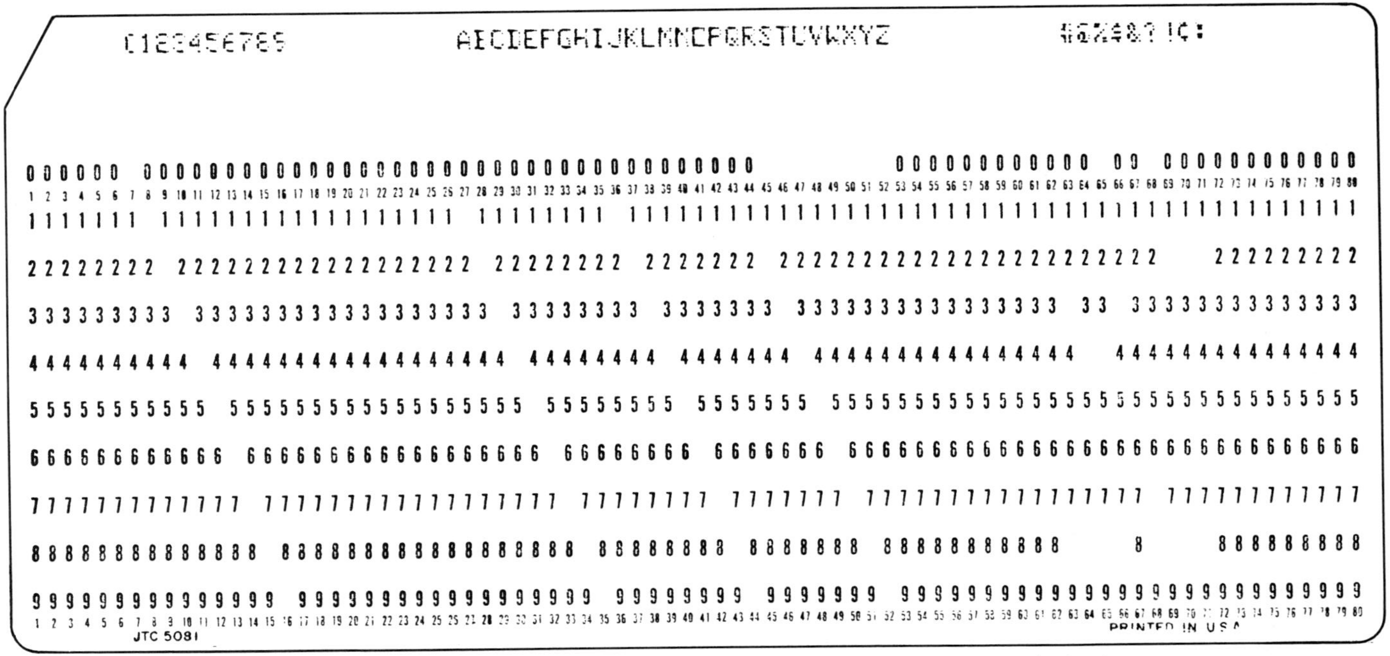

FIG. 1-4 Hollerith Code of Punches for Numerals and Alphabetic Characters (3¼ by 7¾ inches).

to be a hole under the pin. Contact with the mercury (a liquid, but an excellent electrical conductor) completed the electrical circuit to that pin. This record of the absence or presence of holes was the electromechanical process of reading the punched cards.

Using punched cards in this manner, Hollerith devised a way to speed the classification and counting of data from the U.S. Census of 1890. The data included the person's name, age, sex, address, and other statistics. With census data entered on machine-readable cards, it was possible to process the 1890 census data in one third the time it had taken for the manual procedure in 1880. This is only an indication of the time savings available in the computer field. Computers can perform lengthy calculations that would require years by hand. The company organized by Hollerith merged in 1911 with the company that was eventually to become International Business Machines (IBM).

Ex. 1–2

What salary would you ask if you were to substitute yourself for a modern computer doing mathematical calculations?

Large-scale computers are normally rented at a typical monthly rental of $200,000. They can perform 1 million simple additions while an average man is doing one. Thus, to be economically competitive, a man must be willing to work for $200,000 ÷ 1 million = $0.20 per month or $2.40 per year. Time must be allowed for eating and sleeping, which would *bring down the salary to less than $2 per year.*

Despite its great speed and electronic sophistication, the computer is unable to think for itself, which people do with ease. We want to remember throughout our discussion that *computers can't think any more than radios can sing.* Our definition of thinking implies the entrance of an idea into one's mind with or without deliberate consideration or reflection. Both thinking and singing are human functions.

Aiken and Stibitz Electromechanical Calculator—1944

A host of mechanical calculators made their appearance near the turn of the century. The *Burrough's adding machine* appeared in 1885. The acceptance of this machine was widespread and was followed in 1917 by the *desk calculator* which did multiplication and division as well as addition and subtraction. The calculators became electromechanical in 1944 when Howard Aiken of Harvard University developed the *MARK I,* the first large-scale digital calculator. Once the steps in a solution were programmed by code on paper tape, the device would sequence through the calculations without human intervention. It weighed 5 tons and contained

3304 electromechanical relays. Consequently, it was faster than previous calculators. *Relays* are switches that can be opened or closed by an electrical current passing through a magnetic coil. Figure 1–5 is a sketch of a

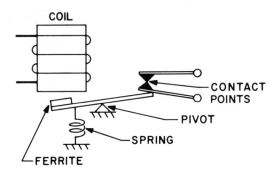

FIG. 1–5   Arrangement of Components in a Normally Closed Relay.

relay that is normally closed, but is switched open by the coil current. The magnetism induced in the armature of the coil attracts a ferrite piece on the end of the relay spring and causes the mechanical opening or closing of the switch contact points. The spring returns the switch to its original state when the signal is absent. Thus, the absence or presence of a signal to an array of relays coils can influence the current paths through the array of associated switches. We will see in Chapter 3 that the characteristics of switching networks are useful for designing computers. The MARK I remained in use for over 15 years before being retired in 1959. Parts of the original machine are on display at the Smithsonian Institution and at Harvard University.

Another man working independently of Aiken envisioned such a calculator at about the same time. He was George R. Stibitz, a research mathematician at Bell Telephone Laboratories. The Stibitz machine, known as the complex number calculator and later as the *Bell Model I,* was placed in formal operation on January 8, 1940. The Bell System could be expected to be in the forefront in developments using relays because a new relay system for switching telephone calls appeared in 1937. Figure 1–6 shows the external resemblance between the Bell Model I and the first crossbar switching system. The Bell computer represented a landmark in reliability in that it could be left running overnight with no one in attendance.

Eckert and Mauchly Electronic Computer—1946

A real breakthrough came in 1946 when *high-speed bistable devices* were used to make the first electronic computer, the ENIAC. We mentioned

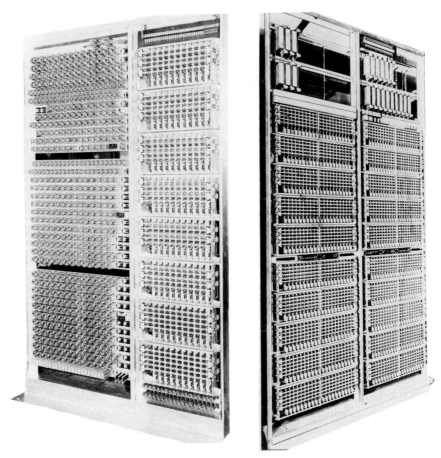

FIG. 1–6   Electromechanical Relay Systems of 1937: (a) Bell Model I; and
(b) Telephone Switching Systems. (Courtesy of Bell Telephone
Laboratories.)

this invention earlier. We'll discuss in Chapters 3 through 7 how bistable
devices are used in computer circuitry. We'll have in mind transistors for
circuits such as the common flip-flop; however, the same general discussion could apply to the vacuum-tube flip-flops used in the ENIAC. Chapter
7 shows that flip-flops are high-speed devices that are stable in either of
two positions: electrically energized or not energized. We'll see that they
are used to store numbers and count electrical pulses. Therefore, the procedure for representing and handling numbers in the ENIAC is still being
used.

Ex. 1–3

What arguments would you advance in favor of bistable devices as compared to the previous 10-position devices?

The major advantages are *speed and reliability*. Obviously, a device can enter state 0 from state 1 in less time than it takes to move through the many intervening positions in going from 3 to 8, for example. Also, *state 0 is separate and distinguishable from state 1,* whereas a multiple-position device might settle midway between 7 and 8 and cause uncertainty about the true position. Therefore, there are advantages in using bistable devices. Some *Russian computers* are designed with tristate devices. Reports blame their choice of devices for the Russian lag in the moon exploration program. Binary numbers are a necessary consequence of bistable devices.

The ENIAC inventors, John Mauchly and J. Presper Eckert, had to overcome the seemingly insurmountable problem of *unreliable* vacuum tubes. Critics argued against the proposed machine, saying that one of the 18,000 vacuum tubes could be expected to fail every 7½ minutes. To prevent this, the designers combed through lot after lot of vacuum tubes to pick especially hardy samples. In the end, they achieved continuous operation for days at a time before a tube would fail. The company formed by Eckert and Mauchly later became part of the UNIVAC Division of Sperry Rand.

Von Neumann Internally Stored Program—1946

The major operational shortcoming of ENIAC was its lack of stored programs. To change the ENIAC program, the engineers rerouted the maze of wires plugged into terminal panels on the front of the machine. In a 1946 technical paper, John Von Neumann proposed that operating instructions, as well as data, be stored inside the computer memory. The first stored program computer was the EDSAC, a British computer that began operation at the University of Cambridge in 1949. This original Von Neumann computer was the model for the MANIAC, which helped the United States to develop the H bomb before any other nation.

The magnetic-core memory is widely used for the internal storage application that Von Neumann proposed 25 years ago. We'll discuss memory devices in Chapter 8. In Chapter 9 we'll discuss *input* and *output* devices for converting the information on coded cards to a form suitable for storage in the internal memory. In Chapter 10 we'll discuss the computer organization and control that decodes the stored instructions and performs the mathematical operations specified by the instructions. Therefore, the internally stored program is a requisite to the high-speed operation of computers having the versatility to solve unrelated problems in succession. A typical large-scale computer may compute your bank balance and then a short time later may analyze Handyman Hardware inventory records.

Brief Account of Computers in the Last 20 Years

During the late 1940s and early 1950s, several electronic computers were developed. Among them were the WHIRLWIND I with the first magnetic-core memory, at the Massachusetts Institute of Technology, and the UNIVAC I, the first commercially available machine.

Transistors, of course, removed the size limitation of the previous vacuum-tube designs. Computers using transistor circuits are classed as *second-generation* computers. *Third-generation* computers are now being produced using integrated circuits.

We won't attempt to name the large number of second- and third-generation computers that were developed. The computer field is immense. For example, over 100 billion punched cards are used each year. The trend is toward faster operation, lower cost, smaller size, and a greater choice of output forms, including sketches, graphs, and spoken words.

Figure 1–7 shows that the operation of a computer begins and ends in the hands of people. The distinguishing characteristics of modern digital computers are

1.   Internal *memory* for storing instructions and data, either of which can be accessed rapidly and processed automatically.
2.   *Control unit* to automatically take specified action depending on the interpretation of the instructions.
3.   *Arithmetic unit* to add, subtract, multiply, divide, compare, and other actions.
4.   *Input* and *output* units to convert between the language of people to a machine-readable code.

All digital computers have the same functional units; however, we know all computers do not have the same capabilities. The more costly computers usually have greater capabilities, generally attributable to greater sophistication of one or more of the functional units. For example, $10,000 systems may have 4096-word memories and $10,000,000 systems may have 240,000-word memories. The arithmetic unit of a small machine may perform multiplication and division with the adder circuit rather than having built-in circuits for that purpose. The larger machines have more built-in automatic operations to save time and provide greater flexibility

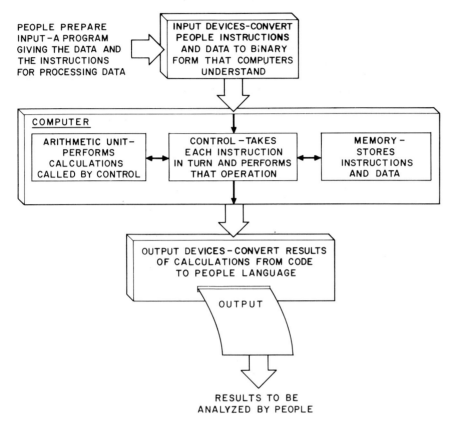

FIG. 1–7 Block Diagram of Units in a Computer System. People are the most important. They formulate the solution and check the answers.

in programming. It is reasonable to expect *a wide range of computer sizes and prices, because there are a wide range of uses.* The intended usage is, therefore, important in choosing the capacity and type of memory, the arithmetic circuits, and the characteristics of the input/output devices.

1.2 COMPUTER LANGUAGES WITH BINARY DEVICES

Electronic devices respond to electrical signals. To make the signals represent information, most digital computers use the *binary code.* The language of the computer is based on a code of high-frequency electrical pulses, or bits, generated and timed by an electronic clock in the computer.

Ex. 1–4

Suppose that the computer is used to arrange vast quantities of data into a specified order. People are supplying the data and reviewing the ordered listing. This task requires language conversions. Figure 1–8 illustrates the necessity for these conversions in the simple problem of

1.   Arranging five decimal numbers in ascending order.
2.   Printing the list.

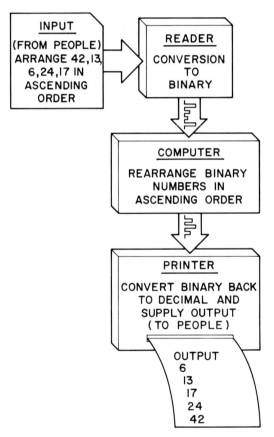

FIG. 1–8   Electrical Pulses, Shown inside the Broad Arrows, in and out of the Computer Represent the Original People Language after Conversion to the Binary Code.

The computer's pulse language can be represented by the two binary digits, 0 and 1. The *1 represents a pulse* and the *0 represents the absence of a pulse.* Using these two symbols, people have developed many different information codes that are used in various parts of the computer. The basic code, though, in most computers is based on the binary number system.

We are familiar with the decimal number system. In normal decimal notation, each digit represents successive powers of 10. For example, the number 253 means $2 \times 10^2 + 5 \times 10 + 3 \times 1$ for hundreds, tens, and units as read from left to right.

The binary number system is different from our conventional decimal system in only one respect—there are *fewer symbols* on which it is based. The symbols 2, 3, 4, 5, 6, 7, 8, and 9 used in the decimal system do not exist as such in the binary system. If 0 is zero and 1 is one, it is logical to call 2 the next number in a table containing only ones and zeros. Thus, two (2) is 10 and three (3) is 11, as shaded in Table 1-1.

TABLE 1–1
First 15 Binary Numbers

Number	Decimal	Binary
Zero	0	0000
One	1	0001
Two	2	0010
Three	3	0011
Four	4	0100
Five	5	0101
Six	6	0110
Seven	7	0111
Eight	8	1000
Nine	9	1001
Ten	10	1010
Eleven	11	1011
Twelve	12	1100
Thirteen	13	1101
Fourteen	14	1110
Fifteen	15	1111

We can manipulate the two symbols in much the same way as we do the 10 decimal symbols. For example, in a decimal number the first column on the right represents units. For numbers larger than can be accommodated in the units column, we have columns to the left, and call them tens, hundreds, and so on. In binary the columns are units, twos, fours, eights, and so on.

Thus, we see the code for representing *numbers* in binary. *Letters of the alphabet* are represented by other binary codes. Chapter 2 presents more details of number systems. However, before going to that discussion, we want to complete the present chapter. Our introduction to computers would be incomplete unless we mentioned analog computers.

1.3   ANALOG COMPUTERS

Electrical computers belong to two large families, *analog* and *digital*. Both are important in the computer field, althought digital computers have a larger scope of uses.

The term "analog" implies an analogy. In computer application it implies the *analogy between the levels of two parameters,* one being measured and the other serving as an indicator of the measured parameter. The computer utilizes convenient electrical variables to represent the measured quantity. Convenient analog signals are *electrical voltage, current, and frequency.* Any of these may represent a *temperature, pressure, velocity,* and the like. The computer processes these electrical signals, either performing a summation, a difference, or other slightly more complex operations. Once it has been experimentally established that the electrical variables are an accurate proportional representation of the measured variables, the computer becomes a tool for studying the overall effect of adjusting the magnitude of one or more of the variables.

For example, suppose that we are using analog computers to study the suspension system of an automobile. After experimental verification of the analog model, we might use the computer to predict the handling response to various-sized simulated potholes.

The fundamental idea of the electrical analog computer was first conceived by D. B. Parkinson and C. A. Lovell of Bell Telephone Laboratories in June 1940. In November 1941, the first system to use the idea, the M9 Anti-Aircraft Gun Director, was submitted to the U.S. Army for testing. By 1943 these 90-millimeter guns were in regular service in Europe and their success was phenomenal. The magnitudes of the *electrical quantities* were selected to be analogous to the *latitude, longitude, and height* of the target. The prediction of target intercept also involved the projectile characteristics and atmospheric conditions. They had to solve two simultaneous equations so that the target and projectile, each moving along its own course, would arrive at the intercept point at the same time.

Special-purpose analog computers are also in widespread use. The most common application is in the design of control systems for chemical and manufacturing plants. The difference between *actual position* (or level) and *desired position* (or level) is detected, processed, and used to adjust conditions to achieve agreement.

We'll discuss in Chapter 9 some of the details in converting analog variables to a digital form and vice versa. Sometimes digital computers are used in conjunction with analog systems. Digital methods are better suited for complex computations that may arise in the analog system. Hence, there exists a need for high-speed conversion in the digital input/output units. These topics appear in Chapter 9 along with a general discussion of input/output units.

2 Number Systems

Computer components are connected into an electrical network with sequences of pulses transmitted in rapid succession through the network. These transmissions are usually in binary form. In Chapter 1 we introduced the symbol 1 to denote a pulse and 0 to denote the absence of a pulse. People are familiar with our everyday language, which at first seems far removed from sequences of electrical pulses. However, we know that information originating from people is understandable by computers.

In getting understandable data to and from the computer, two or more language conversions are required. Computer circuits are designed to quickly handle the conversion from one code to another. This automatic internal feature frees the computer programmer to communicate with the machine using a form of English and decimal numbers. The programmer saves time in solving a problem compared to the undesirable alternative of phrasing the communication in machine binary code.

2.1 CONVERSION BETWEEN DECIMAL AND BINARY

Data accepted by the computer and the answers returned to the programmer are usually decimal numbers. The automatic conversions between decimal and the various binary codes do not involve manual assistance. In fact, the user may not even be cognizant of the conversion details.

In this chapter we'll discuss the basic concepts of number codes. We'll present the steps in the manual conversion process in order that we might better understand why certain binary codes originated. We'll see that some codes can be manually converted by an uncomplicated process, which implies that they can be automatically converted by a simple electrical circuit.

The conversion from binary to decimal is fairly straightforward. The conversion from decimal to binary is a little more difficult. We will approach the two in a manner such that the easy forward operation can be applied in reverse to obtain the conversion from decimal to binary. Table 2-1 is useful in this approach.

TABLE 2–1

Binary Number for Positive Powers of 2

Number	Power of 2	Decimal Number	Binary Number
One	2^0	1	00001
Two	2^1	2	00010
Four	2^2	4	00100
Eight	2^3	8	01000
Sixteen	2^4	16	10000
Thirty-two	2^5	32	100000

Ex. 2–1

Convert the binary number 11010 to an equivalent decimal number. The conversion is the simple operation of adding $1*2^4 + 1*2^3 + 0*2^2 + 1*2^1 + 0*2^0$.

Consider the sum of the numbers in each of the following columns.

Binary		Decimal
00010	=	2
01000	=	8
+10000	=	+16
11010		26

Therefore, 26 is the answer.

Ex. 2–2

Convert 1110 to decimal.
We form the sum of

Binary		Decimal
0010	=	2
0100	=	4
+1000	=	+ 8
1110		14

Therefore, 14 is the answer.

These exercises were fairly easy. Rules exist for conversion in the opposite direction; however, they are confusing and hard to remember. Instead of introducing a whole net set of rules, we'll approach the conversion from decimal to binary as the converse of the procedure used in Exs. 2–1 and 2–2.

Ex. 2–3

Convert the decimal number 26 to an equivalent binary number. (We know the answer from Ex. 2–1.)

In Table 2–1 we see 32 and 16 and know 26 is in between. In the following column containing decimal numbers, we have subtracted 16, leaving 10, which is large enough that 8 can be subtracted leaving 2.

Decimal Number		Binary Number
26		
−16	=	10000
10		
− 8	=	01000
2		
− 2	=	00010
0		11010 = sum = 26

We know the answer is 11010.

The final step is reached when only 0 is left. Of course, these steps of subtracting 16, 8, and 2 from 26 are exactly the opposite to the steps in Ex. 2–1 in which we added these numbers.

We know the answer is 11010.

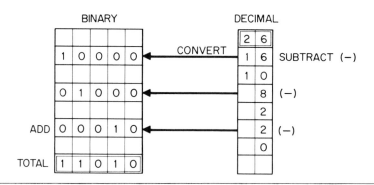

The steps in the conversion to binary can be illustrated by a chart such as the one introduced in Ex. 2–3. We remember from algebra that $2^5 = 32$, $2^4 = 16$, $2^3 = 8$, $2^2 = 4$, $2^1 = 2$, and $2^0 = 1$.

Ex. 2–4

Using the same procedure as in Ex. 2–3, convert decimal 57 to binary. Of course, 57 is between 32 and 64, so we subtract 32, leaving 25, and continue subtracting lesser powers of 2 until 0 is left.

Figure 2–1 shows these steps in the rectangular boxes. Binary ones

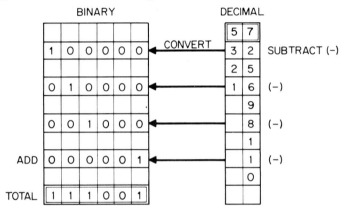

FIG. 2–1   Conversion of Decimal 57 to Binary 111001.

are in positions representing 2^5, 2^4, 2^3, and 2^0, because 32, 16, 8, and 1 can be successfully subtracted from 57. The answer is 111001.

Ex. 2–5

Convert decimal 42 to binary.
The answer is illustrated in Fig. 2–2.

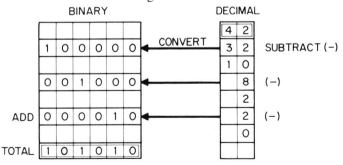

FIG. 2–2   Conversion of Decimal 42 to Binary 101010.

These conversions apply to numbers on the left-hand side of the radix point. In the decimal system the radix point is called the decimal point. Binary numbers are expressed with a binary point. The fractional part of binary number appears to the right of the binary point. Let's develop rules for converting between *binary and decimal fractional numbers*. Our procedure will be the same as for whole numbers except we'll refer to Table 2–2, showing negative powers of 2 rather than Table 2–1.

TABLE 2–2
Binary Fractional Numbers for Negative Powers of 2

Fraction	Power of 2	Decimal Number	Binary Number
One half	2^{-1}	0.500	0.10000
One quarter	2^{-2}	0.250	0.01000
One eighth	2^{-3}	0.125	0.00100
One sixteenth	2^{-4}	0.0625	0.00010
One thirty-second	2^{-5}	0.03125	0.00001

Ex. 2–6

Convert binary 0.11000 to decimal.

The binary number can be represented as the sum of 0.10000 and 0.01000, each equal to a negative power of 2 and a corresponding decimal number.

Binary		Decimal
0.10000	=	0.500
+0.01000	=	+0.250
		0.750

The answer is 0.750.

Ex. 2–7

Let's convert back to binary using the decimal number 0.750. We note that it is between 1 and 0.500. We'll subtract 0.500 and then continue subtracting decreasing powers of 2 until 0 is left (or the round off is minimum). Figure 2–3 illustrates the steps and shows the expected answer, 0.11000.

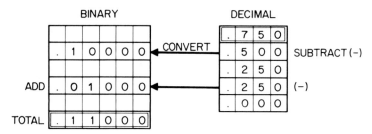

FIG. 2–3 Conversion of Decimal 0.750 to a Binary Fraction.

Ex. 2–8

Convert decimal 25.6 to binary.

This number is composed of an integer and a fraction. Let's draw two charts, Fig. 2–4 showing decimal 25 = 11001 and Fig. 2–5 showing the fraction 0.6 = 0.10011.

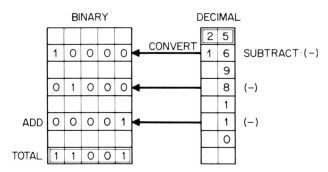

FIG. 2–4 Conversion of Decimal 25 to Binary 11001.

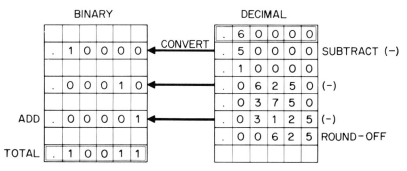

FIG. 2–5 Conversion of Decimal 0.6 to Binary Fraction.

Exercise 2–8 establishes that $25.6 = 11001.10011$. The conversion of 0.6 is not exact because a *round-off error* is present in the binary fraction. The error could be reduced by defining the binary fraction to be longer than the five places we used. Computers typically have 36-place binary numbers in order to minimize the round-off problem. The preceding exercises illustrate that binary numbers are longer than the equivalent decimal numbers.

2.2 BINARY ARITHMETIC

There are four basic rules for *binary addition*:

$$0 + 0 = 0$$
$$0 + 1 = 1$$
$$1 + 0 = 1$$
$$1 + 1 = 0 \quad \text{and 1 to carry to the next column}$$

All except the last rule are identical to the rules for decimal addition. We might have expected that $1 + 1 = 2$; however, the binary system doesn't contain the symbol "two." Having no higher digits, we introduce a carry to the next column on the left and have 10. In the process of adding decimal 1 to 9, we also introduce a carry, because there is no higher digit than 9.

Ex. 2–9

Perform binary addition of $1 + 1 + 1$.
Taking the first two digits, we have

$$\begin{array}{r} 1 \\ + 1 \\ \hline 10 \end{array} \quad \text{and then} \quad \begin{array}{r} 10 \\ + 1 \\ \hline 11 \end{array} = \text{answer}$$

Therefore, $1 + 1 + 1 = 1$ and 1 to carry to the next column. Also, we know from Table 1–1 that binary 11 is equivalent to decimal 3.

Ex. 2–10

Add 111 to 110 and show that the binary sum is equivalent to the sum of the corresponding decimal numbers.

Binary		Decimal
111	=	7
+ 110	=	+ 6
1101		13

In summing the leftmost column, we used our finding that $1 + 1 + 1 = 11$. The answer is 1101, which Table 1–1 *shows is equivalent to decimal 13*.

Ex. 2–11

Add 1101 to 1011.

Binary		Decimal
1101	=	13
+ 1011	=	+11
11000		24

In Ex. 2–11 a carry was obtained in the right column and continued to appear in the other columns to the left. The carry was *generated* in a lower-order column and then was *propagated* through higher-order columns.

These examples have introduced the manual process of binary addition. We're now better able to understand the automatic process. Specially designed circuits automatically handle binary addition. Chapters 3, 4, and 5 are concerned with the fundamentals of circuits.

In Chapter 6 we'll discuss the computer circuitry for adding two binary digits. It is called the half-adder. It is designed to follow the four basic laws of binary addition. A full adder will be shown to be a network of half-adders. Most computers contain several carefully designed full adders, which serve as the heart of the computer for arithmetic operations. We'll see in Chapter 6 that designers give considerable thought to making circuits that perform addition in minimum time. Therefore, it is economically desirable that maximum use be made of the investment in the adder circuitry. In fact, several small computers perform addition, subtraction, and multiplication with the same basic circuit.

To multiply 1101 by 11, some small computers simply add 1101 to itself three times. The final sum is the desired answer.

2.2.1 Subtraction by Two's Complement Addition

Subtraction can be performed by using the basic rules of addition. In general, the method is called *complement* addition. With reference to binary numbers, it is called *two's complement* addition. Specific subtraction rules exist and could be used as an alternative to the two's complement method. However, computer designers, thinking of common usage circuits, have taken the approach that subtraction should be like additional as much as possible.

In subtraction we have the minuend *minus* the subtrahend to yield the remainder.

$$
\begin{array}{r}
\text{Minuend} \\
- \text{ Subtrahend} \\
\hline
\text{Remainder}
\end{array}
$$

In two's complement addition, we content that the minuend *plus* the two's complement of the subtrahend will yield the desired remainder (almost). For this approach to be called valid, the two's complement of a binary number must be obtained by the following steps:

$$
\begin{array}{r}
\text{Minuend} \\
+ \text{ Two's complement of subtrahend} \\
\hline
\text{Remainder (almost)}
\end{array}
$$

Step 1. Complement the number by changing all 0's to 1 (this is called the one's complement).

Step 2. Add 1 to the one's complement.

Ex. 2–12

Find the two's complement of 101.

$$
\begin{array}{ll}
010 & \text{one's complement} \\
+1 & \\
\hline
011 & \text{two's complement}
\end{array}
$$

Ex. 2–13

Subtract 101 from 111, which, of course, is equivalent to subtracting decimal 5 from 7. In the decimal system, 7 minus 5 gives 2, which is 010 in binary. Let's compare this result with the answer we get by two's complement addition.

Decimal	*Binary*			
7	111		111	111
−5	−101	modify →	+ (010) →	+011
2			(+1)	1 010
				omit

The answer is 010, which is 2 in decimal. The desired remainder is obtained by omitting leftmost digit.

Ex. 2–14

Subtract 11 from 111.

Decimal	*Binary*		
7	111		111
−3	−11	modify → +(100) →	+101
4		(+1)	1100
			omit

After omitting the leftmost digit, the answer is 100, which is 4 in decimal.

Curiosity may be arising as to why this trick works. Here is the explanation. Suppose that *A* and *B* in Table 2–3 are binary digits. Except for the 2, the complement addition yields the remainder. Therefore, we omit the 2, which is equivalent to omitting the leftmost digit in this two-digit sum. Regardless of the number of digits in the sum, the *general rule applies that the leftmost digit be omitted.*

TABLE 2–3

Comparison of Two's Complement Sum
and Subtraction Remainder

Subtraction		*Two's Complement Addition*
A		*A*
		(*C*)
−*B*	modify →	(+1)
Remainder		Sum
Remainder = *A* − *B*	where	$C = 1 - B$
		sum $= A + C + 1$
		sum $= A + (1 - B) + 1$
		sum $= 2 + (A - B)$
		sum $= 2 + $ (remainder)

Ex. 2–15

Use complement addition to obtain the remainder of

$$111.01$$
$$-1.1$$

Binary remainder

The solution of this problem is left to the reader. You'll need to derive rules for subtracting fractional numbers by complement addition. The answer is 5.75 in decimal or 101.11 in binary.

2.2.2   Use of Complements to Represent Negative Numbers

Negative numbers are distinguished from positive numbers by introducing a *sign digit* in the leftmost position. The standard convention is *1 for negative and 0 for positive*. Furthermore, the *complement* of the original negative number is usually used. In this form, subtraction becomes the straightforward operation of adding the negative numbers. The overall result is exactly the same as subtraction by two's complement addition.

Ex. 2–16

How would — 6 be stored as a five-place binary number according to the standard convention?

In binary, 6 equals 0110 and the complement is 1001. Placing a 1 in the leftmost position, we have 11001 as the answer.

Ex. 2–17

Subtract 6 from 13 using binary digits.
We know 13 — 6 is equivalent to 13 + (—6).

Decimal	Binary	
13	01101	
+(—6)	+11001	
	⟨1⟩00110	sum
omit	+1	
	00111	= 7 = answer

The term *end-around carry* is a catchy name for the operation of handling the normally omitted leftmost digit of the sum. The end-around carry, of course, achieves the same result as forming the two's complement of the subtrahend before adding the minuend.

The computer designer has two options with regard to storing negative numbers.

1. Store the negative number in complement form and use the end-around carry technique.

2. Store the negative number in true form and build the adder circuitry to form the two's complement (see Section 10.4). With either option the convention for the sign digit is standard.

2.3   BINARY-CODED NUMBER SYSTEMS

The binary number system, which we defined in Table 1–1, is one of several schemes for representing decimal numbers. In Sections 2.3.1 through 2.3.4 we'll discuss four alternative schemes. Two of these, the octal code and the hexadecimal code, result in numbers that are shorter than the equivalent binary number. The binary-coded decimal system is longer but easier to convert. The excess-3 code serves a special purpose. Table 2–5, summarizing the codes, shows that all these systems are based on the two symbols, 0 and 1.

Regardless of the specific code, the computer circuitry is built of two-state devices that react to high-speed sequences of pulses. The answer obtained by the computer depends on the interconnection of devices in the circuit and the composition of the pulse sequence. For example, 00011 and 11010 are different sequences and could be expected to produce different answers.

2.3.1   Binary-Coded Decimal

The *binary-coded decimal* (BCD) is a notation in which the individual decimal digits are each represented by a group of four binary digits. For example, let's represent the decimal number 38 in BCD and compare it with the equivalent binary number.

Binary Coded Decimal	*Binary*
38	38
0011 1000	100110
Eight digits	Six digits

Table 2–5 lists the BCD representation for several decimal numbers. The obvious *disadvantage of BCD* is the extra digits—eight compared

to six for the binary number for this example. Thus, computers using BCD require more storage capacity for each decimal number. Within the computer circuitry, there is continual electrical pulse activity. For example, a sequence of pulses precisely ordered to represent the number 38 may be transferred to the adder. The less costly adders accept the sequence one pulse at a time until the entire sequence is accepted. Obviously, addition will be slower for BCD than for the shorter binary numbers. Therefore, BCD is best suited for applications that don't involve extensive arithmetic operations or high-capacity internal storage.

Ex. 2–18

What number system would you recommend for computing payroll records? Each employee's check is issued according to the mathematical product of hours worked and hourly rate plus overtime pay, minus deductions for taxes, Social Security, and so forth.

The best choice is BCD. After a few simple calculations, the computer has available the employee's pay data. Then each number must be converted to decimal (the system familiar to bank cashiers) and printed on the payroll check.

The *advantages of BCD* have led to its use primarily for applications in which there is concern for the time required to achieve the conversion to or from decimal. A large number of commercial applications are efficiently handled with a BCD system. Payroll processing is one example in which the amount of input/output is large compared to the computation effort. The reverse is true of many scientific problems having a large amount of computation compared to the input/output. Consequently, most machines for scientific applications use the binary system; however, a few use special schemes, such as the excess -3 code.

*2.3.2 Excess –3 Code (or XS-3 Code)

The XS-3 code is a UNIVAC innovation. It is a binary-coded decimal representation in which each decimal digit N is represented by the binary equivalent of $N + 3$ (see Table 2–4). For example, the XS-3 code for decimal 38 is

38
0110 1011

TABLE 2–4
XS-3 Code for Decimal Numbers

Decimal	XS-3 Code
0	0011
1	0100
2	0101
3	0110
4	0111
5	1000
6	1001
7	1010
8	1011
9	1100

The *usefulness of the XS-3 code* originates from the ease with which the nine's complement can be formed. The nine's complement of the decimal subtrahend can be used in subtracting decimal numbers in much the same way that the one's complement is used in subtracting binary numbers. The nine's complement of a digit is 9 minus the digit. The ten's complement is 10 minus the digit or the nine's complement plus 1.

Ex. 2–19

Subtract 4 from 7 using ten's complement addition.

Subtraction		Addition
7	7	7
−4	modify → (+nine's complement) →	(+5)
	(+1)	(+1)
		→(1)3
	omit	

The answer is 3.

Ex. 2–20

From Table 2–4 the XS-3 code of 4 is 0111. The nine's complement of 4 is 5, which is 1000. What rule would you suggest for obtaining the nine's complement in the XS-3 code? Check the rule using other digits.

XS-3 Code *of 4*	*XS-3 Code* *of 5, the Nine's* *Complement*
0111	1000

We see that *the nine's complement in XS-3 is obtained by simply interchanging 1 and 0.* Let's check this general rule using 3. It's nine's complement is 6.

XS-3 Code *of 3*	*XS-3 Code* *of 6, the Nine's* *Complement*
0110	1001

Ex. 2–21

Subtract 4 from 7 using XS-3 code.

Decimal	XS-3 Code		
7	1010		1010
−4	−0111	→ interchange →	1000
3		1 and 0 to	+1
		obtain nine's	(1)0011
		complement	

(omit)

The answer is 0011, which is 3 in BCD.

The procedure for subtracting two decimal numbers using the XS-3 code is summarized as follows:

1. The subtrahend and the minuend are changed to XS-3 code (4 became 0111 and 7 became 1010 in Ex. 2–21).
2. The nine's complement of the subtrahend is found by interchanging 1's and 0's (this gave 1000 in Ex. 2–21).
3. The ten's complement is formed by adding 1 (1000 + 1 = 1001 in Ex. 2–21).
4. The ten's complement of the subtrahend is added to the minuend. The leftmost bit is dropped, leaving the answer in BCD (the answer was 0011, which is equivalent to decimal 3).

The *disadvantage of the XS-3 code* is the same as BCD because both codes require more digits to represent a decimal number than the equivalent binary number.

*2.3.3   Octal Code

The octal notation uses the numbers 0 through 7 and thus has a radix base of 8. The *chief advantage of the octal system* is the ease with which conversion can be made between binary and octal. The conversion is a straightforward process of grouping the binary digits by threes and printing the octal digits. It is quicker for the machine to print and easier to read 1370, an octal number, rather than its equivalent 001011111000. Other examples of octal code appear next and in Table 2–5.

Binary	011	111	001		010	101	000		001	110	100	010	000	101
Octal	3	7	1		2	5	0		1	6	4	2	0	5

The octal code is used primarily for display purposes. For example, vast quantities of binary data are displayed as output in a memory dump. It requires less machine time to convert from binary to octal rather than to decimal. In a memory dump, all or part of the contents of memory are printed upon special request by the programmer. Whenever a program is being developed, the programmer may inadvertently misform some of the steps, leading to errors in the answers. Some errors are hard to find; however, the memory dump helps to some small degree by printing every detail of what the program looked like as the error occurred. The octal code reduces the time and cost involved in displaying the printed information in a memory dump.

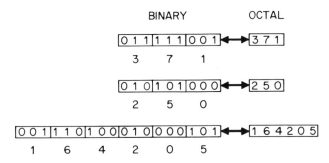

*2.3.4   Hexadecimal System

The hexadecimal system uses the base 16. Each hexadecimal symbol represents a group of four binary digits. Some computers (the IBM 360, for example) use the hexadecimal system for display purposes as an alternative to the octal system. Except for extraordinary operations, such as a memory dump, most machines, including the IBM 360, display decimal information.

Table 2–5 shows the hexadecimal symbols (0 through 9 and A, B, C, D, E, and F) and summarizes the binary-coded number systems. The shaded row shows the various ways of representing ten with from one to eight digit groups. Do you remember the attractive features and intended application of each code?

TABLE 2–5

Summary of Binary-Coded Number Systems

Number	Decimal	Binary	BCD	XS-3	Octal	Hexa-decimal
Zero	0	00000	0000 0000	0011 0011	0	0
One	1	00001	0000 0001	0011 0100	1	1
Two	2	00010	0000 0010	0011 0101	2	2
Three	3	00011	0000 0011	0011 0110	3	3
Four	4	00100	0000 0100	0011 0111	4	4
Five	5	00101	0000 0101	0011 1000	5	5
Six	6	00110	0000 0110	0011 1001	6	6
Seven	7	00111	0000 0111	0011 1010	7	7
Eight	8	01000	0000 1000	0011 1011	10	8
Nine	9	01001	0000 1001	0011 1100	11	9
Ten	10	01010	0001 0000	0100 0011	12	A
Eleven	11	01011	0001 0001	0100 0100	13	B
Twelve	12	01100	0001 0010	0100 0101	14	C
Thirteen	13	01101	0001 0011	0100 0110	15	D
Fourteen	14	01110	0001 0100	0100 0111	16	E
Fifteen	15	01111	0001 0101	0100 1000	17	F
Sixteen	16	10000	0001 0110	0100 1001	20	10

3 Basic Logic Circuits

We are familiar with the terms logic and logical. We have probably made statements to the effect that "considering the events that lead to the situation, *Mr. X used logic to predict the outcome.*" We'll assume that he carefully considered the important events and the sequence of their occurrence. His prediction may have included two or more outcomes with a predicted sequence of occurrence. The dictionary defines logic as a science that is *in accordance with predictions reasonably drawn from events and their sequence.*

The entire principle of the computer is based on the science of logic. In adding binary 011 to 101, the predictable sum is 1000. Mr. X might consider adding the columns of digits starting the sequence with the column on the right. The computer doesn't have a Mr. X; however, the *electrical circuits are interconnected in accordance with the principles of logic* to perform the desired operations. These logic circuits are the center of activity in all functional computer units. For example, the adder is a functional unit contained in nearly all computers. Figure 3–1(a) shows the two binary inputs and predictable output sum.

Of course, *logic circuits are designed to handle sequences of electrical pulses.* Using the standard convention of 1 for pulse and 0 for the absence of a pulse, we show 111 as ⊓⊓⊓→ and 110 as ⊓⊓⌐→ . If there existed a voltmeter with ultrafast response, we could connect it to an output terminal and measure evidence of the electrical pulses.

The binary adder in Fig. 3–1(b) accepts the input pulse sequence and generates the output sum. In serial operation, the two pulses on the right-hand end of the input sequence are transmitted simultaneously through wires to the adder. After a few tenths of a microsecond (called the propagation time), the right-hand pulse of the sum is available as output. The other columns are summed in turn along with the carries between columns. The sum is the final output determined by this logical processing of the

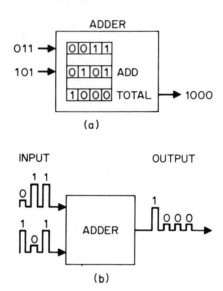

(a)

(b)

FIG. 3–1(a) and (b)   Block Diagram of Binary Adder.

sequence of input information. We'll see in Section 3.1 that the computer clock serves to maintain the proper order of the events. For example, one function of the clock would be to make sure that the final sum is not used elsewhere until all columns have been properly added.

The adder circuit will be discussed further in Chapter 6. Before reaching that point, we plan to discuss the basic building blocks for logic circuits. In this chapter we'll see the importance of the computer clock and AND, OR, NOR, and NAND logic gates which we will define. In Chapters 4 and 5 we'll discuss some of the mathematics that have aided computer designers in achieving the desired circuits with minimum complexity and cost.

3.1   FUNCTION OF COMPUTER CLOCK

The clock is the name given to the circuitry which generates the *electric pulses that serve as the event reference.* The plot in Fig. 3–2 shows

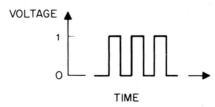

FIG. 3–2   Plot of Pulses Generated by Computer Clock.

the magnitude of the voltage output of a clock as a function of time. We see a series of equally spaced pulses. We'll adopt the convention of attaching an arrowhead to one end of the pulse train and count pulses beginning with number 1 immediately behind the arrow head.

Ex. 3–1

Consider a special circuit that allows every other clock pulse to be transmitted to its output terminals (see Fig. 3–3).

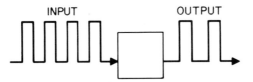

FIG. 3–3   Input and Output for Single-Stage Counter.

Circuits having this repetitive feature can be assembled in stages to form the widely used *counter*. This first stage would be useful in timing operations that could be expected to be completed within the time span of two regular clock pulses. Most operations take longer. In the adder, the final sum may not be available until after 10 or more clock pulses. Therefore, a 10-stage counter would be appropriate. The details of counters are discussed in Chapter 7.

Circuits that modify the regular clock pulse tend to increase the time interval between pulses. The clock pulse has the shortest time interval of all pulses being transmitted in the computer. Therefore, the pulse frequency of the clock is chosen on the basis that the pulse spacing is slightly greater than the time lapse of the fastest operation to be timed. Typical clock frequencies are 1 to 10 million pulses per second.

3.2   SYNCHRONOUS VERSUS ASYNCHRONOUS COMPUTERS

Most computers that have been marketed to date have been of the type called *synchronous*. Each step of an operation is allotted a specific amount of time within which it is to be completed. If it is completed before this time has elapsed, the machine waits. If it is not completed on time, an error occurs. To eliminate the latter possibility, the machine designer must be certain that, even if all environmental conditions are such that they cause the circuit to operate as slowly as possible, enough time has been allotted.

These problems are not present in *asynchronous* computers. In these the completion of one operation signals the beginning of the next. No time is spent in wasteful waiting, and an operation cannot be initiated until its logical predecessor has been completed. The asynchronous computers are more complicated to design and require more components; hence, for cost reasons, few have been marketed.

3.3   LOGIC ELEMENTS AND TRUTH TABLES

The computer is based on simple concepts. You may find this assertion rebuffed by those who visualize the computer as a giant maze of interconnected electrical circuits. In our endeavor to understand the concepts of computers, we will show that the giant maze is composed of a few general categories of circuits—called *functional units*. For example, computers have adders, counters, and registers. These functional units are built of devices that are even more basic.

The *logic element is the basic unit*. It performs the simple operation of accepting one or more input signals and transforming them to yield the predicted output signal. Of course, the sequential order of input signals will establish the sequential order of the output signal. Logic elements are classed as combinational or sequential, depending on whether the output at a specific time is influenced by the order of previous inputs. The *sequential* logic element has memory, in that it retains or remembers one or two previous inputs. The output at a specified time depends on the past input as well as the present input. In Section 7.1 we'll discuss the flip-flop circuit, which is a sequential logic element that is widely used in counter design. It remembers one previous input. A *combinational* logic element accepts one or more input signals and after a few tenths of a microsecond (the propagation delay time) gives a predictable output. The output does not depend on previous values of the input. Examples of combinational logic elements are AND gates, OR gates, NAND gates, and NOR gates, all of which will be discussed in this chapter.

In an integrated-cirucit package, we may not be able to see the tiny logic elements with the naked eye. However, the elements are considered an entity by themselves for purposes of logic design.

The *truth table* is also a simple concept. It is a tabular listing of all possible combinations of input signals and all logically true output signals. We'll be constructing several truth tables in the following chapters. With each table we'll be taking the approach of someone saying, "Let's suppose that we make a list of all possible sequences of events that could affect the situation. Furthermore, let's suppose that we make, alongside, a second list of the logical outcome for each sequence of events." You'll agree that this table leads directly to an assessment of the true significance of the events on the situation. It is a truth table and is very helpful in analyzing and designing logic circuits. It seems reasonable to assume that Eckert and Mauchley established the ENIAC design on simple concepts, such as the logic elements and truth table, before they undertook the lengthy task of sorting the few good vacuum tubes from the batch containing mostly bad ones.

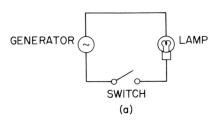

(a)

INPUT	OUTPUT	INPUT	OUTPUT
SWITCH OPEN	LIGHT OFF	0	0
SWITCH CLOSED	LIGHT ON	1	1

(b)   (c)

FIG. 3–4   Logic of a Switch: (a) Circuit; (b) and (c) Truth Tables.

The *simplest logic element is a switch*. When the switch in Fig. 3–4(a) is closed, the light goes on, as could be predicted. This of course assumes no equipment malfunction. In Fig 3–4 (b) the truth table for the switch shows the predicted outcome.

Truth tables usually contain binary symbols for the inputs and outputs. For inputs, we'll use 1 for closed and 0 for open switch; and for outputs, we'll use 1 for on and 0 for off. Figure 3–4(c) shows the truth table with these symbols.

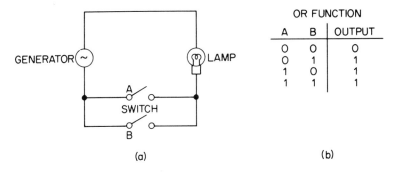

OR FUNCTION

A	B	OUTPUT
0	0	0
0	1	1
1	0	1
1	1	1

(a)   (b)

FIG. 3–5   The OR Function: (a) Switch Circuit; (b) Truth Table.

Consider the *lamp and two switches A* and *B* in Fig. 3–5(a). For this parallel arrangement the lamp is on if switch *A* or *B* is closed. The two switches so arranged give rise to the *OR function*. The output of an OR logic element is 1 when *A or B* is 1, as shown in Fig. 3–5(b). Thus, the name OR function is appropriate.

The two switches can be arranged in series to give another important logic function. The lamp is on if *A* and *B* are closed. The circuit in Fig. 3–6(a) illustrates the *AND function*. The truth table for the AND function

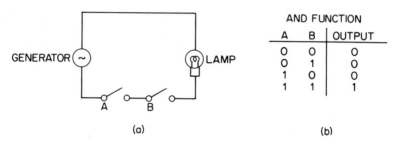

		AND FUNCTION	
A	B	OUTPUT
0	0	0
0	1	0
1	0	0
1	1	1

(a)   (b)

FIG. 3–6   The AND Function: (a) Switch Circuit; (b) Truth Table.

in Fig. 3–6(b) shows the output is 1 when *A and B* are both 1. Otherwise, the output is 0.

We know that all colors of the rainbow can be achieved by mixing the three primary colors, red, yellow, and blue. This concept of *building from a primary basis* also applies to logic-circuit design. In fact, the AND and OR functions, along with one more, the NOT function, can be used by logic-circuit designers to achieve any desired logic operation. In the next two sections we'll discuss the hardware items for achieving AND, OR, and NOT. This chapter concludes with a discussion of the NAND and NOR functions. The logic-circuit designer may choose to build the entire computer logic using only NAND devices. As an alternative, he may choose NOR devices as the primary building blocks.

Some computers in the past were built with AND and OR logic systems using thousands of switches in the form of electromechanical relays. In Chapter 1 we said the 1937 Mark I contained electrical circuits, and logic functions were realized by opening or closing relays in the electrical current paths. These circuits are classified as *branch* type as opposed to the more popular *gate* type.

The lamp in Fig. 3–7 is on if the proper switches are closed to form a path through one of the various branches in the network. Thus, the output is either on or off at least temporarily.

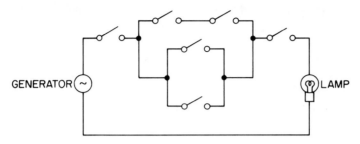

FIG. 3–7 Branch Circuit.

3.4 *AND* GATES AND *OR* GATES

In the years after the Mark I, much of the subsequent development was devoted to the twin problems of speed and reliability. The relay systems were capable of less than 100 operations per second. This speed is very low compared to the speed of today's logic elements, which approach 50 million operations per second. The quest for improved reliability has led to modern computers that run for many days without a mistake.

Ex. 3–2

Compare the output pulses of an OR gate with an OR branch circuit in Fig. 3–8. Suppose that the input pulses are of the form $A = 0101$ and $B = 1101$.

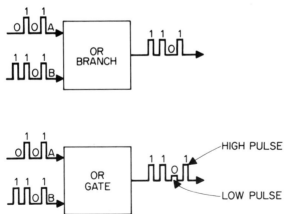

FIG. 3–8 Comparison of Output Pulses for Gate and Branch.

The output pulse of both logic elements is of the form 1101.

We know that the *devices in the modern computer are solid state,* either diodes or transistors. They consist of *logic gates,* which serve the same basic purpose as the branch arrangement of relay switches. The mode of operation of the gate type is slightly different from the on–off operation of the branch type. The transmission path from the input to the output of a switch is either open or closed. The characteristics of transistors and diodes preclude complete closing of this transmission path; hence, the two stable states are on but *never completely off.* The output of a logic gate is therefore *high* or *low.*

The OR function can be achieved by the idealistic circuit in Fig. 3–9(a). A pulse at either input, *A* or *B,* will cause a pulse at the output. However, this circuit has problems.

Ex. 3–3

Assume a pulse of 6 volts is imposed at terminal *A,* causing current to flow. How many current flow paths exist in the Fig. 3–9(a) circuit?

There are three paths, one of which is eliminated in a properly designed OR gate. One path is from *A* to *C;* another path is from *A* through the resistor to ground; and the *undesirable path is from A back to B.*

To *isolate B from A, we introduce two diodes* into the circuit. Diodes impede the current flow in one direction; however, current passes with ease in the opposite direction. The symbol for a diode signifies the preferred direction with an arrowhead. The *OR function* can be achieved by the diode circuit in Fig. 3–9(b). We note the lower diode impedes current flow from *A* to *B,* and the upper diode prevents current flow from *B* to *A.* Therefore, the diodes isolate the input terminals from each other.

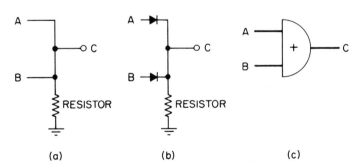

FIG. 3–9   OR Circuits: (a) Idealistic; (b) Practical Diode Gates; (c) Conventional Symbol.

The truth table verifies that the circuit operates as desired. The output voltage is high if we impose a pulse at either *A* or *B*. Otherwise, *C* will be at ground potential.

| *Input* | | *Output* |
A	B	
0	0	0
0	1	1
1	0	1
1	1	1

Circuit designers use a variety of *symbols to represent the OR gate*. We will use the symbol in Fig. 3–9(c).

The *AND gate* can be achieved with diodes as shown in Fig. 3–10.

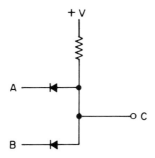

FIG. 3–10   AND Circuit with Diodes.

Ex. 3–4

Assume a pulse of +*V* volts is applied at *B*. What will be the voltage level at *C* if *A* is ground potential (0 volts)? Refer to Fig. 3–10.

Current flows to terminals *A* and *C*. Current will not flow from +*V* through the resistor to *B* because in this example *B* is also at +*V*. The voltage at *C* will be zero for all practical purposes, which is the same as *A*. However, diodes do not completely close the transmission path. Therefore, *C* is slightly greater than at *A*.

The truth table of the AND circuit shows the high–low states that always arise with semiconductor devices.

	Input			Output
	A	*B*		*Output*
	Ground	Ground		Low
	Ground	+V		Low
	+V	Ground		Low
	+V	+V		+V

We can show the same thing with 1 and 0:

Input A	B	Output
0	0	0
0	1	0
1	0	0
1	1	1

We will represent the *AND gate with the symbol in* Fig. 3–11.

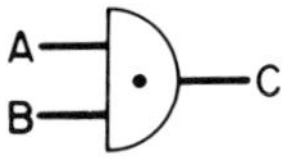

FIG. 3–11   Common Symbol for the AND Gate.

The OR gate was patented by A. W. Horton, Jr., and the AND gate was patented by W. H. Holden, both of Bell Telephone Laboratories.

Ex. 3–5

We know that gates in fences open to provide passage. Do you recognize any similarity between the function of a fence gate and electronic gate, particularly an AND gate?

Yes. The AND gate can be used to open and close the flow of electrical pulses. This gating action can be demonstrated with the AND gate in Fig. 3–11.

We'll assume that a timing pulse is applied to input *A* in Fig. 3–12

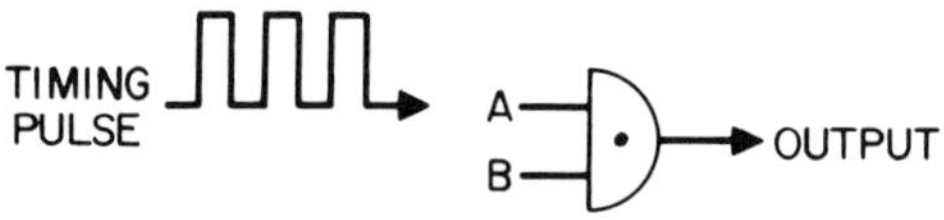

FIG. 3–12   AND Gate Demonstrating Common Application of Timing Pulse.

and a long duration pulse is applied to input *B*. The *gate is opened by the timing pulse,* and the binary value of *B* is passed on to the output. Pulse *B* is gated to the output by *A*.

Ex. 3–6

We mentioned in the first part of this section that diode and transistor circuits can perform many more computer operations per second compared to relay switches. What obvious reason would you give for this?

Answer: Electronic devices have no moving parts.

3.5 *NOT* **GATE**

The fundamental logic operators are the AND, OR, and NOT. We saw in the previous section that two of these can be achieved with diode circuits. However, the NOT gate, sometimes called the *inverter circuit, requires transistors* or some other amplifier. The term "inversion" means to reverse in position. As we might expect, *the output of an inverter is the exact opposite of the input.* The truth table shows this relationship.

Input	Output
Low	High
High	Low

In binary form we have

Input	Output
0	1
1	0

The symbol for the NOT gate will be recognized by those familiar

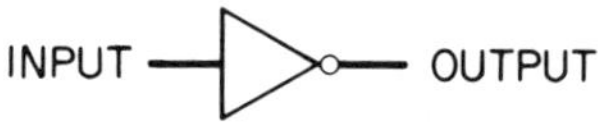

INPUT ——▷o—— OUTPUT

FIG. 3–13   Conventional Symbol for Inverter or NOT Gate.

with radio circuits. It is similar to the symbol for an amplifier. We'll use the little circle on the output side of the symbol to signify a signal inversion. The same circle is used conventionally in the symbol of NOR and NAND because they are inversions of OR and AND. All *these gates require signal*

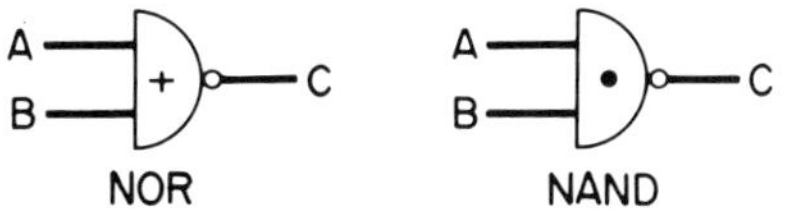

FIG. 3–14   Symbols for NOR and NAND Gates.

amplification, a capability of transistors but not diodes. Let's briefly discuss the transistor.

The *transistor* is probably the greatest invention in the history of electronics. It was of paramount importance in the evolution of the computer. Its invention in December 1947 earned the Nobel Prize for Physics in 1956 for John Bardeen, Walter Brattain, and William Shockley, all of Bell Telephone Laboratories.

Unfortunately, the theory of electronics that describes the physics of transistors is beyond the scope of this book. We will discuss the transistor from the point of view of the electrical-current flow paths between terminals and means for electrically changing these paths to cause the transistor to become an extremely high speed switch. Therefore, the complex theory of the transistor is not being treated here, but, rather, we'll discuss the *practical functioning of the transistor as a switch.*

Transistors are tiny devices that range in size from a pinhead to slightly larger than a pencil eraser. They have three terminals, the base,

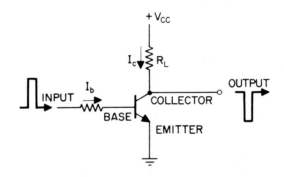

I_b = BASE CURRENT
I_c = COLLECTOR CURRENT
V_{cc} = POSITIVE VOLTAGE

FIG. 3–15   Transistor Inverter Circuit.

the collector, and the emitter, as shown in Fig. 3–15. By connecting the emitter terminal to a ground lead, we realize the common-emitter configuration, which is widely used.

The transistor circuits in Fig. 3–15 can achieve the inversion of the input. Certain things happen in the transistor when a current flows into the base terminal. The *net effect of the base current is to increase the ease with which current flows from the collector terminal* through the transistor to the emitter and then to the ground lead. A high current in the path from the collector to the emitter signifies that the path is *closed* in the same way that a switch would be closed. Similarly, a low collector current signifies that the transistor is acting as an *open* switch.

Ex. 3–7

Construct a table showing whether the current is high or low in each of the flow paths in the transistor for a low and then a high pulse at the input.

Voltage at Input	Base Current	Collector Current	Path from Collector to Emitter	Voltage at Output
Low pulse	Low	Low	Open	High $= V_{cc}$
High pulse	High	High	Closed	Low $=$ ground potential

The truth table for the NOT gate is a condensation of this table.

Voltage at Input	Voltage at Output
0	1
1	0

Ex. 3–8

The symbol commonly used for the NOT gate is the same as the symbol for an amplifier except a small circle has been added to denote negation. Explain why this symbol, shown in Fig. 3–13, is reasonable.

Clearly, *the common-emitter circuit is an amplifier* (both current and voltage), because the level of the output voltage is set by V_{cc}, which could be much greater than the level of the input. We know that amplifiers are devices having higher output than the controlling input.

---

*3.6 *NAND* AND *NOR* GATES

The transistor is so versatile at performing negation that two other gates have come into being and are widely used instead of the AND, OR, NOT set. These are *the NAND and NOR, where N denotes negation*. The name NAND is short for "not AND" and NOR is short for "not OR." The truth table illustrates the result of these negations.

NOR				NAND		
Input				*Input*		
A	*B*	*Output*		*A*	*B*	*Output*
0	0	1		0	0	1
0	1	0		0	1	1
1	0	0		1	0	1
1	1	0		1	1	0

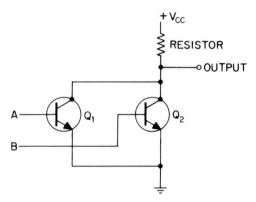

FIG. 3–16   Direct-Coupled Transistor NOR Gate.

The circuit in Fig. 3–16 performs the *NOR function.* Inputs *A* and *B* are connected to the base terminal of transistors Q_1 and Q_2, respectively. The output voltage will be either high (at V_{cc}) or low (at ground potential), depending on whether the current flow path is closed through either transistor.

Ex. 3–9

Assume that a low voltage pulse is applied to input *A* in Fig. 3–16 at the same time that a high voltage pulse is applied to input *B*. Describe the current flow paths through Q_1 and Q_2. What is the output voltage?

We refer to the second and third pulse in the pulse sequence in Fig. 3–17. Either of these depict the situation. The high pulse at input *B* causes a base current to flow in transistor Q_2. We know that the base current closes the path between the collector and the emitter; hence, the output voltage becomes the same as the emitter voltage, which is at ground potential. Therefore, the output voltage is low. Furthermore, we see that the output will be low for all combinations of input voltage levels, except the one case where both inputs are low. Then the path between collector and emitter is open and the output voltage becomes V_{cc}, a high voltage.

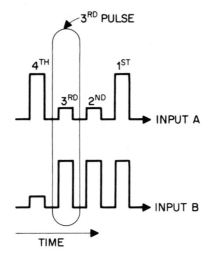

FIG. 3–17   Sequences of Input Pulses.

The circuit in Fig. 3–18 performs the NAND function. The output is at a high voltage level unless both *A* and *B* are high, because the path through the transistors is open unless both base currents are applied.

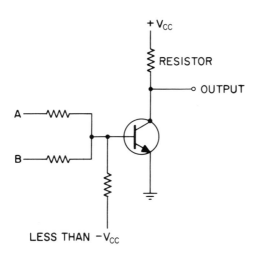

FIG. 3–18   Direct-Coupled Transistor NAND Gate.

These transistor circuits for the NOR and NAND gates are not necessarily (and in fact aren't) the best for high-speed low-power and good noise immunity. Other circuits are better in these respects, but they all perform the logic function of NAND and NOR. They may have more than one transistor in the gate, have diodes, or perhaps, capacitors.

The logic designers take the approach that the logic gate is a "black box." The manufacturer (perhaps Texas Instrument, Incorporated, Motorola, Incorporated, or Fairchield Camera and Instrument, Incorporated) *defines the gate in terms of high-speed, low-power, high noise immunity, fan out* and *fan in.* The *fan out* is the number of circuits that can be supplied with input signals from an output terminal of a gate. The number of elements that one output can drive depends on the power available from the output and the power required by each input. Specifying the *fan out* is analogous to specifying the number of light bulbs that can be lit by a given battery or household circuit. The *fan in* pertains to the number of input signals that can be connected. The number is limited, because the power delivered by too many simultaneous pulses or signals could destroy the input device.

A *logic gate* is a basic building block of computer circuitry. Our discussions for the next four chapters will be concerned with applying gates to achieve a desired logical operation.

4 Concepts of Logic Circuits

Logic circuits have a predictable output. We don't mean to imply that the circuit designers simply measure the output of a given circuit and thereby establish that the output is predictable. The concepts of logic-circuit design enable the designer to carry out *a true design approach*. This approach commences with a description of the function to be performed by the logic circuits. The second step consists of *forming the truth table* relating the inputs and the desired output. The final step in the design is *forming a logic circuit* whose outputs correspond with the list of outputs in the truth table. Ideally, the *circuit is minimized in complexity and cost*.

4.1 BACKGROUND ON BOOLEAN ALGEBRA

The process of designing circuits is largely an art unless some basis or science is applied. The *scientific basis is provided by Boolean algebra,* which was introduced by George S. Boole (1815–1964). This English mathematician published a book in 1854 proposing that his new mathematics could be used to analyze the logical nature and constitution of the human mind. His form of mathematical expressions is loosely akin to the form of the algebraic expressions we encounter in high school albegra. Boolean algebra involves the use of OR, AND for logical addition and multiplication instead of $+$, $\times$ for the familiar case.

The pioneering work by Boole led mathematicians of his period into several new fields of mathematics. However, this early interest preceded the computer era by nearly 100 years.

The *present-day application of Boolean algebra* to switching functions is credited to a 1938 paper by Claude E. Shannon, an employee of Bell Telephone Laboratories. We mentioned in Section 1.1 that the Bell System was developing relay-type computers and switching systems in the 1930s.

The work by Shannon was associated with those developments. Shannon described a technique whereby he could use algebraic expressions to mathematically represent a given combination of switches and relays. The expressions could be manipulated and thereby simplified in much the same manner as ordinary algebraic expressions. Circuits corresponding to the simplified expressions contained fewer relays and hence represented *lower cost* and *higher reliability*. His straightforward technique has been *adopted almost universally* for the design of switching and computer logic circuits, whether they be relays or transistors.

Boolean algebra has greatly improved our capacity for understanding and describing computer circuitry. We would be remiss if we skimmed over a topic so indispensible to computer design.

The AND gate handles two or more input signals and yields one output, which is the logical product of the inputs. Figure 4–1(a) shows an

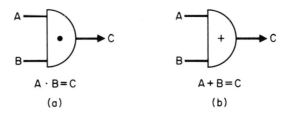

$$A \cdot B = C \qquad\qquad A + B = C$$

(a)   (b)

FIG. 4–1   Boolean Expressions for (a) AND and (b) OR.

AND gate with inputs A and B, and output C. For short, we could represent the gate as $A \cdot B = C$; read A AND B. A few other books use $A \cap B = C$, where $\cap$ is called the cap and read as A INTERSECTION B. We shouldn't reveal our unfamiliarity with the notation by reading $A \cdot B$ as A times B or A multiplied by B. The dot is used in ordinary algebra to denote multiplication; however, it is used here to denote logical multiplication. We are also using the dot in the symbol for the AND gate to distinguish it from the OR gate, which is identified by a plus sign.

The *OR gate* shown in Fig. 4–1(b) yields the logical sum of inputs A and B. The expression $A + B$ is read A OR B and not A plus B. The alternative form is $A \cup B$, where $\cup$ is the cup and read as A UNION B.

The expressions $A \cdot B = C$ and $A + B = C$ look algebraic.

Ex. 4–1

Consider two gates in the same circuit.

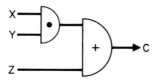

$X \cdot Y$ = output of AND gate
Z + output of AND gate = C
$Z + X \cdot Y = C$

The expression $Z + X \cdot Y = C$ in Ex. 4–1 is definitely algebraic. Let's construct the truth table relating X, Y, and Z to C. For clarity, we'll take two steps and make use of Table 4–1.

TABLE 4–1
Basic Boolean Algebra Relations

Logical Products	Logical Sums
$0 \cdot 0 = 0$	$0 + 0 = 0$
$0 \cdot 1 = 0$	$0 + 1 = 1$
$1 \cdot 0 = 0$	$1 + 0 = 1$
$1 \cdot 1 = 1$	$1 + 1 = 1$

In the first step, we form the truth table for each gate.

AND Gate

Inputs		Output
X	Y	$X \cdot Y$
0	0	0
0	1	0
1	0	0
1	1	1

OR Gate

Input		Output
Z	$X \cdot Y$	C
0	0	0
0	1	1
1	0	1
1	1	1

Therefore, the output is 1 when Z is 1, or X and Y are both 1. In the final step, we form the truth table for all three inputs.

Inputs			Output
X	Y	Z	
0	0	0	0
0	0	1	1
0	1	0	0
0	1	1	1
1	0	0	0
1	0	1	1
1	1	0	1
1	1	1	1

Ex. 4–2

Obtain the algebraic expression and truth table for the circuit in Fig. 4–2.

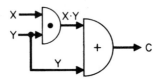

FIG. 4–2   Circuit before Simplification.

We recognize that the output, C, is $Y +$ output of AND gate. Thus, the required expression is $Y + X \cdot Y = C$. To obtain the truth table, you may want to form an intermediate truth table in the two-step approach. For brevity, we'll show the final form.

Inputs		Output
X	Y	
0	0	0
0	1	1
1	0	0
1	1	1

We observe that the output column of the truth table in Ex. 4–2 is identical to the Y column. Therefore, the value of X *is superfluous* to the output, and the X terminal of the circuit can be eliminated. The simplified equivalent to the two-gate circuit is no gates, but rather a direct connection between Y and the output.

4.2   ADVANCING FROM THE TRUTH TABLE TO BOOLEAN EXPRESSION

We want to spend just enough time on Boolean algebra to show that it does form a scientific basis for logic circuit design. Furthermore, the algebraic expression of a logic function can be manipulated to reduce its complexity, which in turn leads to a less complex circuit having fewer logic elements.

To reemphasize the *steps involved in arriving at the logic circuit,* the diagram in Fig. 4–3 illustrates that the process begins with a word description and culminates with the simplified logic circuit.

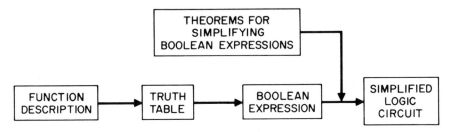

FIG. 4–3 Diagram of Steps in Logic Design Process.

The next chapter presents an orderly process for each step. Before reaching that point, we want to discuss some basic concepts in the inter-relationship between Boolean expressions and logic circuits. We'll use the "backdoor" approach to a certain extent, starting with the logic circuit and working backward to the Boolean expression. As an example, we'll consider the *two-level AND–OR circuit.* We'll present several *basic theorems* that can be applied to simplify Boolean expressions. A proof is given of some of these theorems, including the two *DeMorgan theorems* that form the basis for alternatives to the AND–OR circuits. The alternatives, the *NAND and NOR circuits,* are discussed in Section 4.7.

4.3 TWO-LEVEL *AND–OR* CIRCUITS

Consider the output of the AND–OR circuit in Fig. 4–4(a). The *four vertical lines represent bus bars* having uniform voltage throughout their length. By connecting *inverters* to A and B as shown, we achieve the inverse of A and B, which we'll denote as A' and B', respectively. The *junctions* between the bus bars and the leads to the AND gate are shown as large dots. The term A' can be read A inverse, A negative, or A prime.

The inputs to the upper AND gate are A and B; thus, the output $=$ $A \cdot B$. This signal is passed on to the OR gate along with $A' \cdot B'$ from the lower AND gate. The output of any OR gate is the OR function of the inputs. In this circuit, the inputs are $A \cdot B$ and $A' \cdot B'$. Therefore, the output is $A \cdot B + A' \cdot B'$.

Thus, *a sequence of pulses applied to terminals A and B* will be trans-mitted through the level of AND gates and then through the OR gate to appear as the final output. There is a time lapse between the application of the input and the availability of the output. In this *two-level logic circuit,* the time lapse is the summation of *two propagation delays,* one through the AND gates and the second through the OR gate.

The *output is also a sequence of pulses;* however, the order of "high" and "low" pulses may be completely different than the order of either

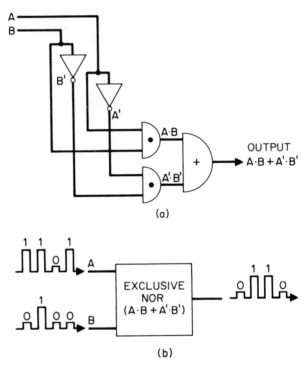

FIG. 4–4 (a) Logic Circuit for $A \cdot B + A' \cdot B'$, Boolean Expression; (b) Output Pulse Sequence of Exclusive NOR with Typical Inputs.

input sequence. The rearrangement in the order is in accordance with the function $A \cdot B + A' \cdot B'$.

Ex. 4–3

Consider that the sequences ⎍⎍⎍⎍⎍⎍ and
⎍⎍⎍⎍⎍⎍ are applied to A and B, respectively.
What is the final output of the circuit in Fig. 4–4(b)?

The truth table for $A \cdot B + A' \cdot B'$ has a 1 in the top and bottom row of the output column.

Inputs		Output
A	*B*	
0	0	1
0	1	0
1	0	0
1	1	1

This function is given the name EXCLUSIVE NOR. Another function, the EXCLUSIVE OR, has the property that the output is 1 if either but not both inputs are 1. The EXCLUSIVE NOR is the inverse.

To find the output sequence, we consider each pulse in the A sequence and pair it up with the proper pulse from the B sequence. The first pair is $A = $ high and $B = $ low; thus, the output is low, as shown in Fig. 4–4(b).

The output is available as soon as the input signals propagate through the two-level logic circuit.

The EXCLUSIVE NOR is one of the 15 logic functions that involve two inputs. Figure 4–5 shows the corresponding 15 circuits. For uniformity in the diagram, the input pulse sequence to all these circuits commences with 00 (low pulses for both A and B) and then, in a binary counting fashion, continues with 01, 10, and 11 for A and B.

The circuits are labeled 1 through 15 and have output sequences 0001 (binary for 1) through 1111 (binary for 15). This figure illustrates that *two-level AND–OR logic is capable of implementing all the logic functions:* 15 functions for two input variables, 31 functions for three input variables, and so on. We note that the last logic circuit shows that the output sequence 111 is obtained with the function $A + A'$. Thus,

$$A + A' = I$$

We have illustrated a basic theorem of Boolean algebra. We *define I as a sequence having all high pulses.* We also *define φ to be a sequence having all low pulses.*

4.4 THEOREMS FOR SIMPLIFYING BOOLEAN EXPRESSIONS

Let's tabulate for ready reference 18 of the basic theorems of Boolean algebra. These appear in Table 4–2. *Each theorem states an equality*

TABLE 4–2
Basic Boolean Theorems

1. $X + \emptyset = X$		2. $X \cdot I = X$	
3. $X + I = I$		4. $X \cdot \emptyset = \emptyset$	
5. $X + X' = I$		6. $X \cdot X' = \emptyset$	
7. $X + X = X$		8. $X \cdot X = X$	
9. $X + Y = Y + X$		10. $X \cdot Y = Y \cdot X$	
11. $X \cdot (X + Y) = X$		12. $X + X \cdot Y = X$	
13. $X \cdot (X' + Y) = X \cdot Y$		14. $X + X' \cdot Y = X + Y$	
15. $X \cdot Y + X' \cdot Y = Y$		16. $(X + Y) \cdot (X' + Y) = Y$	

17. $(X + Y + Z + \ldots)' = X' \cdot Y' \cdot Z' \ldots$ ⎧ De Morgan's
18. $(X \cdot Y \cdot Z \ldots)' = X' + Y' + Z' + \ldots$ ⎩ theorems

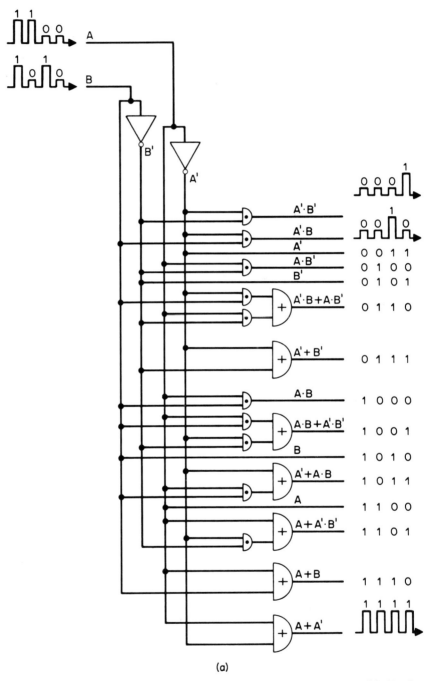

(a)

FIG. 4–5 Logic Functions for Two Inputs: (a) 15 Circuits; (b) Boolean Expressions.

56

FIG. 4–5 *(cont.)*

CIRCUIT	BOOLEAN EXPRESSION	FUNCTION NAME
1	$A' \cdot B'$	NOR
2	$A' \cdot B$	
3	A'	INVERSE OF A
4	$A \cdot B'$	
5	B'	INVERSE OF B
6	$A' \cdot B + A \cdot B'$	EXCLUSIVE OR
7	$A' + B'$	NAND
8	$A \cdot B$	AND
9	$A \cdot B + A' \cdot B'$	EXCLUSIVE NOR
10	B	B
11	$A' + A \cdot B$	
12	A	A
13	$A + A' \cdot B'$	
14	$A + B$	OR
15	$A + A'$	

(b)

between the expression on the left-hand side of the equal sign and the simplified expression on the right-hand side. Upon encountering a lengthy expression, a part of which matches the left-hand side, a prudent circuit designer would obviously use the simplified equivalent as a replacement for the complex expression. By repeating this process for other parts of the expression, we achieve an expression from which the *lowest-cost logic circuit* can be deduced.

Mathematicians deal with theorems and, to us nonmathematicians, they display the habit of *presenting theorems* and then proceeding with the next step of *presenting the proof.* We'll extend them a bit of courtesy by presenting proof of three typical theorems. We'll use the technique of *proof by perfect deduction,* which means that a theorem or statement is true if mathematics can demonstrate that it is true for every case covered.

Ex. 4–4

Consider the statement, "Of all large cities in the United States, Los Angeles is the most distant from New York." Present a proof by perfect deduction.

If we are inclined to approach the proof from a geometric viewpoint, we might unfold a map of the United States and scribe a circle through Los Angeles with the center at New York. We could quickly conclude the proof observing that no large cities lie outside this circle; thus, Los Angeles must be the most distant.

The proof by perfect deduction is different and uses no shortcuts. We would consider the distance from New York to every one of the 20 or so large cities and compare each with the distance to Los Angeles. We could deduce after the lengthy comparison that the theorem was true. All possible combinations would have been considered.

Fortunately, logic circuits operate as high or low; thus, the list of possible combinations is short and well suited to proof by perfect deduction.

Ex. 4–5

Give proof of theorem 5 in Table 4–2, $X + X' = I$. Using the rule that $0 + 1 = 1$ and $1 + 0 = 1$, prove the output pulse is I, as shown in Fig. 4–6. In this proof by perfect deduction, we consider all possible combinations, which are only two.

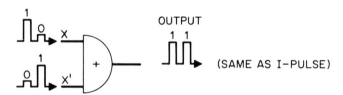

FIG. 4–6   Logic Circuit Illustrating $X + X' = I$.

Ex. 4–6

Give proof of theorem 7, $X + X = X$. We use the rule that $0 + 0 = 0$ and $1 + 1 = 1$. The proof is demonstrated in Fig. 4–7.

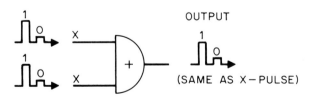

FIG. 4–7   Logic Circuit Illustrating $X + X = X$.

Ex. 4–7

Give proof of theorem 11, $X \cdot (X + Y) = X$. All possible combinations of inputs are shown in Fig. 4–8.

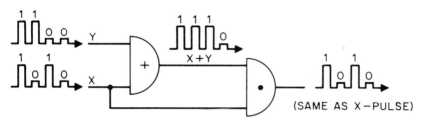

FIG. 4–8   Logic Circuit Illustrating $X \cdot (X + Y) = X$.

*4.5 DE MORGAN'S THEOREMS

Theorems 17 and 18 (a dual set) are worthy of special note because they show that *plus and dot can be interchanged from the right- to the left-hand side* of the equality. This *principle leads to the equivalence* between AND, OR, NOT logic circuits and the preferred NAND or NOR logic circuits.

Two steps are involved in *forming De Morgan's theorems:* for example, refer to theorem 17.

  1.   Addition symbols (on left) are replaced with multiplication symbols (on right).
  2.   Each term (on left) is replaced with its complement (on right).

Ex. 4–8

Present proof of theorem 17.
For two terms we have

$$(X + Y)' \xrightarrow[\text{be equal to}]{\text{assumed to}} X' \cdot Y'$$

Consider the two circuits in Fig. 4–9 showing (a) $(X + Y)'$ and (b) $X' \cdot Y'$. The first circuit is an OR gate followed by an inverter with an input pulse sequence of 00, 01, 10, 11, for X and Y. The other circuit is an AND gate with the inputs inverted to give a pulse sequence of 11, 10, 01, 00 for X' and Y'.

Obviously, the two circuits give the same output; therefore,

$$(X + Y)' = X' \cdot Y'$$

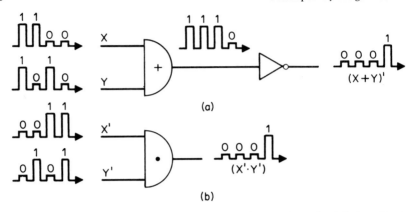

FIG. 4–9   Circuits Illustrating (a) $(X + Y)'$ and (b) $X' \cdot Y'$ Are Equivalent.

The proof illustrated in Ex. 4–8 could be extended to more terms. In general, we have

$$(X + Y + Z + \ldots)' = X' \cdot Y' \cdot Z' \ldots$$

and

$$(X \cdot Y \cdot Z \ldots)' = X' + Y' + Z' + \ldots$$

*4.6   DUALITY OF BOOLEAN ALGEBRA

There is an interesting similarity in Table 4–2 between the odd-numbered theorems and the even-numbered theorems. Mathematicians refer to this similarity as a dual relationship and develop general rules for forming the dual.

The *general rule* covering theorems 1 through 18 specifies that *the dual is formed by*

1. Replacing plus with dot (or vice versa) and then, if either I or $\emptyset$ are present.
2. Replacing I with $\emptyset$ (or vice versa).

Using the principles of duality, the mathematician eliminates the necessity for proving one half the theorems. It is sufficient to prove only the odd-numbered theorems in Table 4–2, because the dual of the theorem follows necessarily.

*4.7   TWO-LEVEL *NAND* CIRCUITS AND *NOR* CIRCUITS

Digital computers are commonly designed with transistor circuits of NAND or NOR gates. We will use De Morgan's theorems to introduce these gates.

Ex. 4–9

Use NAND gates to implement the function

$$X + Y = \text{output}$$

We know the output of a NAND gate is the complement of the *logical product* of the inputs. For example, the NAND gate in Fig. 4–10(a)

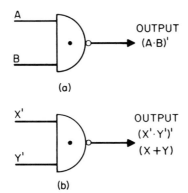

(a)

(b)

FIG. 4–10   NAND Gates for (a) Typical Inputs; (b) $X + Y$.

has output $= (A \cdot B)'$. We are asking for a NAND circuit to handle the *logical sum* of $X + Y$, which, at first look, seems to be *impossible*. However, *theorem 17 holds the clue.* Consider the expression

$$(X + Y)' = X' \cdot Y'$$

which is equivalent to

$$X + Y = (X' \cdot Y')'$$

Therefore, $X + Y$ is the output of a NAND gate having inputs X' and Y', as shown in Fig. 4–10(b).

The output of a *NOR gate is in the form of a logical sum.* Theorem 18 shows that NOR gates can also represent *a logical product*.

Ex. 4–10

Use NOR gates to implement the function

$$X \cdot Y = \text{output}$$

Theorem 18 shows that

$$(X \cdot Y)' = X' + Y'$$

or

$$X \cdot Y = (X' + Y')'$$

The desired output is achieved with one NOR gate in Fig. 4–11.

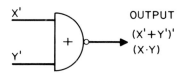

FIG. 4–11   NOR Gate for $X \cdot Y$.

Any logic function can be expressed as *a combination of logical sums and logical products.* We have shown that both of these can be achieved with either NAND gates or NOR gates. The following exercise deals with a function having sums and products. It illustrates one case of the general axiom that *any logic function can be implemented with two-level logic* of either AND, OR, NOT or NAND or NOR.

Ex. 4–11

Consider the function

$$X \cdot Y + X' \cdot Y' = \text{output}$$

Implement this function using

(a)   AND, OR, NOT.
(b)   NAND only.
(c)   NOR only.

(a)   Figure 4–12(a) shows the AND, OR, NOT circuit.

(b)   For NAND gates, the function must be rearranged to eliminate logic sums. We have

$$(X \cdot Y) + (X' \cdot Y') = \text{output}$$

From theorem 17,

$$[(X \cdot Y)' \cdot (X' \cdot Y')']' = \text{output}$$

The required circuit is shown in Fig. 4–12(b). It has three NAND gates with the final stage sometimes called the global NAND gate.
(c)   For NOR gates, the function must be rearranged to eliminate logical products. We have

$$(X \cdot Y) + (X' \cdot Y') = \text{output}$$

Applying theorem 18 to each of the terms in parenteses yields

$$(X' + Y')' + (X + Y)' = \text{output}$$

The NOR circuit is in Fig. 4–12(c).

We note that the output of the last NOR gate in Fig. 4–12(c) is inverted to obtain the desired output. The inverter symbol is shown in the circuit; however, the NOR gate is capable of the inversion function, as shown in Ex. 4–12.

Ex. 4-12

Use NOR gates to implement the NOT function. For an input of X, the output must be X'.
Consider $X + X$. Theorem 7 shows that

$$X + X = X$$

Taking the complement of both sides of the equation, we have

$$(X + X)' = X'$$

The left side is X' (the desired output), and the right side contains only X (the input). The required NOR circuit is in Fig. 4–13(a).
NAND gates can implement the NOT function, also. To illustrate this, let's consider $X \cdot X$. Theorem 8 shows that

$$X \cdot X = X$$

Taking the complement of both sides of the equation, we have

$$(X \cdot X)' = X'$$

The NAND circuit is shown in Fig. 4–13(b).

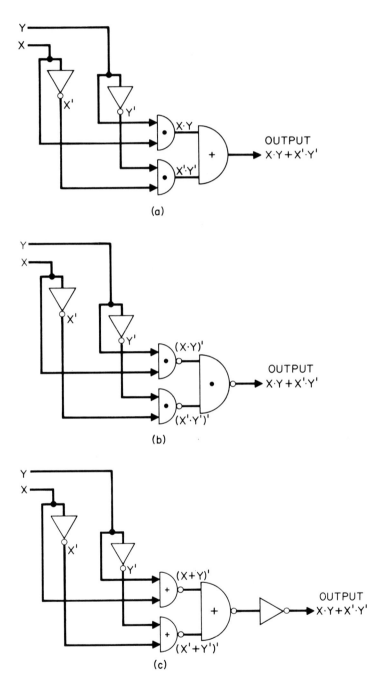

FIG. 4–12 Two-Level Logic Circuit for $X \cdot Y + X' \cdot Y'$ Using (a) AND, OR, NOT; (b) NAND; (c) NOR Gates.

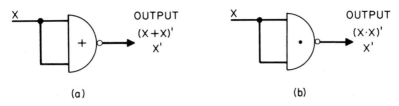

(a)   (b)

FIG. 4–13   Use of (a) NOR and (b) NAND Gates to Achieve the NOT Function.

5 Practical Design of Logic Circuits

We are aware of reports of computers being used to design other computers. It is common practice to use other computers to derive and simplify computer logic circuits. For the computer assistance to be effective, the circuit designer strives to formulate an orderly procedure that can be formed into a computer program. The machine process is extremely rapid. It frees the designer from the manual tasks to pursue general improvements in design procedures and logic concepts.

This chapter details the steps in the manual procedure upon which the machine procedure is based. Both procedures, either directly or indirectly, deal with the Boolean expression of the logic function. This chapter begins with defining the rules for derivation of the expression that can be formed as a sum-of-products or product-of-sums. For example, an expression could be formed as $X' \cdot Y' + X \cdot Y = $ output or $(X + Y') \cdot (X' + Y) = $ same output. The chapter concludes with a discussion of techniques for minimizing circuit complexity and costs, including the Venn diagram and Karnaugh map (pronounced car-no). A third technique, the Quine–McCluskey method, is also discussed as being readily formed into a computer program for use in the machine procedure for logic-circuit design. Hence, it is widely used by designers of complex circuits. For textbook circuits, we prefer a minimization technique that is less elaborate in detail. The Karnaugh map is better suited to our purposes. It works satisfactorily for up to six input variables.

5.1 DERIVATION OF BOOLEAN EXPRESSIONS

A straightforward technique exists for deriving the algebraic expression from the truth table. Consider the truth tables for $X \cdot Y$ and $X' \cdot Y'$.

66

| Inputs | | Output | | Inputs | | Output |
X	Y	X · Y		X	Y	X' · Y'
0	0	0		0	0	1
0	1	0		0	1	0
1	0	0		1	0	0
1	1	1		1	1	0

Take special note of the 1's in each output column, because they lead directly to the algebraic expression. We see that $X \cdot Y$ gives 1 at the bottom of the column and 0 elsewhere, and $X' \cdot Y'$ gives 1 at the top of the column and 0 elsewhere. Consider a truth table having 1 at the top and bottom.

| Inputs | | Output |
X	Y	(What is expression?)
0	0	1
0	1	0
1	0	0
1	1	1

It is apparent that the truth table is represented by the expression

$$(X \cdot Y) + (X' \cdot Y') = \text{output}$$

This logical sum gives output $= 1$ if either product in parentheses is 1. Therefore, the expression gives output $= 1$ at the top and bottom and output $= 0$ elsewhere.

These arguments lead to *general rules* for deriving expressions from the 1's in the truth table. The general expression is a logical sum with

1. The same number of terms as there are 1's in the output column of the truth table.

2. Each term a logical product involving all the input variables.

3. The variables primed for input of 0 and unprimed for input of 1 in that row of the truth table.

Ex. 5–1

Derive the Boolean expression for the following truth table:

Inputs			Output
X	Y	Z	
0	0	0	0
0	0	1	1
0	1	0	0
0	1	1	0
1	0	0	1
1	0	1	0
1	1	0	0
1	1	1	1

There are three 1's; hence, the preceding general rules lead to three terms involving X, Y, and Z or their primes. The desired expression is

$$X' \cdot Y' \cdot Z + X \cdot Y' \cdot Z' + X \cdot Y \cdot Z = \text{output}$$

5.2   SUM-OF-PRODUCTS AND PRODUCT-OF-SUMS

Consideration of 1's in the output column of the truth table leads to a common form for logic functions, the *sum-of-products*.

The 0's in the truth table lead to another useful form. The *product-of-sums* is a convenient form to use in designing NAND gate circuits. We'll develop the general rules for this form and show that they are the dual of the preceding rules.

Consider the truth tables for $X + Y'$ and $X' + Y$.

Inputs		Output
X	Y	$X + Y'$
0	0	1
0	1	0
1	0	1
1	1	1

Inputs		Output
X	Y	$X' + Y$
0	0	1
0	1	1
1	0	0
1	1	1

We note that $X + Y'$ gives 0 in the second row and 1 elsewhere, and $X' + Y$ gives 0 in the third row and 1 elsewhere.

Based on these observations, the truth table

Inputs		Output
X	Y	(What is expression?)
0	0	1
0	1	0
1	0	0
1	1	1

is represented by

$$(X + Y') \cdot (X' + Y) = \text{output}$$

As a general rule, the product-of-sums is a logical product with

1. The same number of terms as there are 0's in the output column of the truth table.
2. Each term a logical sum involving all the input variables.
3. The variables primed for input of 1 and unprimed for input of 0 in that row of the truth table.

Of course, we recognize the preceding truth table from Section 5.1, where we obtained the expression

$$X \cdot Y + X' \cdot Y' = \text{output}$$

which can be shown to be the dual of

$$(X + Y') \cdot (X' + Y) = \text{output}$$

by multiplying the terms in parentheses and using theorem 6 of Table 4–2, which specifies that $X \cdot X' = \phi$ and $Y \cdot Y' = \phi$.

Ex. 5–2

Form the product-of-sums and NAND gate circuit for the following truth table.

Inputs			Output
X	Y	Z	
0	0	0	1
0	0	1	0
0	1	0	1
0	1	1	1
1	0	0	1
1	0	1	1
1	1	0	0
1	1	1	1

We have only two 0's; therefore, we have the product of only two terms:

$$(X + Y + Z') \cdot (X' + Y' + Z) = \text{output}$$

Applying theorem 17 (De Morgan's theorem), we have

$$(X' \cdot Y' \cdot Z)' \cdot (X \cdot Y \cdot Z')' = \text{output}$$

The NAND gate circuit is shown in Figure 5–1.

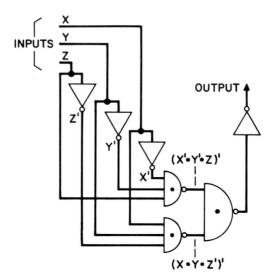

FIG. 5–1   NAND Gate Circuit for the Product-of-Sums, $(X' + Y' + Z) \cdot (X + Y + Z') =$ Output.

The option exists of using the sum-of-products or the product-of-sums. The product-of-sums is in a form that can be readily implemented by NAND gate circuits. However, if the truth table contains less 1's than 0's, we would be wise to use the 1's and sum-of-products. This yields a shorter expression, and it can be rearranged slightly to lead to the NAND gate circuit.

5.3   TECHNIQUES FOR REDUCING CIRCUIT COMPLEXITY AND COST

The unadorned application of the list of theorems in Table 4–2 will usually simplify the Boolean expression and, consequently, reduce the circuit complexity and cost. Occasionally, the designer using this method might mistakenly conclude the process before reaching a minimum. He probably will be bored with the whole concept.

There exists other schemes that are successful and offer some amusement to the user. The *Venn diagram* is a graphical scheme that originates from the illustrations used by students studying the theory of sets and subsets. The *Karnaugh* map is an excellent scheme for up to six input variables and offers a gamelike approach to minimizing the Boolean expression. The *Quine–McCluskey* method is a tabular method that is well suited to automatic computation.

5.3.1   Venn Diagram of Boolean Expressions

Consider a circle and the variable X. The Venn diagram is based on defining the region within the circle to represent X and the region outside to represent X', as shown in Fig. 5–2(a). For a system of two variables, two circles will be needed. The variables X and Y are shown in Fig. 5–2(b). The overlapping circles illustrate the logical sum (OR) and logical product (AND). In Fig. 5–3, crosshatching is used to denote $X + Y$ and $X \cdot Y$.

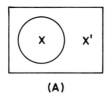   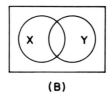

(A)   (B)

FIG. 5–2   Regions in Venn Diagram for (a) One Variable and (b) Two Variables.

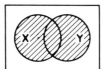   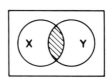

THE REGION WITHIN   THE REGION WITH
EITHER CIRCLE   BOTH CIRCLES
X + Y (OR)   X•Y (AND)

FIG. 5–3   Venn Diagrams for $X + Y$ and $X \cdot Y$.

Ex. 5–3

Draw the Venn diagram for $X + X \cdot Y =$ output.

What simpler expression will achieve the same output?

The diagrams in Fig. 5–4 illustrate the answer. Let's interpret these diagrams.

Figures 5–4(a) and (b) show crosshatching in regions for X and $X \cdot Y$, respectively. Figure 5–4(c) shows a combined diagram to simulate overlaying the separate ones. The region $X \cdot Y$ is double crosshatched.

The desired expression is represented by all regions having either double or single crosshatching. Obviously, this region is simply X. There-fore,

$$X + X \cdot Y = X$$

which agrees with theorem 12.

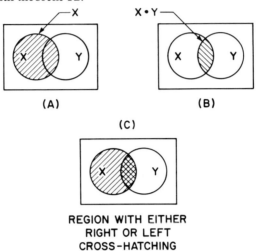

REGION WITH EITHER
RIGHT OR LEFT
CROSS-HATCHING
X+X•Y = OUTPUT

FIG. 5–4   Venn Diagram Illustrating Proof that $X + X \cdot Y = X$ with Cross-hatching for (a) X; (b) $X \cdot Y$; (c) $X + X \cdot Y$.

The Venn diagram is an excellent method for illustrating proof of Boolean theorems. We will show another example to clarify the method.

Ex. 5–4

Consider theorem 18 for two variables $(X \cdot Y)' = X' + Y'$. Let's draw Venn diagrams for the two sides of the equation.

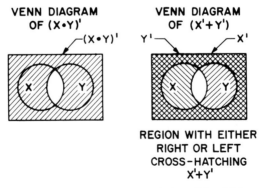

REGION WITH EITHER
RIGHT OR LEFT
CROSS-HATCHING
X'+Y'

FIG. 5–5   Venn Diagram Illustrating Proof that $(X \cdot Y)' = X' + Y'$, One of De Morgan's Theorems.

The two Venn diagrams in Fig 5–5 are equivalent, illustrating a proof that $(X \cdot Y)' = X' + Y'$ or, in general, $(X \cdot Y \cdot Z \ldots)' = X' + Y' + Z' + \ldots$.

5.3.2 Karnaugh Map for up to Six Input Variables

The theorem $X + X' = I$ leads to a useful graphical scheme for textbook exercises in logic-circuit design. The *Karnaugh map* for minimizing algebraic expressions is based on this single theorem.

The map methed illustrates each of the several terms that may be involved in a complex expression. There exist *rules for grouping the terms to simplify the expression*. To develop these rules, we'll take the backdoor approach by starting with a simple expression, adding terms to make it complex, and constructing the map. It should then be obvious that terms shown in the map can be grouped to yield the original simple expression. Consider

$$X = \text{output}$$

Since $Y + Y' = I$, we can multiply by it without changing the output.

$$X \cdot (Y + Y') = \text{output}$$

or

$$X \cdot Y + X \cdot Y' = \text{output}$$

We can increase the complexity by bringing in $Z + Z'$:

$$X \cdot Y \cdot (Z + Z') + X \cdot Y' \cdot (Z + Z') = \text{output}$$

or

$$X \cdot Y \cdot Z + X \cdot Y \cdot Z' + X \cdot Y' \cdot Z + X \cdot Y' \cdot Z' = \text{ouput}$$

The expression now has four product terms involving the variables X, Y, Z, and their primes. Other terms could be added to make the expression longer; however, eight terms is the maximum for three variables. The Karnaugh map for three variables consists of a matrix of eight cells, each identified with a label having 0's and 1's. The labels refer to primed and unprimed variables. It is normal to draw the eight-cell matrix as two rows of cells.

X \ YZ	00	01	11	10
0				
1				

Each product term is plotted on the Karnaugh map by marking the cell having the appropriate label. The top row is labeled 0 and contains those cells to be marked for product terms having X'. Terms having X are plotted by marking a cell in the bottom row. The columns are labeled 00, 01, 11, and 10 to signify the primes and unprimes of Y and Z.

Each cell is labeled by row and column and is marked or unmarked depending on the product terms in the expression being plotted. It is customary to enter the symbol 1 in those cells to be marked and 0 in all other cells. For example, the lower right cell will contain a 1 if the expression has the term $X \cdot Y \cdot Z'$. We have this term and also have $X \cdot Y' \cdot Z'$, which would be represented in the lower left cell. Following this procedure, we represent all four terms in the expression.

The completed map becomes

YZ X	00	01	11	10
0	0	0	0	0
1	1	1	1	1

By encircling the group of 1's, we note that they are in adjacent cells and are all in X but not in X'. Thus, the subcube of four cells illustrates

$$X = \text{output}$$

which, of course, is the original simple expression.

Thus, in the straightforward process for *simplifying complex expressions,* we

    1.   Construct the Karnaugh map.

    2.   Observe the *largest* subcube that can be formed with adjacent cells in a group.

    3. Define the terms in the simplified expression based on the subcube or subcubes (for two or more groups).

Ex. 5–5

Simplify $X \cdot Y \cdot Z + X \cdot Y \cdot Z' = $ output using the Karnaugh map.

X \ YZ	00	01	11	10
0	0	0	0	0
1	0	0	1	1

The two-cell subcube can be represented by

$$X \cdot Y = \text{output}$$

which can be implemented by a single AND gate. The original expression required two AND gates and one OR gate. The cost savings are apparent in addition to the time savings in operation of the single-stage logic compared to the original two-stage logic.

The cells are labeled with a number sequence called the *Gray code*.

TABLE 5–1

Comparison of Binary and Gray Codes

Number	Binary Code	Gray Code
Zero	00	00
One	01	01
Two	10	11
Three	11	10

Table 5–1 shows that each number differs from the preceding number in one place only. Referring to the binary code, we see that both the left and right digits change in going from one to two. With the Gray code, only the left digit changes, which makes it suitable for labeling the Karnaugh map cells. Then adjacent cells can be grouped according to $X + X' = I$.

The *four-variable* Karnaugh map has four rows and four columns, all labeled with the Gray code.

Ex. 5–6

Draw the four-variable Karnaugh map for the expression

$$W' \cdot X \cdot Y' \cdot Z' + W' \cdot X \cdot Y' \cdot Z + W' \cdot X \cdot Y + W' \cdot Y \cdot Z' + W \cdot X \cdot Y \cdot Z' + W \cdot X' \cdot Y \cdot Z' = \text{output}$$

WX \ YZ	00	01	11	10
00	0	0	0	1
01	1	1	1	1
11	0	0	0	1
10	0	0	0	1

We have two four-cell subcubes, giving a simple expression with two terms:

$$W' \cdot X + Y \cdot Z' = \text{output}$$

To form a subcube, we group adjacent cells. It is apparent that cells that touch are adjacent. Other cells are also adjacent. Comparing cells in the left column ($Y = 0$, $Z = 0$) with corresponding cells in the right column ($Y = 1$, $Z = 0$), we see that they differ only by one variable, Y. Therefore, they are adjacent. Also, cells in the top row are adjacent to cells in the bottom row because they differ by only one variable, W.

Ex. 5–7

Draw the Karnaugh map for the expression

$$X \cdot Y' \cdot Z' + W' \cdot X' \cdot Y' \cdot Z +$$
$$W \cdot X' \cdot Y' \cdot Z + X \cdot Y \cdot Z' = \text{output}$$

Two-cell subcube

WX \ YZ	00	01	11	10
00	0	1	0	0
01	1	0	0	1
11	1	0	0	1
10	0	1	0	0

Four-cell subcube

The largest subcubes are a four cell and a two cell, which yield

$$X \cdot Z' + X' \cdot Y' \cdot Z = \text{output}$$

For *five variables,* we draw two four-variable maps, one for the prime and one for the unprimed fifth variable. Consider the variables $V, W, X, Y,$ and Z:

$V = 0$

YZ WX	00	01	11	10
00	1	0	0	1
01	0	0	0	0
11	0	0	0	0
10	1	0	0	1

$V = 1$

YZ WX	00	01	11	10
00	1	0	0	1
01	0	0	0	0
11	0	0	0	0
10	1	0	0	1

It becomes a little harder to visualize adjacent cells; however, by studying the map, we see all the 1's on this map can be grouped into an eight-cell subcube and can be represented by the simple expression

$$X' \cdot Z' = \text{output}$$

To check the answer, place a mark in every cell labeled $X = 0$ and $Z = 0$ for all values of $V, W,$ and $Y.$ The marks should coincide with the ones in the five-variable map.

Six-variables are handled by four Karnaugh maps. Consider the variables $U, V, W, X, Y,$ and $Z.$ The individual $W, X, Y,$ and Z maps would be labeled 00, 01, 11, and 10 for U and $V,$ respectively. *Six variables is approaching the practical limit for the Karnaugh-map method.*

*5.3.3   Quine–McCluskey Method

The Karnaugh map is convenient for three or four variables, but approaches its upper limit for six variables. Computer circuitry usually has at least 10 and may have up to 100 input variables. Clearly, the *task of manually simplifying the logic circuit is limited.*

In 1956, E. J. McCluskey of Bell Telephone Laboratories presented a simplification method suitable for computer solution. This method was a practical application of the theories of M. V. Quine of Harvard University. The concepts of the *Quine–McCluskey* method are used almost universally in logic-circuit design.

We'll manually do an example to introduce the method and then briefly allude to the automatic method. We'll show the steps in the process for dealing with Boolean expressions written as a sum-of-products.

The first step serves to group the product terms according to the number of unprimed variables. There may be several groups, but each group will contain product terms having the same number of unprimed variables. Begin with the group containing the lowest number and draw a line between groups.

Consider the expression

$$W' \cdot X' \cdot Y' \cdot Z' + W' \cdot X' \cdot Y \cdot Z + W' \cdot X \cdot Y' \cdot Z' +$$
$$W' \cdot X \cdot Y' \cdot Z + W' \cdot X \cdot Y \cdot Z + W' \cdot X \cdot Y \cdot Z' +$$
$$W \cdot X \cdot Y' \cdot Z' + W \cdot X' \cdot Y' \cdot Z' = \text{output}$$

The details of the steps follow:

Step 1.   Group terms:

1	$W' \cdot X' \cdot Y' \cdot Z'$
2	$W' \cdot X \cdot Y' \cdot Z'$
3	$W \cdot X' \cdot Y' \cdot Z'$
4	$W' \cdot X' \cdot Y \cdot Z$
5	$W' \cdot X \cdot Y' \cdot Z$
6	$W' \cdot X \cdot Y \cdot Z'$
7	$W \cdot X \cdot Y' \cdot Z'$
8	$W' \cdot X \cdot Y \cdot Z$

Step 2.   Apply the theorem $X + X' = I$ by canceling X from any two product terms that differ from each other by only one variable, X. Such pairs can exist only in adjacent groups. Repeat for W, Y, and Z.

1, 2	W'—$Y' \cdot Z'$
1, 3	—$X' \cdot Y' \cdot Z'$
2, 5	$W' \cdot X \cdot Y'$—
2, 6	$W' \cdot X$—$\cdot Z'$
2, 7	—$X \cdot Y' \cdot Z'$
3, 7	W—$Y' \cdot Z'$
4, 8	W'—$Y \cdot Z$
5, 8	$W' \cdot X$—Z
6, 8	$W' \cdot X \cdot Y$—

Step 3.   Repeat step 2, keeping in mind that a variable can be canceled from two terms if they are alike except for that variable. Also, they must have bars at the same location. Step 2 is repeated until variable cancelation is complete.

1, 2, 3, 7 and 1, 3, 2, 7	— — $Y' \cdot Z'$
2, 5, 6, 8 and 2, 6, 5, 8	$W' \cdot X$ — —
4, 8	W' — $Y \cdot Z$

The Quine–McCluskey method yields the simplified expression

$$Y' \cdot Z' + W' \cdot X + W' \cdot Y \cdot Z = \text{output}$$

Computer programs exist that simplify logic circuits by automatic processing of the three-step method. It is a straightforward procedure to specify that terms be grouped (step 1) and compared with terms in adjacent groups (steps 2 and 3).

Ex. 5–8

Design a logic circuit having three inputs X, Y, and Z; one output that is high for $X = Y$ and low otherwise; and a second output that is high for X less than Z and low otherwise. This comparator circuit is a practical application of the principles in this chapter. Figure 5–6 shows the block diagram.

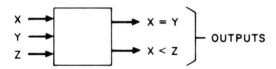

FIG. 5–6 Block Diagram for Comparator Circuit.

This problem definition leads to the truth table

Inputs			Outputs	
X	Y	Z	First	Second
0	0	0	1	0
0	0	1	1	1
0	1	0	0	0
0	1	1	0	1
1	0	0	0	0
1	0	1	0	0
1	1	0	1	0
1	1	1	1	0

The Boolean expressions are

$$X' \cdot Y' \cdot Z' + X' \cdot Y' \cdot Z + X \cdot Y \cdot Z' + X \cdot Y \cdot Z = \text{first output}$$

and

$$X' \cdot Y' \cdot Z + X' \cdot Y \cdot Z = \text{second output}$$

The Karnaugh map shows these expressions can be simplified and in so doing reduce the number of gates in the logic circuit.

		First Output		
X	YZ 00	01	11	10
0	(1	1)	0	0
1	0	0	(1	1)

		Second Ouput		
X	YZ 00	01	11	10
0	0	(1	1)	0
1	0	0	0	0

$$X' \cdot Y' + X \cdot Y = \text{first output}$$

$$X' \cdot Z = \text{second output}$$

The AND, OR, NOT circuits are shown in Fig. 5–7.

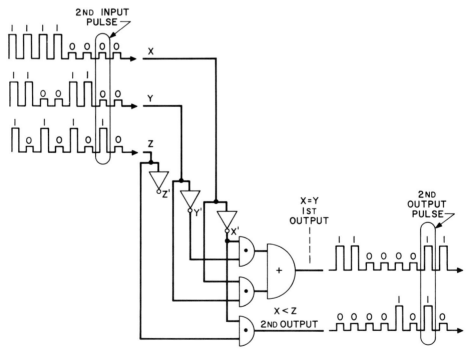

FIG. 5–7   Comparator Circuit.

6 Arithmetic Unit

All arithmetic operations, including addition, subtraction, multiplication, and division, are handled by the arithmetic unit. Most computers have as their main purpose the processing of a set of instructions and executing arithmetic operations on data, all stored in the internal memory. Once the instructions or data are fetched from memory, they typically pass through temporary storage devices called *registers*. For example, the memory-buffer register handles all information immediately before going in or out of memory. Minimum delay in all steps of arithmetic operation determines the worth of a high-speed computer. Therefore, the designer gives considerable thought to the arithmetic unit (see Fig. 6–1).

Addition is a common operation of all computers. A typical instruction may specify that data from a particular memory address (location)

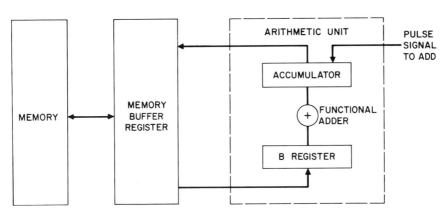

FIG. 6–1 Block Diagram of Information Flow between Arithmetic Unit and Memory.

be transferred to the memory-buffer register and then to the B register. The *arithmetic unit* consists of

> 1.   A specific number of registers, including the *B register* and at least one *accumulator*.
> 2.   Functional units, including a *functional adder* and perhaps a multiplier and divider.

The accumulator is used to temporarily store the result of almost every arithmetic computation. At any given time, the accumulator contains data from a previous operation. Upon the arrival of the pulse signal to add, the functional adder achieves the sum of the contents of the B register and the contents of the accumulator. The sum is usually stored in the accumulator from which it can be moved back to the memory-buffer register and then to memory.

Logic circuits are the basis of all these computer units. In this chapter we'll discuss the logic circuit for the functional adder, beginning with the problem definition, drawing the truth table, writing the algebraic expression, and then showing the adder logic circuit. Chapter 7 is concerned with the logic circuit for registers and counters. These two chapters are intended to show practical application of the orderly procedure for deriving logic circuits.

6.1   LOGIC CIRCUIT OF BINARY HALF-ADDER

Consider the sum of two digits, which we will call X and Y. The rules for binary addition can be expressed as

Case 1	Case 2	Case 3	Case 4	General Case
0	0	1	1	X
$+0$	$+1$	$+0$	$+1$	$+Y$
00	01	01	10	CS

The digits in the answer are symbolized by S and C representing the *sum* of the column and the *carry* to the next column, respectively.

The *half-adder* is the logic circuit for forming the binary addition of two digits. It has two inputs and two outputs.

The truth table has four rows and is obtained directly from the preceding four cases.

Inputs		Outputs	
X	Y	S	C
0	0	0	0
0	1	1	0
1	0	1	0
1	1	0	1

We see the sum column has two 1's; hence, the algebraic expression has two terms (for sum-of-products). The carry is simply $X \cdot Y$.

$$X' \cdot Y + X \cdot Y' = S$$
$$X \cdot Y = C$$

The corresponding AND–OR gate circuit is shown in Fig. 6–2. The

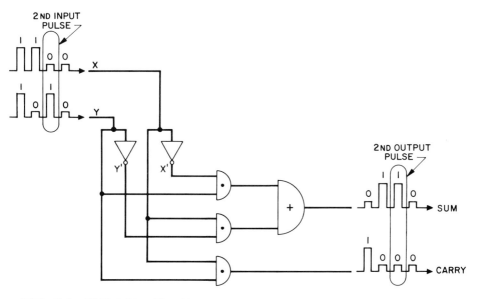

FIG. 6–2   Half-Adder Circuit.

pulse sequence 00, 01, 10, 11 for inputs X and Y propagates through the circuit. The output pulse sequence corresponds to the truth table. For example, the second pulse of the input and output corresponds to the second row of the truth table.

Ex. 6–1

The preceding circuit can be slightly different and we save one gate. We note that $X \cdot Y$ is required for C but isn't used in forming S. Let's rewrite the expression for S to include $X \cdot Y$. We already have

$$X' \cdot Y + X \cdot Y' = S$$

However, $X' \cdot X = \phi$ and $Y' \cdot Y = \phi$. Therefore, they can be added to the expression without changing S.

$$X' \cdot Y + X \cdot Y' + X' \cdot X + Y' \cdot Y = S$$

or

$$(X' + Y') \cdot (X + Y) = S$$

and theorem 18 in Table 4–2 states that $X' + Y' = (X \cdot Y)'$. Thus, $(X \cdot Y)' \cdot (X + Y) = S$ and $X \cdot Y = C$.

Figure 6–3 shows the half-adder circuit derived from these expressions.

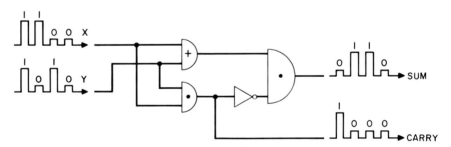

FIG. 6–3   Alternative Circuit for Half-Adder.

6.2   LOGIC CIRCUIT OF FULL ADDER

The *full adder* can handle three digits, as opposed to two for the half-adder. Binary numbers have several digits; for example, the UNIVAC 1108 has 36-digit binary numbers; hence, there are 36 columns to be added. Let's represent the digits in each column by subscripts of X and Y.

$$
\begin{array}{l}
X_0 \ X_1 \ X_2 \ \ldots \ X_{35} \ X_{36} \\
+Y_0 \ Y_1 \ Y_2 \ \ldots \ Y_{35} \ Y_{36} \\
\hline
C_0 \ S_0 \ S_1 \ S_2 \ \ldots \ S_{35} \ S_{36}
\end{array}
$$

Some columns may have a carry to be added to the X and Y digits in that column. In longhand addition we frequently write the carry at the top of the column. Let's write the various subscripts of C at the top of each column.

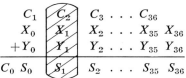

The full adder has three inputs and at least two outputs. It forms the sum and carry for one column in binary addition. Consider the shaded column involving X_1 and Y_1.

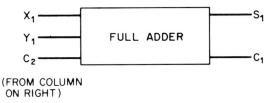

(FROM COLUMN ON RIGHT)

The operation of adding X_1 *to* Y_1 to obtain a sum and carry is familiar. The unresolved operation is adding C_2 to X_1 and Y_1. The full-adder logic circuit is normally a combination of two half-adders:

1. One adds X_1 and Y_1 to obtain an intermediate sum and carry, which we'll call SS_1 and CC_1.
2. The other adds C_2 and SS_1 to obtain S_1 and C_1.

Figure 6–4 shows the full-adder circuit for handling the X_1, Y_1

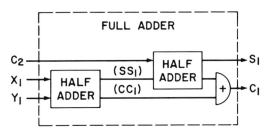

FIG. 6–4 Full-Adder Circuit.

column. If either half-adder generates a carry, the OR gate sends a high pulse to C_1. The output is available after a short time delay for propagation through the adder.

Ex. 6–2

What would be the final output pulse of a full adder in adding the third column from the right?

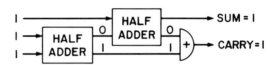

A carry will be generated in the right column and propagate through the third column; hence, the inputs to our adder are all 1's. Figure 6–5 shows the intermediate sum and carry are 0 and 1, respectively. The final sum is 1 and the carry is 1 to the next column on the left.

FIG. 6–5   Pulse Levels in Full-Adder Circuit Handling $1 + 1 + 1$.

6.3   SERIAL FUNCTIONAL ADDER

For a *serial functional adder,* each column of digits is added in turn. All add operations are performed on the same logic circuit. Serial execution permits simpler circuits, thereby reducing cost; but the penalty must be paid in time.

Ex. 6–3

Draw the block diagram and show the timing pulse for a serial adder. Consider

$$
\begin{array}{r}
1\ 0\ 1\ 0 \\
+0\ 1\ 1\ 0 \\
\hline
1\ 0\ 0\ 0\ 0
\end{array}
$$

The pulse sequence for this example is shown in Fig. 6–6. The timing pulse operates the three AND gates to control the flow of X, Y, and C pulses into the adder. For example, the second timing pulse gates the X, Y, and C pulses into the adder. The sum and carry for the second column are available after a short propagation delay. This carry, sometimes called the *carry out,* becomes one of the inputs in adding the third column. Thus, the carry out is delayed one pulse and becomes the *carry in* to be added along with the third pulses of X and Y.

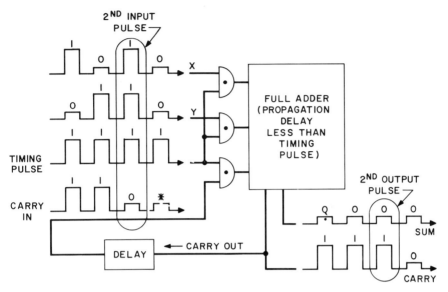

FIG. 6–6   Timing Details of Serial Functional Adder.

An asterisk is shown in Fig. 6–6 over the first pulse of carry in. Because of the delay, the first pulse depends on columns to the right. Assuming that the first pulse represents the rightmost column, then the first carry in is 0.

The answer = 10000 is a combination of sum (all zeros) and the last carry.

The pulse levels shown in Fig. 6–6 exist for only a short time before being replaced by the next pulse in the sequence. Of course, the final answer must exist for a longer time in order that the complete binary number can be transferred to storage or used immediately in the next arithmetic operation. Chapter 7 discusses the details of registers, temporary storage devices. The *shift register* is specially designed for application in the serial functional adder. Binary numbers having 16 to 64 digits are loaded into the shift register in a unique way. For example, a digit may be loaded into the leftmost position. On the next pulse, this digit and all others in the register would be shifted one position to the right, clearing the leftmost position for storage of the next incoming digit. Shift registers in the serial adder accept digits in the sums as they are generated. Also, the input pulses to the serial adder are presented one set at a time; hence, other shift registers are necessary. In Chapter 7 we discuss shift registers for accepting and presenting pulses to adders.

The serial adder is slow by comparison with other devices. For example, the addition of 32-digit numbers takes 52 microseconds on the UNIVAC 9300, whereas 36-digit numbers take 0.75 microseconds on the UNIVAC 1108. As we might suspect, they differ in cost by a factor of 20, a small fraction of which is due to the more capable adder in the 1108. To add 32-digit numbers with the serial adder, the time lapse is 32 multiplied by the propagation time through the adder circuit. This propagation is ideally two logic pulses, resulting in a total lapse of 64 logic pulses.

6.4 PARALLEL-FUNCTIONAL ADDER

For faster operation, several full adders are connected together. The *parallel-functional adder* works quickly on a long number by handling two digits in each column simultaneously. Once this rapid operation is accomplished, the contribution of the carry from the column on the right is processed. The carry operation is disproportionately lengthy unless the adder is properly designed.

*6.5 CARRY RIPPLE

Consider the time lapse in obtaining the sum and carry for the straightforward application of the principles stated so far. The pulse sequences are shown in Fig. 6–7 for adding the following digits on a parallel functional adder.

$$\begin{array}{cccc} & X_0 & X_1 & X_2 \\ + & Y_0 & Y_1 & Y_2 \\ \hline C_0 & S_0 & S_1 & S_2 \end{array} \quad \text{with values} \quad \begin{array}{c} 1\ 0\ 1 \\ +1\ 1\ 1 \\ \hline 1\ 1\ 0\ 0 \end{array}$$

Figure 6–7 shows that the sum is available after six logic pulses. Several notes are shown to describe the occurrences during each logic pulse. The diagram is based on the assumption that the output of a full adder is available within two logic pulses after applying the input.

A delay of six logic pulses is fairly long for an adder that is supposed to be high speed compared to the serial adder. Four pulses are used by the *carry ripple,* which is the name given to the time delay for a carry to propagate through each higher-order position and finally become part of the answer. After two pulses we see that $S_2 = 0$, which is a final value,* and $S_1 = 1$ and $S_0 = 0$, which are intermediate values to be further modified by adding the carry from lower-order positions. During pulse three

* Each final value is temporarily stored in a flip-flop (see page 95) to await completion of the add operation.

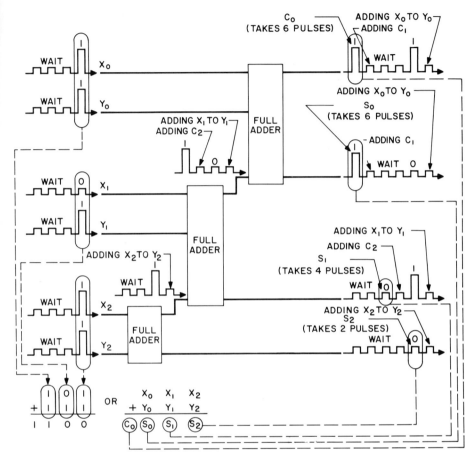

FIG. 6–7 Parallel-Functional Adder with Carry Ripple Takes Six Logic Pulses to Add 3-Digit Binary Numbers.

and four, C_2 is added to the intermediate sum of S_1 and C_1 to obtain a final value of $S_1 = 0$ and $C_1 = 1$. The carry goes forward to the adder handling X_0 and Y_0, and results in the final value of $S_0 = 1$ and $C_0 = 1$ on the sixth pulse.

Ex. 6–4

Consider

$$
\begin{array}{ccc}
1\ 0\ 1 & & X_0\ X_1\ X_2 \\
+1\ 0\ 1 & \text{or} & +Y_0\ Y_1\ Y_2 \\
\hline
1\ 1\ 1\ 0 & & C_0\ S_0\ S_1\ S_2
\end{array}
$$

What pulse sequence will appear on the S_1 terminal?

The diagram in Fig. 6–7 is an aid in finding S_1. After considering that diagram, we can draw the pulse sequence in Fig. 6–8, showing that S_1

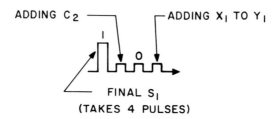

FIG. 6–8   Pulse Sequence on S_1 Terminal of Parallel-Functional Adder for $X_1 = 0$, $Y_1 = 0$, and $C_1 = 1$.

first becomes 0 but finally becomes 1 after four logic pulses.

The timing details of the parallel adder are shown in Fig. 6–9. The operating speed depends on the time delay to span the carry time. The large AND gates and arrows in Fig. 6–9 represent multiple-wire trans-

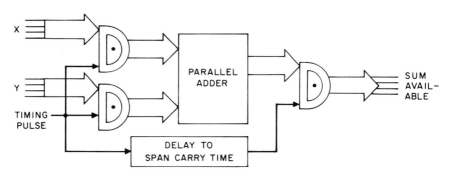

FIG. 6–9   Timing Details of Parallel-Functional Adder.

mission paths. For example, parallel adders have 36 wires and a bank of 36 AND gates, each opened by a timing pulse to allow X and Y to flow to the adder. After the delay to span the carry time, the multiple outputs are gated from their temporary storage in flip-flops to become the final output.

*6.6   LOGIC CIRCUIT OF LOOK-AHEAD CARRY BY GROUPS

A large number of arithmetic operations in a scientific computer are centered around the parallel-functional adder. It is important for high-speed operation that the time delay to span the carry ripple be reduced. The condition of a long ripple in the carry occurs in the following examples:

$$
\begin{array}{c}
1\ 1\ 1\ 1\ 1 \\
+0\ 0\ 0\ 0\ 1 \\
\hline
1\ 0\ 0\ 0\ 0\ 0
\end{array}
\qquad\qquad
\begin{array}{c}
0\ 0\ 0\ 0\ 1 \\
+1\ 1\ 1\ 1\ 1 \\
\hline
1\ 0\ 0\ 0\ 0\ 0
\end{array}
$$

The carry is *generated* in the adder at a low-order position and then *propagated* through the entire bank of adders. Even if we assume the ideal case of two-level logic, a delay of two logic pulses is required for the carry to advance one position. For this five-digit example, the carry would require 8 logic pulses. The sum is available after $8 + 2$ pulses for add $=$ 10 pulses. For a parallel adder handling 32-digit numbers, the sum is available after $62 + 2 = 64$ pulses. Fortunately, it is possible to use extra circuitry to increase the speed of handling the carry. This feature of adders is called *look-ahead carry*. The concept is based on whether an incoming carry or a generated carry from within a group of positions will be propagated out of the group to higher-order positions.

Parallel adders featuring look-ahead carry have two extra terminals, P and G. If either or both digits in a column are 1, then an incoming carry will be *propagated* to the next position on the left. Thus, $X + Y = P$ expresses the logical relationship between inputs and the output, P. There will be a carry *generated* if both X and Y are 1. Therefore, $X \cdot Y = G$. The P and G terminals are necessary along with the regular C and S terminals, as shown in Fig. 6–10.

Time savings are attainable with these extra terminals. Within the time lapse of only two logic delays, outputs are available at the P and G terminals because they are based only on the two input digits. Thus, the *outputs for C, S, P, and G are available simultaneously.*

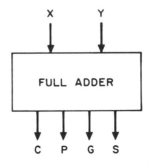

FIG. 6–10   Full Adder with P and G as Extra Terminals Are Used in Parallel-Functional Adders Having Look-Ahead Carry Feature.

The normal procedure to achieve a speedup in the carry is to group the adders for two or more positions (usually about four), as shown in Fig. 6–11.

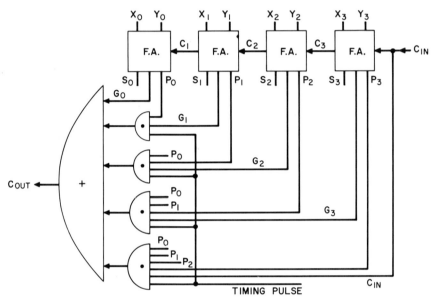

FIG. 6–11   Circuit for Handling P and G Output in a Four-Position Group of a Parallel-Functional Adder Having Look-Ahead Carry Feature.

The carry out for the group is available within two logic delays after arrival of the carry in. In the next group to the left, the look-ahead feature will quickly send another carry on its way. For 36-digit numbers, there would be nine groups of four. The carry out of any group is given by

$$C_{\text{OUT}} = G_0 + P_0 \cdot (G_1 + P_1 \cdot (G_2 + P_2 \cdot (G_3 + P_3 \cdot (C_{\text{IN}}))))$$

Ex. 6–5

Assume that at least one carry is generated. Will it appear as a carry out for the group?

Yes; it will be sent to the next group if it propagates through all positions to the left. Assume that $G_2 = 1$; the carry out is 1 if P_0 and $P_1 = 1$.

The carry in will propagate through all stages in the group if all P terminals have an output of 1. Thus, the carry to the next group, regardless of size, is available in minimum time. The carry situation for each group can be processed in only one pulse after the P and G terminals are set. Thus, the carry time for a 32-digit number would be eight pulses.

Ex. 6–6

It would seem that the carry time can be shortened by using larger groups. Is there a practical limit on the group size?

Yes. The limit is reached when the fan in* exceeds practical limits. Most standard logic gates have fan in limits of eight or less. We see that the bottom AND gate in the preceding circuit has six inputs. The corresponding gate in a five-stage group would have seven inputs.

The practical limit is accessed from the following considerations:

1. The carry time is *eight logic pulses* for a 32-digit number handled in groups of four.
2. The processing of the carry within groups also takes two pulses × four stages = *eight logic pulses* to set the final sums.

Thus, the carry out and all final sums, except for those in the last group, are available simultaneously.

Look-ahead carry by groups increases the speed of operation for the parallel-functional adder. Consider the addition of 32-digit binary numbers:

1. After two logic pulses, the carry and tentative sums are available.
2. After eight more pulses, the final carry out is determined, assuming groups of four.
3. After six more pulses the final sum is set. It takes a total of eight pulses to process the carry within groups, including the leftmost group. However, there is a two-pulse delay in this group before the final carry out in (2) is available.

With the look-ahead carry, the final output is available after a 16-pulse delay, which is considerably less than the 64-pulse delay associated with the carry ripple.

* See Section 3.6 for discussion of fan out and fan in.

7 Registers and Counters

Arithmetic operations involve registers for temporary data storage and counters for timing events. In a functional adder, for example, registers store data words entering and leaving the units. This information is transferred into at least three registers before the computed sum is available. These are the memory-buffer register, B register, and accumulator. Counters generate a continuous sequence of pulses that serve to keep events in the proper time sequence. Timing pulses generally appear as input to AND gates along with the inputs being timed. For example, the timing pulse in Fig. 7–1 causes inputs such as X, Y, and Z to be propagated

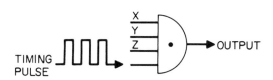

FIG. 7–1   Use the Timing Pulses to Open an AND Gate for Inputs X, Y, Z.

through an AND gate. In a typical application, the counter can generate a pulse to gate the computed sum to the proper register immediately after the preset carry time has elapsed.

Logic circuits for registers and counters are presented in this chapter. The approach is basic and serves as a useful application of the principles of logic design.

7.1 LOGIC CIRCUIT OF FLIP-FLOPS AS BASIC REGISTER UNIT

Registers are storage devices capable of *high-speed* operation. In most applications they are used for *temporary storage,* rather than permanent storage, to take advantage of this speed. Data may be stored only a few microseconds before being transmitted elsewhere and new data stored in its place. Register capacities range from a low of 16 digits to a high of 128 digits.

The *building block of a register is the flip-flop,* which is capable of storing one digit. The flip-flop has two inputs, as shown in Fig. 7–2. The

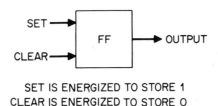

SET IS ENERGIZED TO STORE 1
CLEAR IS ENERGIZED TO STORE 0

FIG. 7–2   Basic Terminals for a Flip-Flop.

output is high or low to indicate the storage of 1 or 0, respectively. The flip-flop has other names, including *latch, toggle,* and *bistable multivibrator.* The term bistable is descriptive because at any given time the device is in one of two possible states. Rapid data exchange gives the illusion that the device is a vibrator.

The first step in designing logic circuits is a word description. The flip-flop circuit is based on the following *rules of operation.*

1. Normally both inputs are 0. For neither input energized, the output remains at its *present state* of either 1 or 0.
2. If SET is brought to 1, the output goes to 1 and remains energized regardless of the present state or subsequent changes in SET. Thus, a short pulse to SET will energize the output for an indefinite time (1 is stored).
3. The output will change to 0 only if CLEAR is energized. Once this occurs, subsequent changes in CLEAR have no effect. The output remains at its present state and can be changed only by SET as described above (0 is stored).

The truth table obviously involves SET and CLEAR. The present state is another condition that influences the output; hence, it is included to give three input variables.

	Inputs		Output
Present State	*SET*	*CLEAR*	
0	0	0	0
0	0	1	0
0	1	0	1
0	1	1	0
1	0	0	1
1	0	1	0
1	1	0	1
1	1	1	0

The *algebraic expression* contains three terms corresponding to the three 1's in the output column of the truth table. Let's use the symbols P for present state, S for SET, and C for CLEAR:

$$P' \cdot S \cdot C' + P \cdot S' \cdot C' + P \cdot S \cdot C' = \text{output}$$

which can be reduced to

$$C' \cdot (S + P) = \text{output}$$

Normally, the flip-flop has two output terminals, one being the complement of the other. The flip-flop circuit can be formed from a combination of AND, OR, NOT gates or be entirely NAND or NOR gates. We'll form the circuits for each of these options.

1. The *AND, OR, NOT gate* circuit is shown in Fig. 7–3.

$$C' \cdot (S + P) = \text{output}$$

2. The *NOR gate* circuit is shown in Fig. 7–4.

$$C' \cdot (S + P) = \text{output}$$
$$[C + (S + P)']' = \text{output}$$

3. The NAND *gate* circuit is shown in Fig. 7–5.

$$C' \cdot (S + P) = \text{output}$$
$$C' \cdot (S' \cdot P')' = \text{output}$$

It is common practice to use a version of the circuit in Fig. 7–6(a) and to illustrate the flip-flop as shown in Fig. 7–6(b).

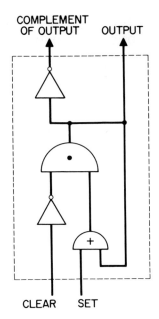

FIG. 7–3   Circuit for a Flip-Flop.

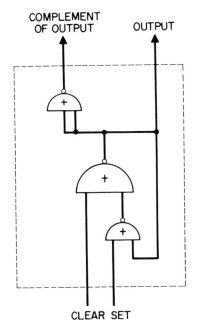

FIG. 7–4   NOR Gate Flip-Flop.

COMPLEMENT
OF OUTPUT   OUTPUT

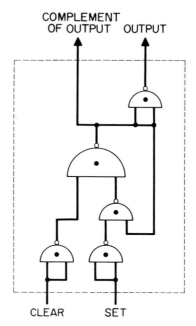

CLEAR   SET

FIG. 7–5   NAND Gate Flip-Flop.

7.2   *N*-POSITION REGISTER

A register is a series of flip-flop circuits used to *store a group* of binary digits. It is apparent that a flip-flop can *store a single* digit. To store a 1, the SET line is energized; to store a 0 the CLEAR line is energized. A register is simply a group of flip-flops. The block diagram in Fig. 7–7(a) illustrates the arrangement for a five-position register.

Binary digits are entered into a register in a two-step operation:

1.   Clear all positions to zero.
2.   Set the appropriate stages to 1.

Ex. 7–1

Suppose that the input terminals of the five-position register in Fig. 7–7(a) receive the pulse sequences shown in Fig. 7–7(b). What binary number is stored in the register after the third pulse?

The *first pulse* clears the register so that 0's are stored in all positions. The *second pulse* enters the binary number 10011. The SET 4 input represents the least significant digit. The *third pulse,* at first glance, would

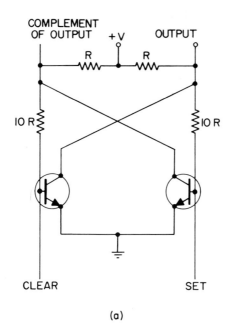

(a)

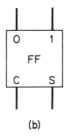

(b)

FIG. 7–6 Flip-Flop: (a) Practical Circuit; (b) Common Symbol.

enter 00111; however, it doesn't. This exercise tests our recall of the rules for flip-flop operation. We remember that once SET is energized, the output remains 1 until CLEAR is energized. Thus, the output of SET 0 remains 1 after the second pulse until CLEAR is energized. The third pulse changes only the output of SET 2 to 1. Therefore, SET 0 = 1; SET 1 = 0; SET 2 = 1; SET 3 = 1; and SET 4 = 1, which gives an answer of 10111.

Registers and Counters

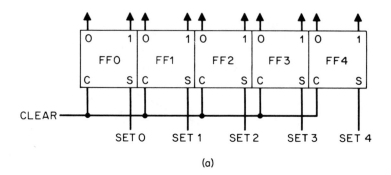

(a)

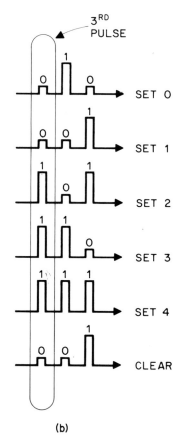

(b)

FIG. 7–7   (a) Five-Position Register; (b) Pulse Sequences Analyzed in Ex. 7–1.

Registers are temporary data-storage devices; hence, data is repeatedly entering and leaving registers. Often the data came from or are going to another register. It is important that *data transfer between registers* be handled easily. Figure 7–8 shows a simple arrangement for simultaneous

B – REGISTER

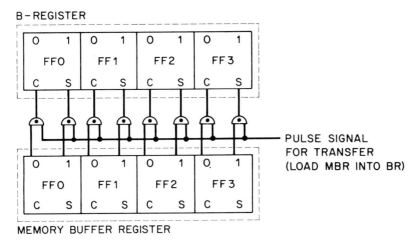

PULSE SIGNAL
FOR TRANSFER
(LOAD MBR INTO BR)

MEMORY BUFFER REGISTER

FIG. 7–8   Parallel Transfer between Registers.

transfer of digits in all register positions. For example, digits are moved by *parallel transfer* from memory-buffer register to the B register in a parallel-functional adder.

Ex. 7–2

Form the one's complement of a three-digit binary number entering a parallel-functional adder.

The one's complement, of course, is formed by changing 1's to 0's and vice versa. It is a common operation to add or subtract the contents of the B register from the accumulator. The one's complement is formed in subtraction operations.

Figure 7–9 shows the arrangement for forming the one's complement of the binary digits being transferred from the B register to the X terminals of the adder. The Y terminals in an actual adder would be connected to the accumulator. The input to the X terminal will be 1 from all flip-flops storing a 1 if adding, or storing a 0 if subtracting.

The pulse signal to add or subtract originates in the computer control section. In Chapter 10 we discuss the execution of the programmer's instruction that leads to *generation of control signals*.

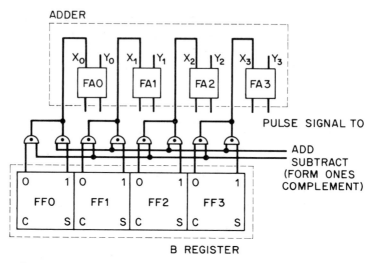

FIG. 7–9 Transfer of B Register Contents to Adder.

7.3 SHIFT REGISTER

In Chapter 6 we mentioned that the input data to the serial adder are presented one digit at a time from the B register and the accumulator. The output data are accepted in a similar fashion by another register, or perhaps by the unfilled flip-flops in the accumulator. The shift register is specially designed to present input data or accept output data of serial units.

In the B register, for example, the binary digit stored in each flip-flop will be *shifted one position* each time a shift pulse is applied. Figure 7–10

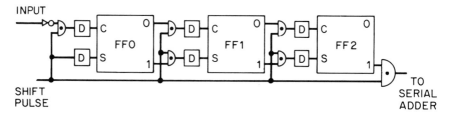

FIG. 7–10 Shift Register.

shows a register that shifts rightward. Of course, the digit in the right position enters the adder.

The three-position register in Fig. 7–10 has AND gates that open on each shift pulse to let signals pass. The net result is to transfer the contents of each flip-flop to the adjacent flip-flop on the right. Thus, *digits are transferred to the right* and replaced with other digits from the left. The delays are introduced to prevent the incoming replacement digits from affecting the situation until enough time has elapsed to be sure that the contents of a given flip-flop are in transit to the right. The output of this flip-flop on the right is connected to an AND gate that also opens upon receipt of the shift pulse to transfer the right digit to the adder.

Shift registers can be constructed so the left position is filled by a pulse sequence from another source at the same time that pulses are being transfered from the right. For example, the adder output may be entered into the left positions of the accumulator. Eventually, the adder output may fill all positions and be ready for the control signal to add the new contents of the accumulator and the B register.

Shift registers may be constructed to shift left rather than right. Regardless of the construction, they function so that each digit is shifted each time a shift pulse is applied.

7.4 LOGIC CIRCUIT OF BINARY TRIGGERS AS BASIC COUNTER UNIT

A counter is a device which *records the number of events* that have occurred. During each event, at least one of several output terminals changes state from *high* to *low* or vice versa. After the changes, the binary combination appearing at the outputs represents a particular state that is different from the state before the event, after the next event, or, perhaps, after the next several events. For example, consider a counter with two outputs, both of which are initially low, making the initial *binary combination 00*. After the first event we will assume one output becomes high: *binary state 01*. The second event might change that output to low and the other output to high: *binary state 10*. The succession of binary combinations 00, 01, 10, *and finally 11* is obviously *binary counting*.

The input to a counter is normally the equally spaced *pulses from the clock*. The counter changes state after each of these pulses. Figure 7–11 shows the sequence of output states for a *two-position counter*.

In a typical application, the output pulses are used to open AND

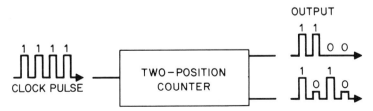

FIG. 7–11   Pulse Output for a Two-Position Counter.

gates to allow signal transmission at the proper time. For example, the
bottom output in Fig. 7–11 could be used to open an AND gate every
second clock pulse. We mentioned earlier that the final sum from an adder
was available after 16 pulses; hence, a four-position counter is needed. The
basic building block for the counter is the *binary trigger*. We remember
that the flip-flop is the basic building block for the register. In fact, the
binary trigger is derived from the flip-flop by adding a T *terminal*.

Counters record the number of changes in the input state. The logic
in the trigger is designed to give a *change in state when a positive-going
signal is applied to the T terminal*. Of course, the signal amplitude must be
of sufficient level to energize the flip-flop. The truth table for the trigger
shows that the present state is changed to a new state for $T = 1$.

Inputs		Output
Present State	T	New State
0	0	0 (no change)
0	1	1 (energize SET)
1	0	1 (no change)
1	1	0 (energize CLEAR)

The logic circuit must be designed so that SET is energized when
$T = 1$ and present state $= 0$. CLEAR is energized when $T = 1$ and
present state $= 1$. Figure 7–12(a) shows that the logic circuit consists of

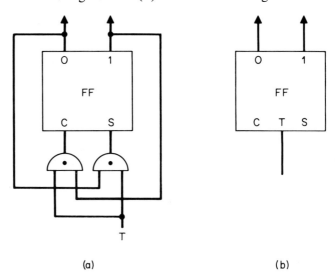

(a)   (b)

FIG. 7–12   Binary Trigger: (a) Gates for Handling T Terminal; (b) Common Symbol.

two AND gates connecting the T terminal to SET and CLEAR. The binary trigger is usually shown diagrammatically, as in Fig. 7–12(b).

7.5   *N*-POSITION BINARY COUNTERS

Counters have one trigger flip-flop for each binary position. Clock pulses enter the trigger associated with the lowest-order position. Its output is connected to the T terminal of an adjacent trigger.

Consider the output (and complement) of a trigger with a clock pulse input as shown in Fig. 7–13.

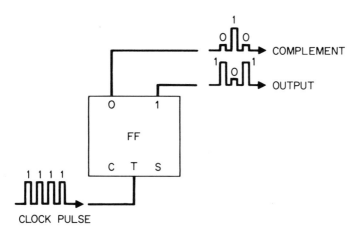

FIG. 7–13   Pulse Outputs for Binary Trigger.

For four input pulses there are only two output pulses, because the interval between pulses has doubled. There is an output pulse for every other clock pulse. The frequency of the output is one half that of the input. The frequency of an electrical signal normally refers to the number of pulses per second, as shown in Table 7–1.

The counter generates several signals having frequency that is $\frac{1}{2}$, $\frac{1}{4}$, $\frac{1}{8}$, . . . of the clock frequency.

The clock pulses in most computers are somewhat higher in frequency than 1 megahertz. Assuming a clock pulse of 4 megahertz is the trigger input, we know the output frequency will be 2 megahertz. This signal or its complement could be connected to the T terminal of another trigger to give an output of 1 megahertz. An *N*-position binary counter is formed by interconnecting triggers in this manner. Actually, the complement of the output is used.

The three-position binary counter shown in Fig. 7–14 has three

TABLE 7–1
Frequency of Electrical Signals

Pulses per Second	Frequency	Time Interval between Pulses
1	1 hertz	1 second
1000	1 kilohertz	1 millisecond
1,000,000	1 megahertz	1 microsecond

output terminals that change from 000 to 001, to 010, . . . , and so on. After seven pulses, all outputs would be high or in state 111, which the binary number for 7.

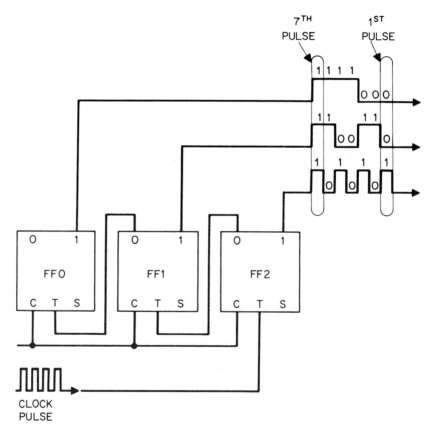

FIG. 7–14   Pulses Showing the Principles of Binary Counting.

Several stages could be added to the counter to increase the counting range. For example, a four-position counter can handle 16 binary counts.

What is the eighth state for the three-position binary counter in Fig. 7–14?

The eighth pulse causes the contents to change from 1 to *0 in FF2*. The complement of the FF2 output becomes 1. This positive-going pulse causes the contents to change from 1 to *0 in FF1*. By similar arguments, we see there will be *0 in FF0*. The net combination of these actions yields an *answer of 000*. The counter is cyclic, returning to its *original state after every sequence of 8 pulses*.

*7.6 PARALLEL BINARY COUNTERS

Now that we understand the general operating characteristics of a binary counter, we can discuss the logic design for other configurations. The counter in Fig. 7–14 can be designed for *greater flexibility*.

The limited flexibility of the counter in Fig 7–14 can be illustrated. The counter is normally CLEARED to 000 before commencing a count. We may want to start the counter at a binary state other than 000. Suppose that the present state is 011 where FF2 contains 1, FF1 contains 1, and FF0 contains 0. The *interaction between triggers* causes trouble if we attempt to enter 0 in FF1, for example. As soon as FF1 changes state, a positive-going pulse will appear at its complement output and cause an *unwanted change* in the state of FF0. Thus, we attempted to change from 011 to 001 but instead changed to 101.

The *parallel binary counter* can be started at any desired state by energizing the appropriate SET terminals. The clock pulses are connected directly to AND gates at the individual *T* terminals, as shown in Fig. 7–15. A delay is necessary in the transmission path from the trigger output. If the trigger changes state, the change will be delayed from entering the AND gate until shortly before the next pulse. The operation of the parallel binary counter is covered in Ex. 7–4.

Consider the three-position parallel counter in Fig. 7–15, which contains 011 where FF2 contains 1, FF1 contains 1, and FF0 contains 0. What will be the binary state after the next input pulse?

In the present state both AND gates are open. Thus, the next pulse enters the *T* terminal of all three triggers and they all change state, going from 011 to 100. The counting continues in sequence, as shown in Fig. 7–16.

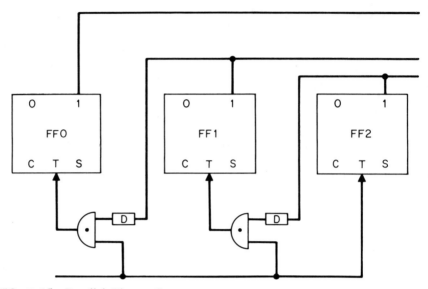

FIG. 7–15 Parallel Binary Counter.

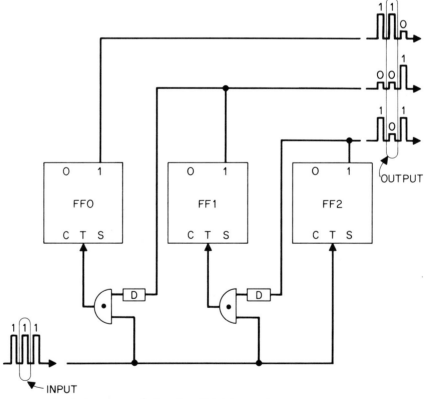

FIG. 7–16 Pulse Outputs for Parallel Binary Counter.

108

*7.7 LOGIC CIRCUIT OF ENCODERS AND DECODERS

The language of people is converted to one of the binary codes by a logic circuit called an *encoder*. The reverse operation is accomplished by a *decoder*. Thus, binary-coded information is involved in both instances; it is the output of an encoder and the input to a decoder. For example, logic circuits are used to convert decimal digits into binary numbers and vice versa. Other circuits are used to convert to and from binary-coded decimal digits. Exercise 7–5 presents the logic circuit for converting decimal digits to binary-coded decimal digits.

Ex. 7–5

Design a logic circuit to convert the decimal digits 0 through 9 to binary-coded decimal digits for storage in a four-position register.

The circuit will have 10 input terminals, one for each decimal digit, and four output terminals, one for energizing each of the flip-flops in the register. Thus, we can construct the truth table.

Inputs	*Outputs*			
9 8 7 6 5 4 3 2 1 0	*SET FF0* (Eight's)	*SET FF1* (Four's)	*SET FF2* (Two's)	*SET FF3* (Unit's)
0 0 0 0 0 0 0 0 0 1	0	0	0	0
0 0 0 0 0 0 0 0 1 0	0	0	0	1
0 0 0 0 0 0 0 1 0 0	0	0	1	0
0 0 0 0 0 0 1 0 0 0	0	0	1	1
0 0 0 0 0 1 0 0 0 0	0	1	0	0
0 0 0 0 1 0 0 0 0 0	0	1	0	1
0 0 0 1 0 0 0 0 0 0	0	1	1	0
0 0 1 0 0 0 0 0 0 0	0	1	1	1
0 1 0 0 0 0 0 0 0 0	1	0	0	0
1 0 0 0 0 0 0 0 0 0	1	0	0	1

Using the sum-of-products, we obtain the following expressions for the outputs:

$$\text{Unit's} = 1 + 3 + 5 + 7 + 9$$
$$\text{Two's} = 2 + 3 + 6 + 7$$
$$\text{Four's} = 4 + 5 + 6 + 7$$
$$\text{Eights's} = 8 + 9$$

These expressions lead directly to the logic circuit shown in Fig. 7–17.

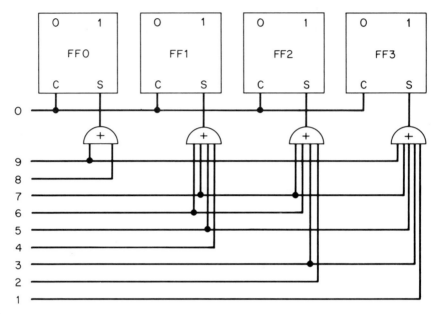

FIG. 7–17   Circuit for Encoding Decimal Digits to Binary-Coded Decimal
Digits.

Sometimes a teletypewriter is used to enter the decimal digits. The operator simply depresses the appropriate key on the keyboard. For example, if the 9 key is depressed the 9 input terminal is energized, and the net effect is to store 1001 in the four-position register.

Decoders are used in every computer to convert some previous encoding. For example, the decimal numbers 23 and 35 may have been encoded and then added. The decoder converts the sum to the original decimal language.

8 Memory

Instructions and data are moved from memory to the control unit or arithmetic unit where operations are handled at an extremely high speed. Data in the B register of the arithmetic unit can be added to the accumulator contents in a few millionths of a second. The control unit processes incoming instructions at an even higher rate. With this incredible speed, the computer appears to be capable of over 100,000 additions per second. However, the cost limitation of computer design causes the practical level to be 10,000 to 50,000 operations per second. During each operation cycle, a significant amount of time is devoted to fetching the data from the computer memory.

Memories having the shortest *cycle time* are the most costly and, therefore, are used sparingly. Cycle time is defined to be the interval of time required to fetch a data word and then return the memory control to the original state ready for the next fetch signal.

The give and take in designing for low cost, high capacity, and high speed have led to a variety of memory elements. Punched cards, paper tapes, and magnetic tapes offer low cost per stored digit. With this economic virtue, these storage methods are the most used despite their disadvantage of having the longest cycle time. Electronic flip-flops are high-speed memory devices. Advancements are being made constantly in the manufacture of lower-cost electronic circuits, and some memories are electronic.

The *magnetic-core memory* is a reasonable compromise between speed and cost. It is based on principles observed by high school physics students in magnetizing an iron strip to have a north and south pole. The poles can be reversed by remagnetizing in the opposite direction. Iron retains magnetism and its direction; hence, the principle can be used to store binary digits. One direction could be defined to be 0 and the opposite direction could be 1.

The first computer having a magnetic-core memory was the Whirlwind I, which was built by the Massachusetts Institute of Technology in 1955. Since then, the use of this memory concept has become so widespread that computer memories are often called "core" for short. Most of our discussion on memory elements is on magnetic-core devices.

Data for other memory devices are presented in Table 8–1 for comparison. Metal oxide semiconductors (MOS) memories are nearly the same cost per digit as magnetic core. Compared to core, they are smaller, faster, and operate on lower power. Metal oxide semiconductor memories are used in the IBM 370 computers.

8.1 COMPARISON OF MEMORY AND STORAGE DEVICES

There is a general tendency in the computer field to use the short terms, memory and storage, to differentiate between internal and external units. The main *memory* is composed of internal elements that are working in fetching and storing instructions during program execution. It combines with the control and arithmetic units to form the central processor. In most memories, the elements retain binary information by magnetic effects.

Storage devices are a broad category, which includes everything outside the central processor plus the functional registers within the processor. External storage is used to transfer information to the internal memory in most program runs. This buffer function is normally assigned to magnetic-tape units. Auxiliary storage is used in situations where it is desired to extend the capacity of the internal memory. Magnetic discs and drums are well suited for this application.

The concept of virtual memory is based on using magnetic discs to extend the core memory to nearly 20 million digits. Ninety-eight to ninety-nine percent of this capacity is on the discs. The real memory is a typical capacity internal memory. During a processing run with virtual memory, data groups that are active stay in the internal memory. Groups are moved to the discs within a moment after becoming inactive. The back-and-forth movement necessitates a fairly complex interface between the disc and the internal memory. These extra logic circuits keep track of memory addresses and disc addresses of each group. Most IBM 370 computers are equipped with virtual-memory provisions. Other manufacturers also use the virtual concept; in fact, they used it for nearly 10 years before IBM.

Programs are formed on a stack of low-cost punched cards. The cards contain the data and the instructions for processing those data. The information on the punched cards usually is transferred to magnetic tapes for fast transfer to internal memory. In general, buffers compensate for the difference in data-handling rate when transferring data from one device

6 ROM - What is it used for, what is its cycle time (Cycle Time)

7 Instruction Word - what does it contain?

8 Execution of Instruction

   Instruction cycle - Decode OP - Fetched & decoded OP

   Execution cycle - Obtained data addressed & performed OP function.

Quiz

Ch 1

Ch 7   Registers, memories (difference)

Ch 8   1, 2, 3

Ch 10   1, 2, 3, 4, 5.

Ch 11   1, 2, 3, 4.

How to Design Your Own Computer, P. 1, 2, 3, 4, 5.

Fig. 1, 2, 3, 4

Mostec   P. 1, 2, 3, 30.

1   History   (Babbage) (Von Neumann) (Hollerith) (Univac) (IBM)

2   What makes up a computer/calculator?

3   "   Data Flow?

     "   (Register, ALU, Data paths.

4   CPU - Data Flow, control, & R/W
         ↳ Registers ALU   (Command)

to another. With the tapes doing the buffering, the internal memory is loaded with less waiting. The internal memory exchanges data with electronic flip-flop registers in the arithmetic unit. The various stages of memory help circumvent the unwieldly differences in operating speed between two stages. Of course, it is uneconomical for programmers to commence with storages more costly than punched cards.

In the remaining sections in this chapter we discuss the cost, speed, and capacity of memory elements and present the fundamentals of magnetic-core memories. Magnetic tapes, discs, and drums also are discussed.

In physical appearance the external storage units are a large-scale version of familiar audio equipment in home entertainment systems. The magnetic tape resembles the stereophonic recording tape; the magnetic disc resembles a stack of phonograph records; and the magnetic drum resembles the antique phonograph cylinders. Further details on their configuration and operation are given in Sections 8.4 through 8.6.

8.1.1   Function Versus Cost

Binary digits are stored in groups that are assigned to one of the thousands of memory locations. These groups are fetched to the central processing unit, where the arithmetic unit rapidly performs the operation specified in the coded program. The next operation could involve data from a memory location (address), which may be out of the sequential order. Therefore, it is imperative that the internal memory be *random access,* meaning that the time to fetch data is not dependent on the address of data most recently fetched. It is obvious that magnetic tape is not random access, but rather sequential access. The adjacent group of data on the tape can be fetched quicker than data several feet away on the tape. The advantages of random access are provided in semiconductor and magnetic-core memories. For most practical purposes, drums and discs also are random access.

The manufacturers of memory units advertise the operating speed by quoting the access time or the cycle time, and sometimes both. The *access time* is the delay between when memory receives a control signal calling for data and when the data become available. The *cycle time* is the time lapse for the memory to fetch (or store) a group of data and then return to a state ready for the next fetch (or store) signal. The cycle time is a direct measure of the operating speed and will be used in our discussion. We'll use the abbreviations 1 μs and ms for one millionth of a second and one thousandth of a second, respectively. The access time is usually about one half the cycle time. We'll avoid using access time as a gauge of memory speed. It probably originated as an advertising gimmick.

Table 8–1 summarizes the speed, capacity, and cost information for memory units. The information gives us an approximate scale for comparing memory characteristics.

TABLE 8–1

Speed	*Capacity*
Very High Speed	*Large Capacity*
(Cycle time less than 1 μs)	(10 million binary digits or over)
Electronic devices such as flip-flops make very high speed registers and small memories. Semiconductor memories have cycle times ranging from 0.05 μs for bipolar devices to 0.5 μs for MOS devices.	Magnetic tape stores 200 million binary digits per reel at a cost of 0.00002 cent/digit. Magnetic disc pack stores 200 to 160 million digits at a cost of 0.005 cent/ digit. Magnetic drum stores 4 to 200 million digits at a cost of 0.1 cent/digit. Magnetic disc and MOSFET store nearly 20 million digits at a cost of 0.05 cent/digit.
High Speed	
(Cycle time to 10 μs)	*Medium Capacity*
Magnetic-core memories have cycle times ranging from 0.5 to 2.0 μs.	(0.1 to 10 million binary digits) Magnetic core is typically 0.26 million digits. Storage cost is approximately 6 cents/digit.
Medium Speed	
(Cycle time greater than 1 ms)	*Small Capacity*
These storage devices usually serve as auxiliary or external memory. The approximate cycle time of magnetic drum is 8 ms; magnetic disc is 20 to 60 ms; and magnetic tape is as low as 3 ms for the next group of digits in sequence. Tape is slower for nonsequential fetches.	(100,000 binary digits or less) Electronic devices are limited to this capacity because of cost, which is approximately 15 cents/digit.

8.1.2 Matching Memory Device with Application

Semiconductors, magnetic cores, tapes, discs, and drums all perform well in their respective missions. Some devices are better suited than others to particular applications. For example, bulk storage is a job for magnetic tape. Our census and tax records are stored on hundreds of reels of magnetic tape. Access to these data would take several minutes, which might appear slow compared to 1-μs cycle time for magnetic core. However, few taxpayers are in a hurry to have their records reviewed. The operator would order the tape from a storage rack, take it to a tape reader, and advance the tape in the reader to the inch or so of tape where our tax data are recorded.

Let's consider another memory device that is well suited to it's application. Operational registers are high-speed devices for transferring information to and from the arithmetic unit. These electronic devices are discussed in Chapter 7.

8.1.3 Internal Memory and External Storage

Figure 8–1 illustrates the interfacing of internal memory with external storage and the input/output devices. In this diagram, magnetic-tape units are used as buffers, and discs and drums are used as auxiliary storage. Buffers and auxiliary storage units are optional to the basic operation of

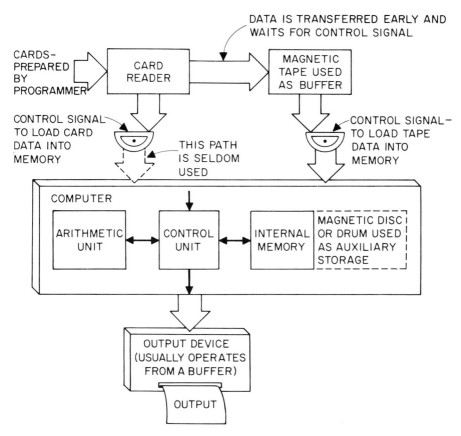

FIG. 8–1   Interfacing Storage Devices with Internal Memory.

the computer. Most large-scale computers systems have five to ten magnetic-tape units and a disc or a drum unit.

Auxiliary storage devices handle programs or data that exceed the capacity of the internal memory. The information in auxiliary storage may contain both short-term and long-term segments of data and programs. For example, steps 5602 through 5928 of a program may be stored on a disc for the short time it takes to complete the preceding steps. When ready, the stored steps would be transferred to the internal memory.

In the case of virtual memory, the continuous exchanges make the external storage an effective expansion of the internal memory. Programmers are free to formulate programs that require nearly 50 times the real capacity of internal memory. The compiler and controller function to move information back to the proper memory address before it is needed.

8.2   MAGNETIC-CORE MEMORY

The magnetic-core memory in a large-scale computer usually occupies a volume approximately the size of a filing cabinet. Binary digits can be stored on each of the millions of small ring-shaped pieces of magnetic material. These cores are smaller than the head of a pin.

Binary digits, 1 or 0, are stored according to fairly simple magnetic principles. The familiar bar magnet has a north and south pole defining the direction of magnetism. The polarity can be established by applying an electrical current through windings around the bar magnet. The polarity can be reversed by reversing the direction of the current.

The direction of magnetism in the ring can be either clockwise or counterclockwise. The direction can be reversed by reversing the direction of current flow in a wire threaded through the ring. This two-state existence is compatible with the 0 and 1 concept of the binary number system. Thus, one binary digit can be stored on each core.

8.2.1   Random Access of Two-Dimensional Core Arrays

The magnetic-core memory is configured in an ingenious layout that permits any group of stored digits to be fetched with the same ease as any other group. This desirable feature is termed *random access,* meaning that the time required to access a randomly selected memory location does not depend on the location most recently accessed.

The random-access property is achieved by threading the proper wires through each magnetic ring. All rings are threaded in exactly the same manner. The magnetizing currents are carried by wires called *drivers.* Two drivers are used, each carrying current $I/2$. These are called X and Y drivers.

Currents beyond the *threshold level, I,* cause the core to be magnetized even after the current is removed. Thus, only a short time pulse is needed to permanently magnetize the core and thereby store a 1 or 0. This stored digit can be changed by another pulse of current in the opposite direction, provided it is beyond the threshold level.

Ex. 8–1

Is the magnetic core permanently magnetized by a current below the threshold level? For example, consider a current of $I/2$.

No. Ferrite material must be saturated with the magnetic flux induced by the current-carrying wire. Otherwise, the magnetic state of the ferrite returns to the original state as soon as the current flow ceases. This physical phenomenon is used in designing the *magnetic-core memory for random access.*

The array size in most computers is 64 by 64, containing 4096 core elements. The 3 by 3 array in Fig. 8–2 illustrates the random-access feature of the larger arrays. The *coincident-current* selection technique is based on applying one half the threshold current to all the core elements

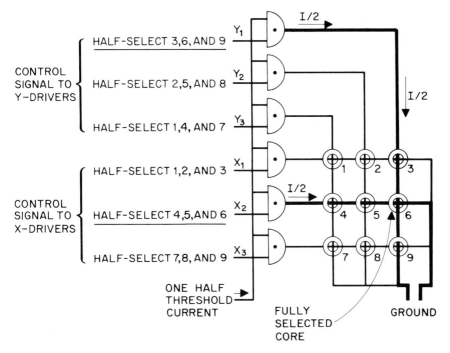

FIG. 8–2 Random Access to Cores by Coincident Current Selection.

in a selected row and a selected column of the array. One core element will be in both the selected row and column; therefore, it will receive the full threshold current. In Fig. 8–2 we see control signals to X_2 and Y_1 cause current $I/2$ to be gated to the middle row (X_2 driver) and the right-hand column (Y_1 driver). These core elements are half-selected. Core element number 6 is *fully selected* and remains magnetized even after the pulse is terminated. Any core element can be selected with the same ease. For example, control signals to X_3 and Y_3 cause core element number 7 to be magnetized.

The terms *read and write* are used to refer to the operation of extracting and entering binary digits into memory. With the coincident-current technique, writing into core memory is straightforward. It takes only 0.2 to 0.5 μs for the write operation. The read operation takes longer. Despite the best efforts of designers, the read is a *destructive read,* because the stored digits in the core are erased and consequently must be rewritten after the read. The cycle time is 1 to 2 μs for the read, rewrite, and then return to the original state ready for the next read.

The read operation uses the two driver wires and a *sense wire,* which is threaded through all the cores in an array. For example, a single sense wire would be threaded through all 4096 core elements in a 64 by 64 array. Sense wires are used to determine whether cores in the array contain a 0 or 1. The magnetic devices cause a pulse of current to flow in the sense wire if any of the cores suddenly changes in magnetic state.

The contents of a particular core are read by applying $I/2$ to the X and Y drivers that are threaded through that core. The direction of the driver current is such to cause the core to become magnetized in the direction corresponding to the 0 state. If the present state is 1, the driver current will cause a sudden change in the direction of magnetism as the core changes to the 0 state. This action causes a pulse of current in the sense wire. On the other hand, the driver current will not change the core to 0 if it is already 0. Thus, we have a current pulse for core content of 1 and no pulse for core content of 0.

Any core in the array can be read with equal ease by selecting the appropriate X and Y drivers. The magnetic-core memory is, therefore, random access for both read and write.

The read operation destroys the contents of the core because, regardless of the previous state, the new contents will be 0 state. It is essential that information be retained after it has been read.

A bank of flip-flops holds the contents and awaits the rewrite phase of the read operation. This rewrite step is straightforward. The core's state, being observed by the sense wire, can be amplified and used to set a pair of flip-flops associated with that particular row and column. The read and rewrite are completed before commencing the next read cycle. Of course, the cycle time includes the total time lapse.

8.2.2 Random Access of Three-Dimensional Core Arrays

The basic building blocks of core memories are 64 by 64 arrays. Each array has X and Y drivers and a sense wire.

Consider the binary number 011. Would it be wise to enter the store number on a single array? For example, would you recommend storing the 0 in core number 4, the 1 in core number 5, and the other 1 in core number 6? The answer is no for reasons that will become obvious. We'll see that it is wiser to store one digit in each of three arrays.

The assembly of core arrays into a memory has given rise to the term .computer word. In everyday writing, we group letters into words. The *computer word* is the fundamental unit for storing binary digits. Common word lengths are 16, 24, 32, and 36 digits plus one or two extra digits for error-detection purposes.

Core memories are arranged for simplifying the reading and writing of computer words. The arrays are assembled into a three-dimensional arrangement. The number of arrays is equal to the number of digits in the computer word.

The driver windings are interconnected between arrays. For example, a current of $I/2$ applied to X_2 of the top array flows through in the series connection to the X_2 driver of all arrays in the stack. The same sort of series connection is used for the Y drivers.

Suppose that 011 are the first three digits of a word to be stored in the X_2Y_3 position of the top three arrays. A current $I/2$ applied to both X_2 and Y_3 will cause 1's to be written in each of the three top arrays in the X_2Y_3 position. However, for writing 011, we should have 0 in X_2Y_3 position of the top array.

A fourth wire through each core is therefore needed. This line is called an *inhibit wire* and is supplied with an opposing current $I/2$ on those selected lines where a 0 is desired. The opposing current inhibits the writing of a 1. Computer words are written in the three-dimensional arrangement of arrays by applying opposing $I/2$ to the inhibit drivers for each array where 0 is desired, while writing 1 with the X and Y drivers. The inhibit and sense functions usually are achieved with one wire. A switch connects the wire to the sense amplifier during a read and to the inhibit driver during a write.

In summary, the arrays normally contain 4096 cores in a 64 by 64 arrangement. Larger arrays, due to the longer wires, are slower and more easily disturbed by noise sources. A 4096-word memory contains the same number of arrays as there are binary digits in the word. A entire 36-digit word can be fetched or stored by applying current to one X driver and one Y driver. Each array has a sense wire and an inhibit wire. The read operation causes a pulse of current to be induced in the sense wire of all arrays storing a 1. All digits in a word are 0 after reading, which effectively destroys the contents. Flip-flops hold the original information for a fraction of a microsecond and then the information is rewritten into the core memory. The write operation consists of storing a 1 in all 36 cores in a particular XY position and at the same time applying an opposing current to the inhibit wires in those arrays where a 0 is desired.

The overall size of core memory is larger than we might expect from the miniature size of the individual core elements. A memory storing 32-digit words on 64 by 64 arrays is about the size of a double fist. The package includes the cores, driver wires, and the combined sense and inhibit wires. The overall size of a functional three-dimensional memory is nearly 10 times the size of the basic unit. The larger size results from the volume of logic circuits that are needed to control the read and write operations. Figure 8–3 illustrates the various packages surrounding the central core unit.

8.3 FUNDAMENTALS OF MAGNETIC RECORDING ON TAPES, DISCS, AND DRUMS

The common storage devices are based on changing and detecting the direction of magnetic flux at tiny spots on a thin layer of magnetic material. Thin coatings are applied to smooth surfaces that are nonmagnetic. The backup surface does not absorb flux from the magnetic film. Thus, brief pulses of current are sufficient to create one of the two states of flux. The present magnetic state remains after the electronic current that produced it has vanished; therefore, permanent magnetic storage exists.

Magnetic tapes, for example, are made by depositing a layer of magnetic material on plastic tape. Binary information can be kept indefinitely on magnetic tapes or can be erased and the tapes used again for recording new information. The same fundamental phenomenon applies to discs and drums as for tapes. These generally have shorter cycle times and operate satisfactorily as an auxiliary storage device. File shelves can hold an immense quantity of tape-recorded data in a small physical volume.

The magnetic read/write head consists of a split ring formed of high-permeability material around which a coil is wound. The permeability of this core is a measure of the ease with which magnetic fields can be rapidly induced. The direction of current flow through the coil determines whether 1 or 0 is recorded on the storage device. Figure 8–4 shows the relationship between the head and the recording surface.

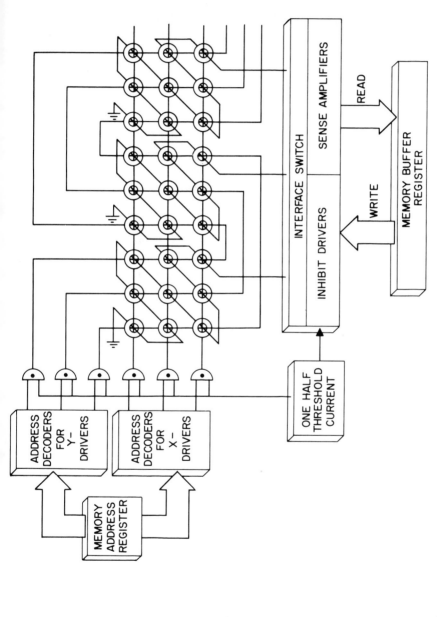

FIG. 8-3 Function Units in Three-Dimensional Core Memory.

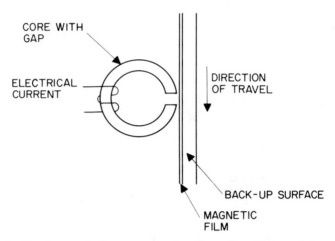

FIG. 8–4 Fundamental Components for Recording Binary Information on Magnetic Storage Devices.

The core provides an easy path for the flux; however, the ring is split with a small gap, usually 0.001 inches wide. At this point, the flux must bridge the gap by passing through the film. Coupling exists through the magnetic material on the tape, disc, or drum in close proximity to the recording head. The head actually does not touch the surface; otherwise, wear would be a problem.

The dimensional aspects of the head-to-surface separation are a critical feature of magnetic recording devices. If the head moves too far from the surface, the recorded signals are weaker. The critical separation necessitates manufacturing the rotating parts to precision dimensions. An operating unit is also affected by thermal expansion, vibration, and bearing wobble.

In tape units the write head has two gaps, one for writing the binary information and the other for immediately reading the record to detect errors. Defects in the film or write head would be in evidence by any discrepancy between the input pulse sequence to the write head and the delayed output pulse sequence from the read head.

The read operation is the reciprocal of write. The magnetic material moves past the reading head (in some cases it is the same head as used for writing). A magnetized spot will couple flux to the split ring. The coupled flux will be sensed by the coil winding and then amplified. Usually, the coil has a center tap with one set of terminals for reading and a heavier gauge set for supplying current in the writing operation.

8.4 MAGNETIC DRUMS

The magnetic material for recording information may be coated on the periphery of drums ranging in size from a few inches to a few feet in diameter. In operation the drum rotates continuously to give a linear velocity at the head that is constant, but may range from 15,000 to 30,000 inches per second, depending on the drum design.

The read/write heads are stationary and usually in a row aligned with the drum axis. Each head records on a track around the drum periphery. Small drums have 15 to 20 tracks and the corresponding 15 to 20 heads. Larger drums have 300 to 400 tracks. For a typical packing density, each inch of track can be magnetized with 600 to 1200 spots (600 to 1200 digits per inch). The reading or writing from a given spot or group of spots can take place at any time as the drum rotates. The location of

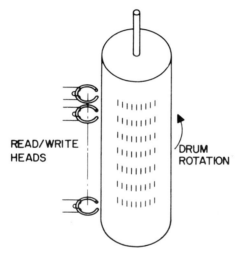

FIG. 8–5 Magnetic Drum with One Read/Write Head per Track.

records is identified by a coded address, which refers to the angular position of the drum relative to the row of heads. One track of the drum is used exclusively as a timing record of the angular position.

The timing track in conjunction with a binary counter provides a means for locating data on the drum. The counter would be set to zero at the same position each time the drum revolves, and advanced one count for each pulse read from the timing track. Say location 1010 is to be read. A register would be loaded with 1010 and compared with the counter contents. The counter will eventually reach 1010, at which time the read would begin and perhaps end at another preset address.

In normal operation the drum is exchanging information, in batch quantities, with the internal core storage. Thus, the access time is important; otherwise, unacceptable delays would be encountered in commencing the processing of each batch. The access time could be as long as it takes for one drum revolution. On the average the access time is one half a drum revolution. Table 8–1 lists a cycle time of 8 ms, which corresponds to 3750 revolutions per minute.

Various schemes exist for achieving faster access. The most obvious method is faster rotation. Speeds of 10,000 revolutions per minute are common. A more expensive approach is using several heads at various positions on the track.

Drums are used for auxiliary storage in applications where the advantages of speed and capacity justify the extra cost over discs. Drums are effective internal memory devices in small-scale computers. They usually are classed as random-access devices, and are handy enough that many medium-scale and most large-scale computers have a drum unit in the basic configuration.

*8.5   MAGNETIC DISCS

In magnetic-disc storage, data is recorded on a layer of magnetic material that is deposited on flat discs. Storing and fetching of binary information proceeds quickly without sequencing through all the records that are filed on other discs.

Magnetic-disc storage is useful for storing master files in data-processing applications. For example, an existing master file for inventory control can be updated quickly to reflect new orders, sales, or other transaction information. Discs and tapes are used to buffer input and output data and for temporary storage of instructions to be transferred to the internal memory at a later time. Discs account for 98 percent of the immense capacity that is addressable in virtual-memory computers. Signals from logic circuits in the central processor unit are continually causing data exchange from the disc to the internal memory. Transfers must be completed before the information is needed in upcoming computations.

Data are stored on the disc in circular tracks that are spaced approximately 0.02 inch apart. The tracks are concentric rather than spiral as are phonograph records. Also, there are no grooves. The packing density along the track is comparable with the drum and typically is 1000 digits per inch. A single recording surface has 200 to 500 tracks and can store from 5 to 50 million binary digits.

The IBM 2311 discs storage drive has six 14-inch discs. It has 200 tracks on each of 10 recording surfaces and a total capacity of 43 million digits. The data transfer rate is 1.25 million digits per second. Figure 8–6 shows the 2311, which is a basic unit in the configuration of the IBM 360

FIG. 8–6   Forty-Million Digits Can Be Stored on This IBM 2311 Disc Storage Unit. (Courtesy of IBM)

Model 20 computer. Further details of this data-processing computer are given in Section 11.3.

The discs in a typical unit are assembled into a disc pack, which is usually a stack of six or nine discs. Spaces of $\frac{1}{2}$ inch are provided between discs. The discs are precisely finished aluminum, with magnetic iron oxide suspended in a plastic binder providing the magnetic film for recording data. Both sides are used, except for the top and bottom discs, which have recordings on only the inside surfaces. Discs are typically 1 to 2 feet in diameter.

Discs that are dropped or severely jolted may be permanently damaged. It is advisable to call the manufacturer to have the pack checked for dimensional changes and film condition.

The access arms move radially in and out between the discs in the space provided. The access time for a given rotation speed and disc diameter is primarily dependent on the number of access arms that are provided. The lowest-cost units have only one arm. It has a read/write head for the bottom of the arm and another for the top. Thus, data can be recorded on the under surface of the disc to give two recording surfaces per disc. To access another disc in the pack, the arm is withdrawn radially, moved vertically to the desired disc, and then extended to the proper track. The head would be brought into near contact with either the top or bottom disc surface.

The head, of course, does not contact the surface; otherwise, wear would be a problem. Most manufacturers use a flying head for magnetic-disc systems. The head is shaped to glide along on a cushion of air that naturally adheres to the rotating disc. Fast-acting mechanisms have been designed to force the head into or out of the air cushion. The preferred scheme is a compressed air-operated piston to force the disc head toward the surface of the disc.

For faster access, additional read/write heads and arms are used. A typical arrangement is one in which an arm is provided for each pair of recording surfaces. This improvement eliminates the time lapse for vertical movement from disc to disc. The average time for radial movement can be reduced by adding additional arms to serve the same disc, some serving the inner tracks and others serving the outer tracks.

*8.6   MAGNETIC TAPES

The magnetic tape is the most popular medium for high-speed data recording. Every medium- and large-scale computer has one, and probably many, magnetic-tape units.

Most television and movie cameramen can't resist the urge to film a bank of tape units. The action includes starting, reversing, whirling at high speed, stopping, and then restarting. After many exposures, the viewing audiences have the mistaken impression that the cabinets with the two whirling reels are the heart of the computer. A typical magnetic-tape unit is shown in Fig. 8–7.

To produce magnetic tape, microscopically small particles of iron oxide are mixed with a binding agent and uniformly applied to the surface of long strips of flexible plastic. The plastic base is about as thick as cigarette paper; the magnetic film is approximately one third that thickness. Recording occurs in the ferromagnetic film with a read/write head that is similar to those used for drums and discs. Tape widths typically are $\frac{1}{2}$ inch with 7 tracks to 1 inch with 14 tracks. A full reel contains approximately 2400 feet of usable tape.

The IBM 2401 has nine tracks and moves the tape at a velocity of 18.75 inches per second (slightly over 1 mile per hour). The data transfer rate is 120,000 or 240,000 digits per second, depending on the method of recording. The faster data rate is obtainable with an in-flight error-correcting provision for a single track. The basic tape unit can handle

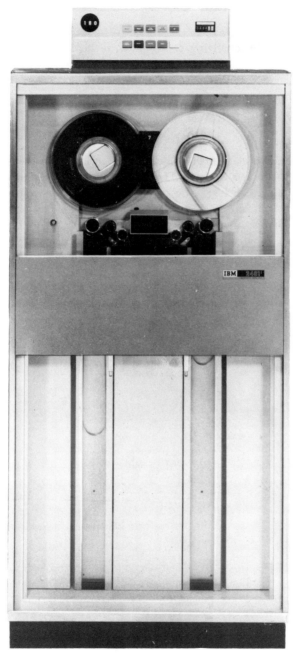

FIG. 8–7   IBM 2401 Magnetic Tape Unit. (Courtesy of IBM)

seven-track tapes by changing the read/write heads and a section in the tape control unit.

The use and operation of the magnetic-tape units are based on the sequential-access feature of the unit. Tapes are most effectively used in situations where long sequences are read or recorded. This basic characteristic is one of the differences between tapes and the (almost) random-access drums and discs.

The tape drive mechanism functions differently than the drives for the other magnetic storage devices. The tape is stopped except when data is being accessed or searched. The drum and disc rotate continuously with the data being electronically gated in or out at the desired times. Thus, the tape drive mechanism must be capable of fast starts and short stops; otherwise, excessive lengths of tape and time would be wasted in sluggish operation.

From the standing start, tapes are able to be accelerated to velocities of 50 inches per second in approximately 1 ms. These operating speeds would not be attainable unless the inertia of the reels was prevented from affecting the rapid changes in tape velocity. Various schemes are used for isolating the reels from the driven tape. The method illustrated in Fig. 8–8

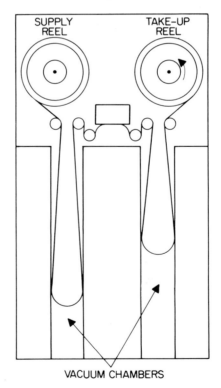

FIG. 8–8   Low-Inertia Tape Transport.

is effective. Slack lengths of tape are provided on either side of the read/ write head. An air vacuum gently holds the tape in place and maintains the slack. The tape is transported by a rotating capstan. Brakes are applied for fast stopping. After a sudden start, the slack in the left-hand vacuum chamber is momentarily reduced as the capstan accelerates. Slack is reapportioned by the vacuum immediately after the critical start-up.

In Section 11.3 we mention that information appears on tape in groups called records. A block is several records. A gap of approximately 0.6 inch separates the records. The tape drive is given an all-out test in stopping and restarting to read the next record without infringing on data outside the interrecord gap. It is more practical to start and stop in the larger gap between blocks.

The biggest advantage of tape over the drum and disc is the ease with which the tape can be removed and stored for future use. This feature has contributed to the widespread use of magnetic types as permanent storage for vast quantities of data. For example, one reel of tape can hold as much data as 480,000 punched cards. It weighs only 4 pounds and takes little shelf space.

Magnetic tapes are often used in the input/output link between the computer programmer and the central processor. The prepared tape could be the input information, which includes the input data and the computer codes stipulating the procedure for processing the data.

9 Input/Output Devices

Information can be exchanged between the central processing unit and the external world. Inputs coming from people are handled by punched-card equipment, paper or magnetic tape units, keyboards, or optical and magnetic character readers. Inputs are communicated to a computer from other computers or from machines in a data-collection system. Each end of a channel between digital computers has a communication adapter to enter the transmitted information in a form that is compatible with the adapter at the receiving terminal. Digital signals can be transmitted thousands of miles over telephone lines, but precaution is always taken to send extra digits in order to check that unwanted electrical disturbances don't introduce errors at the transmitter, along the line, or at the receiver. Analog signals are the common output of measurement instruments in a data-collection system. Analog-to-digital converters are placed in the communications path ahead of the transmitter.

Inputs from people and machines are the only meaningful sources of information. They require completely different techniques and equipment items. Sections 9.1 and 9.2 discuss inputs from people and machines, respectively. Output equipment is discussed in Section 9.3, and error-detecting methods are discussed in Section 9.4.

9.1 INPUTS FROM PEOPLE

In normal activity a general-purpose computer is processing programs and data that have been composed by a person. In most cases these inputs originate with the manual exercise of using a keypunch machine to enter alphabetic letters and numbers in coded representation on paper tape or punched cards. This hardware coding is followed by a software coding that restructures the information to make it understandable by the computer.

130

We'll see in Chapter 12 that the important translation in this final step is performed by a special program called the compiler.

The information that is encoded on the paper tape or cards bears a column-by-column resemblance to letters of the alphabet and decimal numbers. The name *alphanumeric code* is descriptive of the characters that can be represented on the cards or tape.

The eight-track code is common for *paper tape;* however, five-, six-, and seven-track tapes are also used. A row of feed-sprocket holes is provided on all blank tapes. These reference marks serve to index the tape through the read and punch operation. Figure 9–1 shows a length of paper tape passing under a punch.

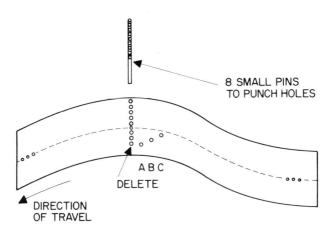

FIG. 9–1   Punching Eight-Track Alphanumeric Code on 1-Inch Paper Tape.

The small size of the punch unit makes it feasible to mount it on the side of a conventional keyboard. It is about the size of a closed fist. By pressing a key the operator causes the coded representation of that character to be punched on the tape. In case of a typing error the tape is back-spaced, and the erroneous information is overwritten with a "delete" character. As Fig. 9–1 shows, this special key places a punch in all tracks. The control unit for the tape reader ignores the delete character; thus, it serves as an eraser of sorts. Rewrites are done on blank tape in sequence and ahead of the error. A segment of tape can be removed and replaced with a correct version, but a rather touchy splicing operation is required.

Punch rates of 300 characters per second are available. At these high speeds, the chad that has been punched out has a tendency to clog the punches unless special design care is taken.

In small computer units the major source of input data is from paper tape. The source tape is typically 20 to 100 feet long. When the program is submitted for a processing run, a second long tape having the compiler program is read into memory, and then the source tape is read. A short object tape is generated, which has the machine codes that correspond to the programmer instructions in the source tape. Manipulating these tapes can take several minutes for a slow-speed read. Fortunately, faster units are available.

Tapes are read by mechanically or photoelectrically sensing the presence of holes. Low-cost units use a *star wheel* with points that are exactly 0.1 inch apart, so that as it rolls it presses through holes that may be in the tape. An electrical circuit is completed through the point in contact with a

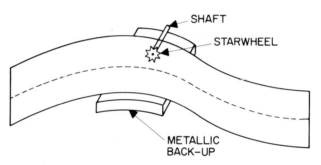

FIG. 9–2   Concept of Mechanical Paper-Tape Reader.

metallic backup to signal the absence or presence of holes. An 8-track tape would have eight star wheels and, of course, the drive sprocket. The reading rate is slow at 30 characters per second. This reader advances the tape at 3 inches per second. At this rate, a 100-foot compiler tape takes nearly 7 minutes to read.

High-speed paper-tape readers reach 1000 characters per second and use a *photoelectric cell* for each track. The purpose of the sensors and the logic principles for decoding the tape are the same as for the mechanical readers. The photoelectric cells are switched on by light passing from a source and through a punched hole. The tape is transported past the sensors by a take-up reel that rotates and accepts tape from the supply reel. They have a capacity of 1000 feet.

The Hollerith *punched card* has 80 columns and 12 rows for square punches. They are manufactured by the billions from paper material that is 0.007 inch thick. The card dimensions are $7\frac{3}{8}$ by $3\frac{1}{4}$ inches and cost $2 to $3 per thousand. Figure 9–3 shows a typical card reader and punch. A hopper on the top back of this IBM 2520 can hold up to 1200 cards. Two

FIG. 9–3   Card Read-Punch, Model 2520. (Courtesy of IBM)

stackers are on the top front of the device to accept the completed cards. The punching and reading rates are 500 cards per minute, which translates to 670 characters per second and is a lower data rate than the photoelectric paper-tape reader. Faster card readers attain speeds of nearly 2000 cards per minute.

Punched cards for source programs are prepared with a *low-speed punch* that is integral with a special keyboard. The keying action produces a column of punches and types the character at the top of the column for easy reading of the card. Keys are provided to feed completed cards to the receiving hopper and move another card into position for punching. In case of a typing mistake, the erroneous card can be replaced by retyping. The device has provisions for reading and duplicating a card. Mistakes in the middle of a card statement can be corrected by duplicating the entire card up to the error, retyping the miskeyed characters, and then continuing the duplication.

Cards have advantages that make them preferred by programmers over paper tapes. The basic disadvantage of the tape is the difficulty of making changes. Unless you master in-tape splicing, a new tape must be duplicated to incorporate changes.

Buffering schemes are used to smooth the data flow from card and tape readers. It has become popular to interface several computer users with the central processor on a time-sharing basis. Using elaborate buffering and control provisions, the operating system accepts transmitted data directly from a *keyboard unit* as the information is keyed. This mode of input circumvents the need for cards or tape. Output is retransmitted to the keyboard unit, where it is printed on a sheet of paper.

For nearly 20 years designers have sought for and developed machines that will accept for the computer *information* as it exists *in everyday form*. The objective is to reduce costs and circumvent the possibility of keying errors in human transcription of the documents. Success has been immediate in some applications and there have been a series of generally steady improvements in others. New possibilities are on the forefront. We'll discuss the concept of machines that read from documents and listen to speech.

The *magnetic character reader* in Fig. 9–4 is used to interpret the

FIG. 9–4   Magnetic Character Reader, Model 1419. (Courtesy of IBM)

special magnetic numbers on bank checks. This application has been a successful method to identify the transaction from the original document. The character can be recognized as being one of the ten numbers in the set.

Optical character readers (OCR) have many potential applications, and with continued progress in hardware design it could make the keyboard operation obsolete.

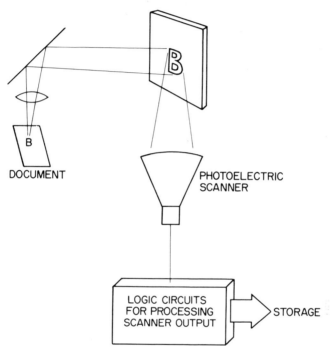

DOCUMENT

PHOTOELECTRIC SCANNER

LOGIC CIRCUITS FOR PROCESSING SCANNER OUTPUT

STORAGE

FIG. 9–5   Basic Components in an Optical Character Reader.

Most OCR units are designed to function with a specified set of characters. The IBM OCR units accept documents that are produced on the Model 1403 printer. It operates with a set of 48 characters.

The sketch in Fig. 9–5 shows the concept of the OCR. The optical arrangement enlarges the image of the digit under consideration. The image is scanned by a photocell, which detects bright and dark patterns. By comparing the patterns observed by the scanner with the template patterns, the OCR establishes whether the scanner is viewing a permissible character. The next character is found by moving 0.1 inch to the right (for documents printed on the Model 1403).

Handwritten *documents* obviously require a more capable machine and, in fact, logic circuits or programs that apply the mathematics of pattern recognition. Writers have a free-swinging liberty in character shapes, sizing, and spacing. Design progress is understandably slow in this area. The U.S. Postal Service has a prominent need for an OCR to automate mail sorting. They have units that read the ZIP code on typed addresses.

The theory of pattern recognition has been applied to an input device that can interpret the sounds in the voice. Work is underway on this concept at Bell Telephone Laboratories. Eventually the device might serve in the two-way exchange of words between people and machines. It may be used in automatic shop-at-home service by giving the customer a limited opportunity to inquire about the features, price, and availability of merchandise.

9.2   INPUTS FROM INSTRUMENTS IN DATA-COLLECTION SYSTEMS

Rockets and other complex, expensive, engineering adventures are given an exhaustive performance evaluation during development. The testing continues into the critical prototype stages, and with each application in the case of moon rockets. Several dozen sensing probes monitor pressure, temperature, stress, voltage, and the like. These instruments generate electrical outputs that are analogous in magnitude to the parameter being measured. Data from space rockets must be processed immediately, if compensation adjustments are to be made in any parameter that is drifting toward danger. Digital computers are well suited for processing these data; however, there must be a conversion from the electrical outputs to a digital basis. The measurements are transmitted to the computer after being individually reformed by special circuits. These are called *analog-to-digital converters*. For example, the input to an A/D converter might be 12 volts, a value that is analogous to a measurement such as a 6000-pound load. The output of the converter could be the digits of the binary number, 110 for 6.

High-speed conversions from analog to digital are slightly involved; however, conversions in the opposite direction are easy. The simple circuit in Fig. 9–6 is a *D/A converter*. The output is 12 volts when the two left-hand inputs are energized to represent the two 1's in 110.

The principle of this resistor ladder can be used to achieve the less obvious conversion from *analog to digital*. The input and output exchange roles, and the terminals of a counter are connected in place of the switches. Figure 9–7 shows the concept of an analog-to-digital converter. The ampli-

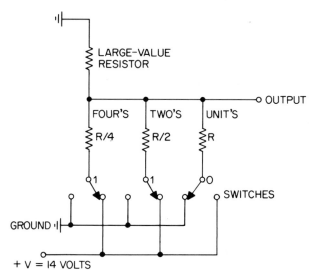

FIG. 9–6 Digital-to-Analog Converter that Yields an Output of 12 Volts for Switches Registering Binary 110.

fier and flip-flop combine to stop further acceptance of the clock pulses by the counter when the voltage at that level builds from −7 volts up to zero. The instant the voltage becomes positive the flip-flop is theoretically cleared, and the clock pulse is blocked. For an input of + 5 volts, it takes exactly five clock pulses to stop the clock. These pulses, of course, cause 101 to be registered on the counter. It is common to rely on a counter to convert from analog measurements.

9.3 OUTPUT EQUIPMENT

Unlike the slow keypunch operation that began the input cycle, the output equipment is typically high speed. Those who hunt-and-peck the keys are particularly amazed by the output printer, because some of these machines can print 1400 lines per minute with up to 120 characters per line. It would take the combined effort of over 500 skilled typists to equal this production. We'll discuss printer concepts and introduce the cathode-ray tube for displaying output information.

Some interesting mechaincal designs are exhibited in *high-speed printers*. They all serve to bring the hardened steel impressions of the characters in contact with a ribbon and in turn with the paper in the appro-priate line and position. Figures 9–8 and 9–9 show the *chain and the*

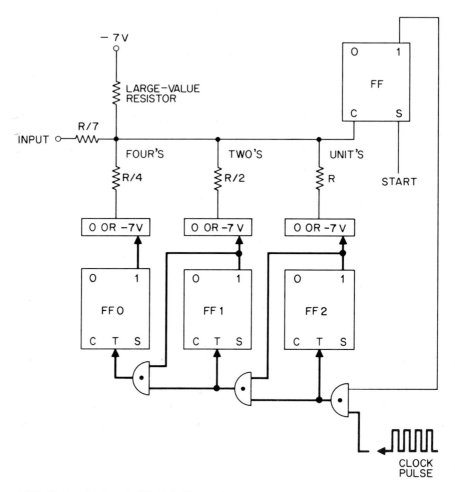

FIG. 9–7 Analog-to-Digital Converter.

rotating drum that are the two most common line-at-a-time methods. In both units the paper is advanced upon receipt of the line-feed control signal. We'll see in Chapter 15 that programmers specify the handling of line feed. A line is printed by a group of tiny hammers that strike the ribbon and paper in the positions were characters are specified. The hammer blows must be timed with the motion of the drum or chain. For example, the letter B is printed in the fifty-eighth column by striking with hammer 58 at the instant that the letter B whirls past. The wait is extremely short because the rotating speeds are high and the character sets are repeated several times in each revolution. The chain on the IBM 1403

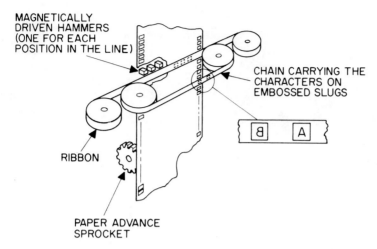

FIG. 9–8   Chain Printing Mechanism.

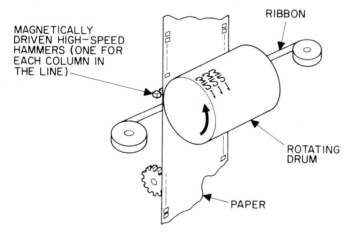

FIG. 9–9   Rotating-Drum Printing Mechanism.

printer is composed of five 48-character sets. Index markers are imbedded into the chain at the start of each set. This printer is shown in Fig. 9–10.

The paper advances in the printer so rapidly that tearing becomes a real problem. For example, the printer can skip lines at the rate of 33 inches per second, which is about half the normal walking pace. Sprocket drive holes are on each side of the paper. The printer in Fig. 9–10 shows the paper supply in the bottom. This fan fold is common because the pages bend naturally at the easily torn perforations.

FIG. 9–10   High-Speed Printer, Model 1403. (Courtesy of IBM)

Electrostatic printers offer compactness and quietness and are used in many small printers. An inspection of some documents will reveal that the characters are formed by a series of tiny dots. The concept of electrostatic printing is illustrated in Fig. 9–11. The paper is specially treated to react to the heated probes and leave a small burnt dot. By using small grids, the concept in Fig. 9–11(a) produces superb character shapes.

Cathode-ray tubes (CRT) are essential displays for the computer users who want to enter into manipulations on the solution as it is being formed. Information is readable from the face of the CRT and appears like a television screen. In a typical application the user may be studying the architectural features of a buildings. It might be decided to reshape prominent members and then use the CRT to display the instant renova-

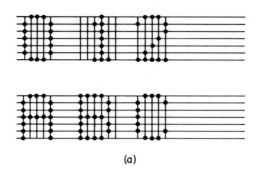

(a)

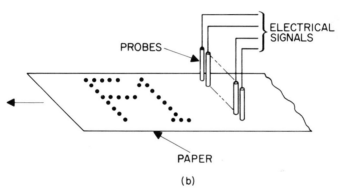

(b)

FIG. 9–11 (a) Character Formation by Tiny Dots and (b) the Principle of Electrostatic Printing.

tion. Of course, this exercise utilizes a stored computer program that may be quite extensive. Automobile designers use the CRT in three-dimensional styling reviews.

Characters can be displayed on the CRT for easy reading of results and messages. The stored program might cause a message or a result to appear for the user's review. In the interactive mode the message can be answered and further questions asked. Some school students have their exams and classroom instruction displayed on a CRT.

Figure 9–12 shows the concept of *projecting characters* on a CRT. An electron beam originates at the electron gun and travels to collide with phosphorus particles on the inside of the evacuated tube. The glow from the energy transfer during this collision is visible on the screen. The beam is shaped in cross section by the first deflection system, which directs the

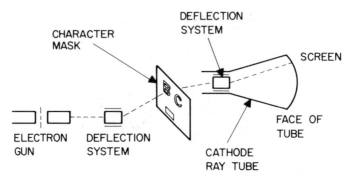

FIG. 9–12   Principles of Cathode-Ray-Tube Display.

beam to pass through a particular area of the character mask. Beams that are masked through B appear as B on the display screen. The second deflection system positions the character on the screen. Of course, the phosphorus glow lasts for several milliseconds, in which time the screen can be filled with other characters before beginning the reenergizing cycle.

9.4   ERROR-DETECTING CODES

The scope of data communications is illustrated in Fig. 9–13 by the bank of tape units that are in view along with the Dataphone 4800 data communications set. The tape units can read 150,000 binary digits per second and the data set can transmit 4800 digits per second. These transmissions can be carried by telephone lines to distant terminals or computers. It is physically impossible to design equipment or communications networks that are error free.

For example, a speck of foreign matter on the tape could momentarily clog the read head. An electrical disturbance at points along the transmission line or in the switching system could nullify a portion of the pulse sequence. Data-processing systems are prone to errors because they rely on several input/output units and, also, accept data from remote stations.

Effective methods have been developed that yield almost 100 per cent reliable reports as output, despite the occasional appearances of an error. These error-detecting methods are economically preferred over an all-out witch hunt for every mechanical or electronic source of malfunction.

The concepts basically consist of checking salient features of short groups of data pulses. If the check gives evidence of an error, there are alternative courses of action that automatically preclude further use of the faulty data. In some schemes the data are corrected by the machine and the processing continues. In other cases the operator can be signaled to stop

FIG. 9–13   Dataphone 4800 in the Foreground of a Typical Bank of Magnetic Tape Units. (Courtesy of Bell Telephone Laboratories)

the run, fix the problem, and then restart. A third alternative is to discontinue processing of the present record, print a message to that effect, and commence immediately with the next record. Payroll processing files are separated into individual records of each employee. The overstepped records would be handled on a second run or by manual methods.

The *parity code* is used in one of the simplest forms of error checking. An extra binary digit is attached to a small group of digits. The value of this parity digit is 0 if the total number of 1's in the group is odd. If the number of 1's is even, the parity digit is 1 to make the total always odd.

The arrays in Fig. 9–14 have parity digits in the left-hand column and bottom row. Can you locate the error in the array in Fig. 9–14(b)?

The error in the bottom, right-hand corner of Fig. 9–14(b) can be detected and corrected. Of course, a double error in a column or row could not be detected. The digits in these arrays could be from a seven track magnetic tape. The alphanumeric code for the tape is based on maintaining odd parity.

The 4-out-of-8 code is also popular for error detecting. It is based on forming a group of 8 digits to have exactly 4 one's. The 2-out-of-5 code is

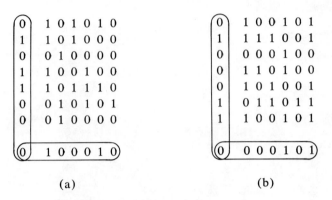

(a)   (b)

FIG. 9–14   Parity Code for Rows and Columns.

one of the earliest attempts at error detection. It was used in telephone
signaling.

10 Basic Computer Controls

The user of the computer prepares a program giving the data and the instructions for processing those data. We have discussed the bulk of the equipment that is involved in processing a program. The input devices deliver the coded instructions and data to the internal memory by way of, perhaps, magnetic tape as an auxiliary store and then through a buffering device. The internal memory becomes the source of data being added, subtracted, multiplied, or divided in the arithmetic unit. The newly formed sums, products, and so on, may be returned to the internal memory to await further processing or eventual transfer to the output device. The instructions are interpreted by the control section. In processing a typical program, control signals cause numerous transfers of data between the internal memory and to and from the arithmetic unit. We mentioned previously that the central processor unit was composed of the internal memory, the arithmetic unit, and the control section.

In this chapter we will describe how the control section functions to execute the programmer's instructions. The presentation is intended to show that the control section is a group of logic circuits which coordinates the function of the hardware devices and other logic circuits to form an operating computer. This is probably the most interesting topic in an introductory course in computer design. It provides for a fairly good understanding of the operation of a basic computer. Among other things, we will describe the processes involved when the machine is handling a typical arithmetic exercise. Specifically, we will evaluate the quadradic $256 * (52)^2 + 317 * 66$ using only four basic instructions.

145

10.1   INSTRUCTION WORD

The term *control section* refers to those circuits affecting the interpretation of instructions and the application of the proper commands to the logic circuits, memory systems, and input/output devices.

The *interpretation of the instruction* means that a logic circuit has been designed to have a predictable output depending on the input. In this case the input is the instruction, and the output is the interpretation.

INSTRUCTION ⟶ CONTROL SECTION ⟶ INTERPRETATION

Ex. 10–1

Consider a machine to turn on a light by typing the instruction "TOL". At least in principle, the preceding chapters describe logic design for circuits to light a bulb if, and only if, the keys of a teletypewriter are pressed in the order "TOL". The logic circuits to interpret instructions of this category can be permanently wired.

The computer word is the fundamental unit of storage. The binary bits composing a word are stored in a single address in the memory. A magnetic-core memory having a 20-digit word in three-dimensional assembly would have 20 core arrays, one digit in each planar array.

The programmer's instructions and data appear in memory as *instruction words and data words*. The data words may have a sign digit as the leftmost bit, 0 for positive numbers and 1 for negative numbers. The remaining digits in the word would then represent the binary code of the original decimal number. For example, the data word may have 20 digits and be structured as shown in Fig. 10–1.

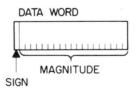

DATA WORD

MAGNITUDE

SIGN

FIG. 10–1   Data Word Format.

The *instruction word* is composed on an operation code and an operand address. The operand is the name given to the data involved in an operation. Figure 10–2 shows an example of instruction word structure.

In general, a *single-address computer* performs those instructions called for by the programmer by beginning with the instruction word stored at some specified location in memory. The contents of this location are interpreted and the operation called for is executed. Instruction words continue to be taken from the memory locations in sequence unless a *halt* or *branch* instruction is encountered. The branch instruction specifies that processing continue but from another memory location not in sequence with the instruction preceding the branch.

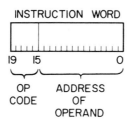

FIG. 10–2   Instruction Word Format.

The instruction word format for the UNIVAC 1108 is shown in Fig. 10–3.

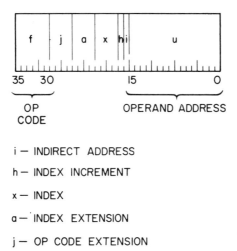

i — INDIRECT ADDRESS

h — INDEX INCREMENT

x — INDEX

a — INDEX EXTENSION

j — OP CODE EXTENSION

FIG. 10–3   UNIVAC 1108 Instruction Word.

The instruction word for the UNIVAC 1108 has a single operand address. Many computers are single-address machines; however, multiple-address machines exist.

OPERATION CODE	ADDRESS OF OPERAND

SINGLE - ADDRESS INSTRUCTION

OPERATION CODE	ADDRESS OF OPERAND (A)	ADDRESS OF OPERAND (B)

TWO - ADDRESS INSTRUCTION

OPERATION CODE	ADDRESS OF OPERAND (A)	ADDRESS OF OPERAND (B)	ADDRESS FOR RESULT

THREE - ADDRESS INSTRUCTION

OPERATION CODE	ADDRESS OF OPERAND	ADDRESS OF NEXT INSTRUCTION

ONE - PLUS - ONE ADDRESS INSTRUCTION

The *longer instruction words* imply increased dimension for the storage medium. The single-address instruction for the UNIVAC 1108 requires 36 digits with a 16-digit operand address. This word can be accommodated with 36 planar arrays in the magnetic-core memory. A comparable two-address instruction would require $36 + 16 = 52$ planar arrays. The additional cost tends to be offset by improved operating speed, because the operation code is interpreted fewer times. With the two-address instruction, the exercise of multiplying $A \times B$ would be handled with one step rather than by two separate single-address instructions.

The *one-plus-one address machines* are a slight variation of the two-address machine. The IBM 650, using this format, processes instructions from a magnetic drum, and hence the location of the next instruction affects the memory access time. Hence, we avoid the situation of the next instruction passing under the read head and then incurring a time delay of one drum revolution until it becomes available again. The sooner the location of the next instruction is known the better are the chances that the desired location will pass under the read head, either while the present instruction is being interpreted or immediately thereafter. This reduction in access time can be optimized automatically with cleverness in the assembler design. The next instruction can be assigned to one of the addresses that naturally passes under the head immediately after the present instruction has been interpreted.

The longer instruction words are more common on computers using magnetic tapes, discs, or drums. The length of the word is not a major limitation when these devices are used as the internal memory. Section

11.3.3 shows that IBM 360/20 computers operate with single-address or multiple-address instructions. Machines handling these mixed lengths are common.

10.2 SYMBOLIC CODED INSTRUCTIONS

Symbolic coding is defined to be the process of writing instructions in an assembly language using symbols for operation and address. The *assembler* is defined to be the software designed to convert symbolic instructions into a binary form suitable for execution on a computer. The assembler provides error messages and other diagnostic information to the programmer to help him develop an operating program.

Very seldom will two computer manufacturers use the same assembler. Thus, an assembler is unique for each machine. A few years ago the programmer learned the symbolic coding for his machine, a knowledge that quickly became obsolete when a new model appeared, having a different assembler. These frustrations have been alleviated somewhat with the FORTRAN, COBOL, and other languages, which are basically applicable to several machines.

An example of symbolic coding is illustrated in Table 10–1. These symbolic codes are only a part of the 140-instruction repertoire of UNIVAC 1108.

TABLE 10–1

Partial Listing of Instruction Repertoire of UNIVAC 1108

Symbolic Code	Description of Operation
SA	The number in the accumulator is stored in the operand address.
SNA	The negation of the number in the accumulator is stored in the operand address.
SZ	Zero is stored in the operand address.
LA	Loads the operand into the accumulator.
AA	The operand is added to the number in the accumulator and the sum is stored in the accumulator.
AU	Add Upper. The operand is added to the number in the accumulator and the sum is stored in an adjacent register. The contents of the operand address and the accumulator are unchanged.
MI	The operand is multiplied by the number in the accumulator and the 72-digit product is stored in the accumulator except for 36 least significant digits, which are stored in an adjacent register.

Symbolic Code	Description of Operation
TZ	Test Zero. The next instruction in the normal sequence is skipped if the operand is zero.
TNZ	Test Nonzero.
TP	Test Positive.
TN	Test Negative.
TE	Test Equal.
TNE	Test Not Equal.
TLE	Test Less than or Equal.
TG	Test Greater.
J	Jump. The next instruction is read from the operand address.
JZ	Jump Zero. The next instruction is to read from the operand address if the accumulator is zero. Otherwise, the next instruction is in sequence.
JNZ	Jump Nonzero.
JP	Jump Positive.
JN	Jump Negative.
SLJ	Store Location and Jump. The next instruction is to be read from the operand address. The "jump from" address is retained for future use.
AAIJ	Allows all input/output interrupts and jumps to operand address.
LX	Load X. The operand is loaded in the index portion of the instruction word.
AX	Add to X. The operand is added to the index and the sum is stored in the index.
LIC	Load Input Channel. The input data are loaded into memory, starting with operand address.
DIC	Disconnect Input Channel.
LOC	Load Output Channel. The contents of memory are transferred to an output device starting with operand address.
NOP	No Operation. Proceed to next instruction in sequence.
HKJ	Halt.

Ex. 10–2

We infer from Fig. 10–3 that each symbolic representation of the OP codes in Table 10–1 has a corresponding six-digit binary code. Let's suppose that binary codes 000001 through 000100 are used to represent AA, MI, SA, and LA, respectively. These symbols appear in the shaded rows of Table 10–1 and, also, in Table 10–2 along with our assumed binary code. Let's use this information to illustrate the computation of 256 * $(52)^2 + 317 * 66$.

TABLE 10–2

Four UNIVAC 1108 Instructions with Assumed Binary OP Code

Symbolic Code	OP Code in Binary	Description of Operation
AA	000001	The data word in the memory address given by the address part of the instruction is added to the number in the accumulator. The sum is stored in the accumulator. In short, we might say the operand is *added* to the number in the accumulator and the sum stored in the accumulator.
MI	000010	The operand is *multiplied* by the number in the accumulator and the results are stored in the accumulator and an adjacent register.
SA	000011	The number in the accumulator is *stored* in the operand address.
LA	000100	The operand is *loaded* into the accumulator.

Assume for our example that the decimal numbers have been converted to binary and stored in memory addresses 5 through 8.

The number 52 is stored in binary form in memory address 5.
The number 256 is stored in binary form in memory address 6.
The number 317 is stored in binary form in memory address 7.
The number 66 is stored in binary form in memory address 8.

We desire to store the result in memory address 9.
In symbolic coding we have:

LA	5	Loads 52 into accumulator
MI	5	Forms $(52)^2$
MI	6	Forms $256 * (52)^2$
SA	9	Stores $256 * (52)^2$ in address 9
LA	8	Loads 66 into accumulator
MI	7	Forms $317 * 66$
AA	9	Forms $252 * (52)^2 + 317 * 66$
SA	9	Stores desired result in memory address 9

In binary form the sequence of instructions would appear as shown in Fig. 10–4.

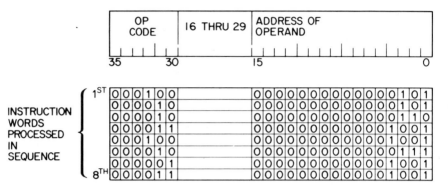

FIG. 10–4   Binary-Coded Instructions for Evaluating a Quadratic Expression.

Only four different instructions were necessary in the above example. However, computer designers typically provide the logic circuits for 30 to 150 basic instructions. As we said, UNIVAC 1108 has 140.

10.3   INSTRUCTION AND EXECUTION CYCLES

In a broad sense an operating computer is either performing the instruction or the execution cycle. These two cycles comprise the entire elapsed time during which the computer is functioning.

Instruction Cycle	*Execution Cycle*
The instruction word is fetched[*] from memory (in binary), interpreted, and the operand address is transferred to the memory-address register.	The operand is fetched from memory and the operation called for by the operation code is performed upon the operand.

The execution cycle follows the instruction cycle except in special cases. Upon the completion of both, the next instruction word is processed. We will see in Section 10.5.1 that special instruction words do not call for an execution cycle.

The control section causes numerous terminals to be energized in proper sequence relative to the clock pulse. For example, the I terminal is energized during the instruction cycle. This identification of events is the *first step in distributing the clock pulse* to the desired output terminals. The logic circuit with the outputs defined in Fig. 10–5 is commonly known as the timing pulse distributor.

Therefore, *each clock pulse is identified* as being in I or E and T_0, T_1,

---

[*] The term "fetch" means to obtain data from a memory device. It is the opposite of "store."

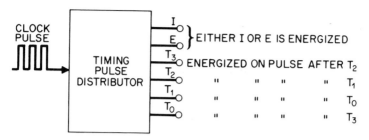

FIG. 10–5   Timing Pulse Distributor.

T_2, or T_3. In Fig. 10–6 the first four clock pulses are in the instruction cycle and each one is labeled. In Section 10.5 we'll describe in detail what functional units are active during each pulse. For example, information is read from memory during the pulse labeled I and T_0.

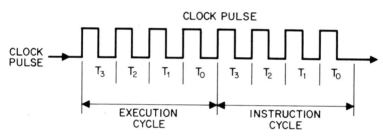

FIG. 10–6   Labeling Clock Pulses.

Obviously, we have a ring-around-the-rosy effect of counting from T_0 to T_3 and then back to T_0. Appropriately, *ring counter* is the name given to the logic circuits for generating this pulse sequence. The ring-counter circuit is shown in Fig. 10–7. The sequence starts with the counter being cleared. We remember that the output of the trigger flip-flop changes state for every positive-going pulse applied to the T terminal. The first pulse will cause FF1 to change from the 0 state to the 1 state. FF0 will be unaffected until after that change. On the next pulse FF0 will change to the 1 state and FF1 will change back to the 0 state. Thus, we see that the T_1 terminal will be energized on the second pulse, and so on. After T_3 becomes positive, the sequence automatically begins with T_0.

10.4   CONTROLLING ARITHMETIC OPERATIONS

The functional units (registers, adders, memory, counters, and input/output) are involved in performing the operations specified by the programmer. The following example introduces the control section.

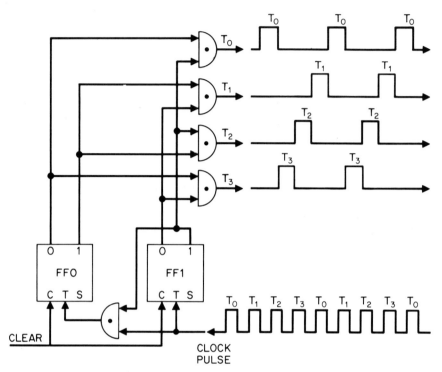

FIG. 10–7 Ring-Counter Circuit.

Ex. 10–3

The instruction word calling for data addition is typical of those handled by the control section. During execution of most instructions, data words will be transfered between registers. We'll assume for example that data must move from the memory-buffer register (MB) to the B register (BR) at precisely the time the E and T_1 terminals are energized by the ring-counter pulse. This is a typical command for the logic circuits in the control section.

Inputs to the control section include the timing pulse and another pulse established by the OP code digits. The broad line, shown in Fig. 10–8 carrying the OP code, signifies parallel paths for transferring all digits to the decoder simultaneously. The control section circuits are simply logic circuits, which by definition have predictable outputs.

The several outputs shown in Fig. 10–8, of course, are routed to the proper connection in the vicinity of the functional unit being controlled. We show only one end of this path. For example, the lower terminal is

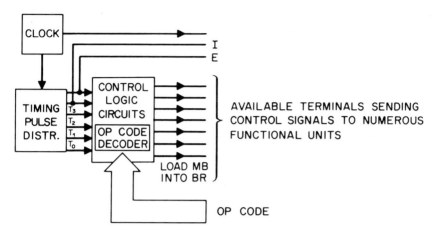

FIG. 10–8   Control Section Input and Output Signals.

labeled **LOAD MB INTO BR**. The other end would be in the vicinity of the B register and be so labeled. In the usual case, it is connected to an AND gate for opening paths between functional units.

In our data addition example, the **OP** code causes the control section terminal **LOAD MB INTO BR** to be energized during the time interval E and T_1 This signal opens an AND gate and permits the desired data transfer.

Control signals in a computer are somewhat analogous to strings in a puppet act. In both cases they *control an activity,* whether it is transferring data, setting flip-flops, or moving puppet limbs. In Ex. 10–3 we discussed the concept of handling an instruction word calling for data transfer. The control signals are predictable at any point in time for a given operation code. These outputs cause data to be transferred or operations to be performed.

Figure 10–9 shows the data transmission paths (broad lines) and control signal that are used in *handling instruction words.* The numbers shown alongside the registers indicate a 6-digit OP code and a 16-digit operand address. The UNIVAC 1108 has this format (see Fig. 10–3). The diagram shows several familiar units, such as memory, registers, and counters.

The new units in Fig. 10–9 function as follows:

1. The read and write flip-flops are used to fetch and store information in memory.

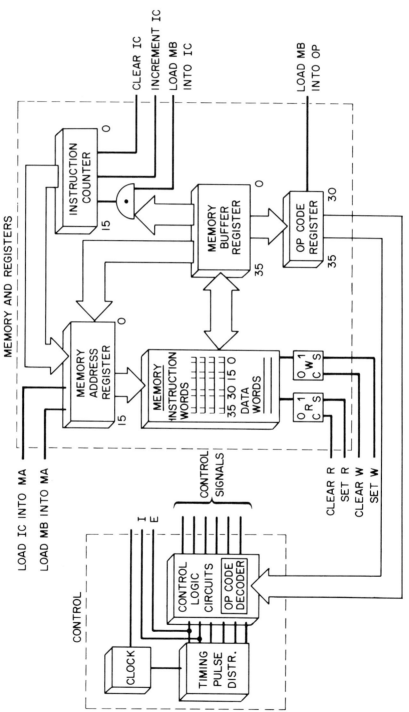

FIG. 10–9 Circuit for Handling Instruction Words.

2. The memory-address register (MA) contains either the address of data to fetch or store or the address of the next instruction. Upon receipt of the command SET R, the contents of the memory location specified by MA will be transferred to the memory-buffer register.

3. The memory-buffer register (MB) is used to temporarily hold information from memory. Considering that MB contains the 36-digit instruction word, we see in Fig. 10–9 that digits 30 through 35 will be transferred to the OP code register, and 0 through 15 will be transferred to the instruction counter.

4. The instruction counter contains the location of the next instruction to be executed.

5. The OP code register temporarily holds the OP code, which is immediately transferred to the OP code decoder to be interpreted.

These devices perform their designed mission upon receipt of the proper control signals. Clearly, the units in Fig. 10–9 can process instruction words. They will be active during the instruction cycle. Data words are handled during the execution cycle. Let's introduce the functional unit arrangement for performing arithmetic operations on data words. Then we'll be prepared for Section 10.5, where we discuss the details of control command sequences for typical symbolic codes.

Arithmetic operations are common. Addition and subtraction are handled by the familiar units (B register, accumulator, and adder) in Fig. 10–10. The control signals are shown that are appropriate for performing arithmetic in one channel of a parallel functional adder. We'll assume the adder is designed to form the sum of the data in the B register and accumulator. The signal LOAD MB INTO BR causes a parallel transfer between those registers. Next, a signal on the line labeled ADD will gate the contents of the B register into the adder. Other adder inputs are from the accumulator and, of course, the carry in from the full adder on the right. After sufficient delay to span the carry time, the ADD signal opens gates to transfer the final sum to the accumulator.

Figure 10–10(b) shows that a few additional logic gates are all that are necessary for handling *subtraction with the same circuit* as addition. The possibility of common circuits was our motive in Chapter 2 when we defined subtraction by *two's complement addition*. The circuits in Figs. 10–10(a) and (b) are exactly alike except for two extra gates and a delay in the path carrying the SUBTRACT signal. The gates present the complement of the digit in the B register to the full adder. As we remember, two's complement addition consists of minuend plus subtrahend complement plus 1 in the *rightmost column*. The circuit in Fig. 10–10(b) represents one of several columns being added. If it represented the rightmost column, of course, a 1 would appear as an input to that full adder.

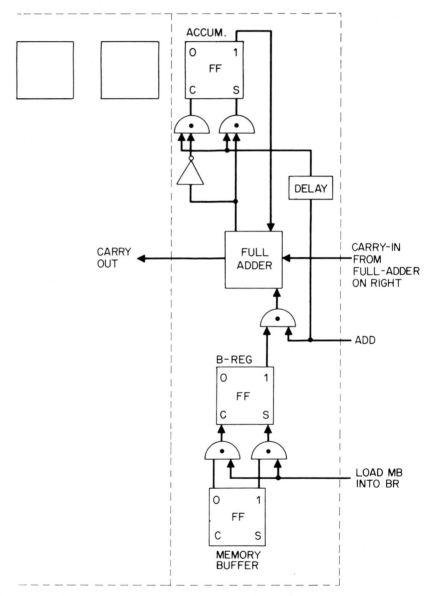

FIG. 10–10(a)   Circuit for Handling Addition. Only One Channel Shown.

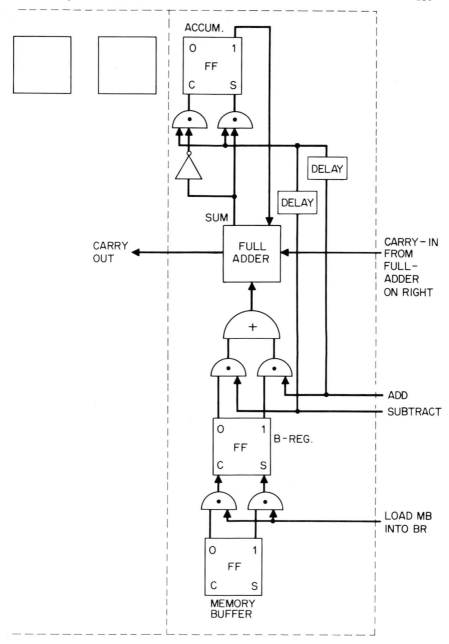

FIG. 10–10(b)   Circuit for Handling Subtraction and Addition.

Ex. 10–4

The functioning of the elements in Fig. 10–10(a) is illustrated by an addition example.

1	*1*	1	Carry in
1	*0*	1 1	Contents of accumulator
+1	*1*	0 1	Contents of memory buffer
11	*0*	0 0	Sum stored in accumluator

Consider the digits in the shaded column. Our circuit of a full adder and three flip-flops is one of many parallel channels for transferring data from MB through BR to the adder. Let's find whether the correct sum is stored in the accumulator.

In our example, the processing begins with

accumulator flip-flop = 0
MB flip-flop   = 1
carry in   = 1   (this digit is available after propagating through the columns on the right)

Control Signals	*Action Taken*
LOAD MB INTO BR	The 1 in MB is transferred to BR
ADD	The full adder is presented 1 from BR and 0 from the accumlator and eventually 1 from the carry-in line; we know $1 + 0 + 1$ gives sum of 0 and carry out of 1
ADD (delayed to span the carry time)	The sum is 0 and causes the accumulator flip-flop to be cleared

Therefore, *the desired result is achieved*: carry out = 1 and the accumulator flip-flop contains 0.

The control signals achieve the desired arithmetic operation, provided the signals are activated in the proper sequence. For example, we see from Fig. 10–10 that the signal LOAD MB INTO BR must be activated before the signal ADD for the proper data to be added. We will see in Section 10.5 that both these signals are activated in the execution cycle and in the proper sequence.

10.5 INSTRUCTIONS FOR TYPICAL OPERATIONS

The complete sequence of instructions is shown in Table 10–3 that causes the data in memory address XX   YY to be added to the data in the accumulator and the sum stored in the accumulator. The symbolic code for this operation is AA for the UNIVAC 1108 (see Table 10–1). The instruction word, consisting of the OP code and operand address, is the binary coded form of | AA | XX   YY | and stored in address XNYN.

TABLE 10–3

Sequence of Signals for Arithmetic Operations

Time	*Control Signals to be Activated*	*Explanation*
I and T_0	SET R	The *read flip-flop is set* and causes $+Im/2$ to flow through the XN and YN selection wires of the core array. Thus the instruction word in memory address XN YN is transferred to memory-buffer register.
I and T_1	LOAD MB INTO OP CLEAR R	The *OP-code* part of the instruction word is transferred to the *Op-code* register and the read flip-flop is cleared. (Note: Before *I* and T_2, the OP code is interpreted by the OP-code decoder. Thus, all succeeding steps in *I* and *E* will depend on the decoder output.)
I and T_2	INCREMENT IC	The *instruction counter is incremented* to XN YN + 1. (Note: The OP code did not call for a branch; therefore, INCREMENT IC is automatic and normally done during *I* and T_2.)
I and T_3	LOAD MB INTO MA CLEAR I, SET E	The *address* part of the instruction word (XX YY) is transferred from the *memory-buffer register* to the *memory-address register*. The sequence enters the execution cycle.
E and T_0	SET R	The *read flip-flop is set* and causes the data word in memory address XX YY to be transferred to the memory-buffer register.

Time	Control Signals to be Activated	Explanation
E and T_1	LOAD MB INTO BR, CLEAR R	The *data word* is transferred to the *B register* as the first step in forming the sum of the contents of the B register and the accumulator.
E and T_2	ADD	Each *full adder forms the sum* of the contents of the B register and the accumulator [see Fig. 10–10(a)]. The look-ahead carry feature would be used for high-speed parallel adders. The final sum is placed in the accumulator.
E and T_3	LOAD IC INTO MA, SET I, CLEAR E	The location of the *next instruction* is transferred from the instruction counter to the *memory-address register*. The instruction flip-flop is turned on and the execution flip-flop is turned off.

Another typical operation is storing the number in the accumulator in the operand address. The symbolic code is SA for the UNIVAC 1108. (We'll assume that SA is the next instruction after AA.) The sequence of operations is shown in Table 10–4.

TABLE 10–4
Sequence of Instructions for Storing Data Word

Time	Control Signals to be Activated	Explanation
I and T_0	SET R	The read flip-flop is set. The instruction word in memory address XN YN + 1 is transferred to the memory-buffer register.
I and T_1	LOAD MB INTO OP CLEAR R	The *OP-code* part of the instruction word is transferred to the *OP-code register*, and the read flip-flop is cleared.
I and T_2	INCREMENT IC	The instruction counter is incremented to XN YN + 2.

Time	Control Signals to be Activated	Explanation
I and T_3	LOAD MB INTO MA CLEAR I, SET E	The *address* part of the instruction word is transferred from the memory-buffer register to the *memory-address register*. The sequence enters the execution cycle.
E and T_0	LOAD AC INTO MB, SET W	The *data word* in the accumulator is transferred to the memory buffer register and then into *memory* upon setting the write flip-flop.
E and T_1	CLEAR W	The *write flip-flop is cleared.*
E and T_2		*Extra time* is available for writing into memory.
E and T_3	LOAD IC INTO MA, SET I, CLEAR E	The location of the *next instruction* is transferred from the instruction counter to the *memory-address register*. The instruction flip-flop is turned on and the execution flip-flop is turned off.

The sequences of operations for adding and storing data are compared in Fig. 10–11. We see that similarities exist. For example, all operations correspond identically during the instruction cycle. Both sequences serve to fetch and interpret the instruction word and transfer the operand address to the memory-address register. Also, the instruction counter is incremented and ready to be transferred to the memory-address register during the T_3 portion of the execution cycle.

We notice that the READ operation is called for twice in the sequence for adding and once in the sequence for storing. With the magnetic-core memory, the read operation destroys the contents of that memory address; therefore, the original contents have to be rewritten and sufficient time has to be allocated for this automatic operation. We see that SET R is called for in adding during I and T_0; however, no further read or write is called for until E and T_0, which is sufficient time for the reestablishment of the original memory contents. Three time intervals elapse before the sequence moves into the execution cycle; therefore, the destructive-read feature of the magnetic-core memory is a less severe shortcoming than we might have thought at first glance.

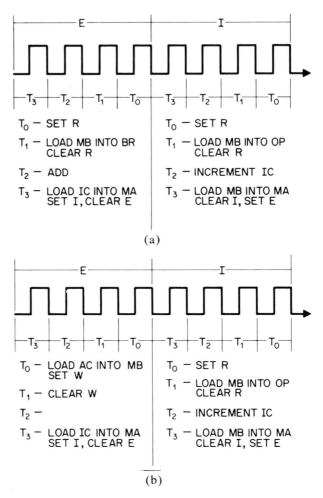

T_0 — SET R

T_1 — LOAD MB INTO BR
        CLEAR R

T_2 — ADD

T_3 — LOAD IC INTO MA
        SET I, CLEAR E

T_0 — SET R

T_1 — LOAD MB INTO OP
        CLEAR R

T_2 — INCREMENT IC

T_3 — LOAD MB INTO MA
        CLEAR I, SET E

(a)

T_0 — LOAD AC INTO MB
        SET W

T_1 — CLEAR W

T_2 —

T_3 — LOAD IC INTO MA
        SET I, CLEAR E

T_0 — SET R

T_1 — LOAD MB INTO OP
        CLEAR R

T_2 — INCREMENT IC

T_3 — LOAD MB INTO MA
        CLEAR I, SET E

(b)

FIG. 10–11   (a) Microcommands for Adding; (b) Microcommands
for Storing.

Ex. 10–5

In Tables 10–3 and 10–4, the signal LOAD MB INTO MA is activated during I and T_3. Could it be during I and T_2?

The answer may not be immediately obvious, so let's review magnetic-
core operation. The logic circuits that handle the automatic rewriting are
outside the basic control section. They activate flip-flops that briefly hold
the data being read until the read operation is finished (CLEAR R), and
then the contents of the flip-flops are rewritten back into the memory-

address register. Thus, it is important that the contents of the memory-address register are not changed immediately after CLEAR R. In both the ADD and STORE sequences the CLEAR R is followed by INCREMENT IC and then LOAD MB INTO MA. Therefore, we see that the *answer is no*.

The sequence of operations that follow I and T_1 is dependent on the operation specified by the operation code. The operation at I and T_2 need not be INCREMENT IC should the operation code specify something different. The branch or transfer instructions are the two common instruction words that lead to peculiar sequences that do not have the INCREMENT IC operation at I and T_2.

10.5.1   Branch or Transfer Instructions

Normally, the next instruction word is in sequence; however, the *branch or transfer instruction alters the sequence.* The formal program may call for the next several instructions to be jumped or, perhaps, a backward jump to repeat a sequence of instructions. The IF and GO TO statements are two FORTRAN statements that involve the branch or transfer instruction.

There are two types of branch instruction, *unconditional* and *conditional*. They are defined in Table 10–5, from which we see that we need to

TABLE   10–5
Defining Branch Instructions

Unconditional Branch	*Conditional Branch*
The address portion of the memory-buffer register is transferred to the instruction counter. The appropriate signal is LOAD MB INTO IC.	The control signal is either LOAD MB INTO IC or INCREMENT IC, *depending on the sign* of the data word in the accumulator. Most machines are BRM (Branch on Minus). Thus, a positive number in the accumulator means that the contents of the instruction counter will simply be incremented by 1. For a negative number, the proper signal is LOAD MB INTO IC.

consider the sign digit in the accumulator in order to establish the appropriate sequence of operations in the conditional branch. The UNIVAC 1108 is capable of executing the instruction JN (Jump Negative). The sequence of operations for a typical branch on minus is listed in Table 10–6.

TABLE 10–6

Sequence of Signals for Branch on Minus
(negative numbers have sign digit $= 1$)

Time	Control Signal to be Activated	Explanation
I and T_0	SET R	The instruction word is read and transferred to the memory-buffer register.
I and T_1	LOAD MB INTO OP, CLEAR R	The OP-code part of the instruction word is transferred to the OP-code register, and the read flip-flop is turned off.
I and T_2 — and sign digit equal 0	INCREMENT IC	The instruction counter is incremented. The sign digit of the data word in the accumulator being 0 does not call for a branch.
I and T_2 — and sign digit equal 1	LOAD MB INTO IC	The address of the next instruction word is transferred from the memory-buffer register to the instruction counter. The sign digit is 1; therefore, we want to branch rather than take the next instruction in sequence.
I and T_3	LOAD IC INTO MA	The location of the next instruction is transferred from the instruction counter to the memory-address register. The E flip-flop is not turned on because we want to fetch the next instruction word; therfore, the execution cycle is not needed.

Ex. 10–6

Assume that an instruction word is located in memory address XN YN. Compare UNIVAC 1108 symbolic codes for conditional and unconditional branches to this address.

From Table 10–1 we see J XN YN is an unconditional jump and JN XN YN specifies a jump on the condition that the accumulator is negative.

The unconditional branch has a slightly different sequence of operations. At I and T_2 the instruction counter is loaded with the contents of the memory-buffer register.

The instruction counter is used in the execution of every instruction word. We see it must be designed to either be incremented or loaded with the contents of the memory-buffer register. Therefore, let's consider the design of a four-digit instruction counter that will be

1. Either incremented on command INCREMENT IC; or
2. Loaded with the contents of the memory buffer register on command LOAD MB INTO IC.

This circuit is shown in Fig. 10–12. The components are familiar. The terminal labeled BRANCH would be activated when the OP code specifies an unconditional branch or a conditional branch agreeing with the sign digit.

*10.6   INDEX REGISTERS

The pulse distribution unit maintains a count and, thereby, distinguishes between time frames in the execution and instruction cycles. For example, an output of T_3 and E flip-flop set identifies the last of four frames in the execution cycle.

Index registers also maintain a count. They contain binary digits that represent the number of times that a particular set of calculations is to be performed. The index-register contents would typically be reduced by one count each time the set is repeated. When the count diminished to zero, the index register has served its purpose; then the next instruction in sequence is fetched.

An index register holds a number that can be added or subtracted from the address portion of an instruction word to form an *effective address*. The UNIVAC 1108 designers have devised symbolic codes (Table 10–1) that bring their index registers into action. We could use those codes in the following example; however, the UNIVAC 1108 has several complications in the instruction word that warrants our presenting a simpler code for a hypothetical machine. We'll consider an instruction word in which the *two leftmost digits designate the index register*. Thus, our hypothetical machine could have up to three index registers, one being register 01 and the other two being 10 and 11. The normal situation is 00, signifying that the instruction word is processed in a routine manner.

Figure 10–13 shows the index digits on the left of the OP code and the operand address. We'll assume that *index register 01 is being used* by the programmer for the present example. We define three additional symbolic codes:

LX—Load Index. Load the operand address into the index register. For example, $\boxed{01 \mid LX \mid 49}$ means the number 49 is loaded into index register 01.

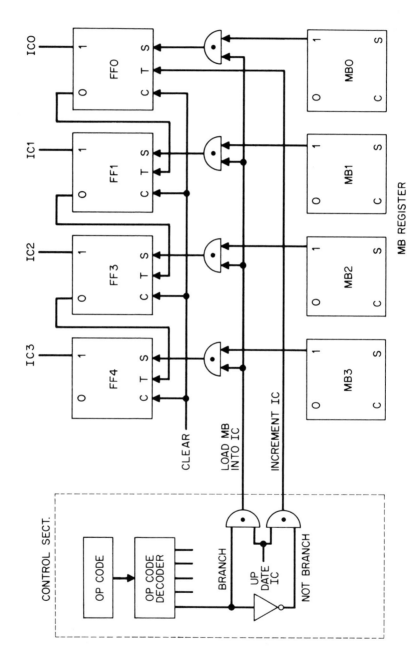

FIG. 10–12 Circuit to Load Next Instruction Address into Instruction Counter.

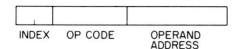

INDEX   OP CODE   OPERAND
ADDRESS

FIG. 10–13   Instruction Word Having 2-Digit Index Register Designation.

> BRI—Branch and Index. For example [01 | BRI | 60] means the contents of index register 01 are decreased by one and at the same time a branch is made to address 60. The next instruction word will be fetched from address 60 unless the index register contains all zeros. Then the next instruction is in sequence.
> FEA—Fetches data from an effective address. For example, [01 | FEA | 150] means the data is fetched from memory location (150 + index register 01 contents).

Ex. 10–7

We promised that index registers would keep count of repeated operations. Which symbolic code has this purpose?

It should be apparent from considering these three codes that the basic objective of maintaining a count is achieved by the symbolic code BRI. We see in it the provision for stepping the count down by one each time it is processed, and finally the count has proceeded until the index register contains all zeros. Then the next instruction in sequence is performed.

Let's consider a detailed example to show the way the index register enables the programmer to specify repeated calculations. A sequence is shown, and we'll attempt to explain what is taking place.

Ex. 10–8

Consider the following six instruction words stored in memory address 21 through 26. What happens if we process the sequence?

Four of the instructions will be processed several times, so let's clarify events the first time through.

Address in Memory	Instruction Word	Comments on First Time Through
21	[01	LX	49]	Loads number 49 into IR 01
22	[01	FEA	150]	Fetches data word to be added from address 199

Address in Memory	*Instruction Word*	*Comments on First Time Through*
23	00 | AA | 200	Adds to form current total
24	00 | SA | 200	Stores the current sum
25	01 | BRI | 22	Index register contents reduced to 48 and branch to address 22
26	00 | HKJ | 0	Halt (not processed until later)

Thus, we see that the instruction 01 BRI 22 continues the recycling to memory address 22 until the index register contains all zeros. Then the sequence will halt with the instruction in address 26. The net result of the repeated maneuvers is to form the sum of all the data words in memory addresses 150 to 199 and place the final sum in address 200.

Let's look at what happens on the second and third time through the sequence. Table 10–7 lists the contents of index register 01, the contents of the instruction counter, and the data read/write address.

Therefore, the data words in address 150 through 199 are added together, and the final sum is stored in address 200.

10.7   SUMMARY

Computers are designed to perform several relatively simple operations. The instruction repertoire (140 for UNIVAC 1108) is carefully chosen to yield a machine that is flexible and rapid. The purchaser or lessee wants assurances that the machine, perhaps costing millions of dollars, can handle his present programs and those in the future.

The basic repertoire is permanently wired. We mentioned in Chapter 1 that permanent wiring was a severe handicap with the ENIAC of 1946. It calculated trajectories of artillary rounds but couldn't handle any other problems. The unique feature of modern computer flexibility is brief instructions that are likely to be a small part of almost an infinite number of problem solutions.

To build confidence, it is said that "the longest journey begins with a single step." To build a general-purpose computer, we might say that the most difficult problem can be solved with many simple steps. With the incredible speed of electronic devices, instructions such as "add" and "store" take less than one millionth of a second. Therefore, we see that a billion operations can be processed within minutes.

Throughout these first 10 chapters we discussed computers as being made of logic circuits with input and output pulse sequences. Sketches were

TABLE 10-7

Address in Memory	Instruction Word	Contents of Index Register			Contents of Instruction Counter	Address of Data Read/Write		
		1st Time	2nd Time	3rd Time		1st Time	2nd Time	3rd Time
21	01 | LX | 49	49	—	—	22	—	—	—
22	01 | FEA | 150	49	48	47	23	199	198	197
23	00 | AA | 200	49	48	47	24	200	200	200
24	00 | SA | 200	49	48	47	25	200	200	200
25	01 | BRI | 22	48	47	46	22 (Unless index register 01 is all zeros, then 26)	—	—	—
26	00 | HKJ | 0	—	—	—	—	—		

drawn to illustrate how several logic circuits altered the input pulse to achieve the desired output. These illustrations depict the real situation, because computer inputs and outputs are electrical pulses.

We have attempted in Chapter 10 to show how functional units are controlled in basic computers. We shouldn't be overconfident in our new-found knowledge and begin designing our version of UNIVAC 1108. Before singlehandedly launching a drive at a giant, we should be fore-warned. Few people completely understand the many features of a large-scale computer.

11 Concepts of Stored Programs

Computers are truly general purpose in their ability to handle unrelated problems in rapid succession.

The computer operator starts the computer running by pushing the appropriate buttons. The run usually begins with the transfer of input data and instructions for processing those data from an input device to the internal memory. The information, of course, is transferred in the form of an electrical pulse sequence. In the typical application of payroll preparation, the input may consist of payroll data (hours worked, pay rate, etc.) and instructions on how to calculate and print paychecks. After a few minutes or even seconds, the computations are finished and the operator makes ready for the next run. Compared to the succeeding run, it may involve completely different parameters and conditions. A lot has happened to streamline activity in a computer since the late 1940s when computers were designed for special tasks. The operator, usually a scientist in that era, had to reroute a vast maze of wires in order to handle a different task with the early machines.

Today's computers are flexible because they operate from internally stored programs. To handle a different category of problem, the operator, usually a clerical specialist, pushes the button to load a different program. Not all features of the computer can be changed. There exists a vast amount of permanent wiring in the form of logic circuits. Each circuit is designed to do a simple operation such as add, subtract, and so forth. This *instruction repertoire* generally consists of at least 30 and up to 200 permanently wired operations. The system is useful because most problems can be solved by the proper combination of these simple operations. For example, most mathematical problems involve the operation of adding data to form sums.

173

11.1 GENERAL FEATURES OF COMPUTER SYSTEMS

All general-purpose computers operate on stored programs. A *program* is a sequence of instructions specifically arranged to accomplish a given task. The programmer formulates the solution to a particular problem by using steps in the program that can be handled by one or more of the basic instructions. In simple solutions the steps may be processed one at a time in the same sequence as they appear in the program. Working from a stored program, the computer can decide on the processing sequence during the run. By handling *decisions* and acting accordingly, the computer is more useful. The robot in Ex. 11–1 is one illustration of the usefulness of machine decision making.

Ex. 11–1

Suppose that a robot is designed to handle packages of various sizes and weights. Let's consider the robot is programmed to (1) move to a package, (2) grasp and pick it up, (3) move back to the unloading area, and (4) lower it into place and release. Can you think of how its usefulness might be enhanced by a stored program?

Yes; all four basic steps can be performed more efficiently because a robot having a stored program could handle decisions and could be reprogrammed easily for another assignment. For example, in performing step (1) a well-designed robot would move to the closest package and then on return trips move further to those remaining. The robot may be programmed to decide during step (2) whether the package is too heavy or light enough that two can be carried. It may be programmed to decide before step (3) that the package is the large crate that should be delivered to a separate unloading area. It may decide before step (4) that the box is the small but heavy box that should be gently lowered on a foam pad to protect the fragile contents.

The robot in Ex. 11–1 used an instruction repertoire limited to move, grasp, pick up, lower, and release. However, with a stored program it takes on human-like flexibility. Computers are robots also except that they handle electrical pulses instead of packages. Certain packages caused the robot to reach decisions on what to do in the next step. Any change from the basic robot routine corresponds to processing a different block of instructions from another location in the stored program. In an analogous manner, certain pulses cause the computer to reach decisions that establish the sequence of processing instructions.

Other information is effectively stored in the internal memory. The manufacturer usually furnishes directions that govern the hardware while the program is being loaded and processed. The *operating system* is a set of programs that guide the computer in the performance of its tasks. Control of the input/output units is a typical function of the operating system. In some computers the operating system is limited to fundamental functions of activating the reader and printer at the beginning and end of the program, respectively. In expensive computers the user wants to make maximum use of his investment; hence, the operating system becomes more elaborate. The ultimate in present use is probably the time-sharing operating system that allows many programmers to use the computer simultaneously. This complex system occupies a sizable portion of the internal memory, leaving less for the program being run.

The term general-purpose computer, of course, in literal translation implies that many different types of problems can be handled by the machine. Computers are properly classified as general purpose that can perform the following categories of operations:

1. Process instructions in prescribed sequence.
2. Locate binary digits in memory or on input channel and transfer them to another unit.
3. Perform arithmetic operations.
4. Store the results of operation.
5. Formulate branch-type decisions by comparing sign or magnitude of two data words. Process sequence in different order depending on decisions.
6. Repeat sequences a specified number of times.
7. Accept input and generate output information.

The decision-making feature of computers gives the programmer freedom to break, skip, and jump between program steps to obtain the desired answer. It's easy to lose track of the sequence after several decisions. We know the computer will follow exactly the steps it is given. Our poorly charted course will lead to incorrect answers. Some programmers construct a *flow chart,* which is a graphical representation of the chosen paths between operations. Flow charts are a tool to help the programmer comprehend and explain the interrelated paths to others (see Section 12.2).

This chapter introduces two general-purpose computers. The IBM System 360 Model 20 is typical in several ways with other computers used in *data-processing application.* The IBM 360/20 is the least expensive of the 360 series; hence, it is widely used in data-processing work where the computations are brief on each input item. Approximately 75 percent of the computers used in university courses are the IBM 360/20; hence, it is chosen here so the text will supplement class work with the college or university computer.

In this chapter an overview is given of the UNIVAC 1108, which is further discussed in Chapter 10. The UNIVAC 1108 is discussed because we get a look at another manufacturer's computer, which is typical of machines for lengthy computations in *scientific applications.*

11.2 PRACTICALITIES OF COMPUTER SYSTEMS

There are thousands of applications for computers, and over 1 million people working with computers as programmers: analysts, operators, engineers, scientists, and administrators. It would seem the usefulness of computers is unlimited; however, computers are sometimes misused by being placed on jobs that are too small, too poorly defined, or, perhaps, even unnecessary. Some administrators, wanting to be a part of the "in" generation, advocate computers for the wrong applications.

We'll list the general categories in which computers are widely and effectively used. There are other categories and other applications, some of which you may uncover if you choose a computer career.

Computers are well suited for the general category of applications that have a *repetitious* procedure. It is a simple task for the programmer to specify repeated processes for sections of the program. A number is stored in an index register and decreased each time the section is processed. When the number diminishes to zero, the processing continues at another section. People become bored with repetitive actions; hence, the computer assistance is a relief of their boredom. To uncover applications, be aware of repetitive tasks that are necessary. In some situations they may not be handled manually at present because they would make an undesirable boring assignment.

Computers are used in applications that involve *voluminous data.* Using classifiers, recording, or summarizing routines the programmer can build a mountain of data and then literally look for a "needle in the hay stack." These data-processing applications are numerous. Examples include the data maintained by the U.S. Census Bureau, Internal Revenue, airlines, telephone companies, banks, accounting departments, and universities. It isn't likely that we'll uncover entirely new situations in which there exists the need for establishing a giant data bank. Our efforts are more effectively directed to finding worthwhile uses for the existing data records. For example, the census data contain billions of facts. Judgment and ingenuity are needed to establish what should be classified and summarized. All that is gleaned from a data bank is not gold. Useful information can be made available to administrators, planners, and legislators, as well as the broad class of buyers and sellers.

Computers are useful in applications requiring *instantaneous analysis.* A familiar example is a space rocket test and launching. Thousands of measurements may be monitored because they represent levels of voltage, stress, temperature, and the like, that are critical to the test or launch. The computers can be rapidly analyzing these data and recommending corrective action. Clearly, there are no alternatives for computers in on-line processing of a high-speed activity. By on-line we mean the input units are transferring data directly to a running computer. In the test–launch applications, the transfer is accomplished as the data are measured. The human contribution is extremely valuable, because otherwise all conceivable malfunctions and disturbances from the ordinary must be anticipated to preestablish an all-encompassing course of action.

Computers are used in the solution of engineering problems having *numerous equations and parameters*. It relieves engineers from laborious hand calculations and frees them for more creative tasks. New applications are being uncovered continuously. Engineers are finding solutions to problems that were too lengthy for manual solutions. Also, engineers welcome the opportunity to apply preprogrammed solutions to their problems. These user programs are a challenge to formulate and perfect. To be frank, some are poorly conceived or solve problems seldom encountered in real life. The good user programs are valuable. Examples are programs for analyzing stresses in bridges or other structures and programs for finding the economic advantages of alternative courses of action. Numerous equations and parameters may be involved in both these examples of user programs. Good user programs are needed in several applications. They can be prepared and sold like a book or a piece of artwork.

11.3 INTRODUCTION TO IBM SYSTEM 360/20

The Model 20 leases for less than $3000 per month. Thus, it is affordable by educational institutions and medium-volume data-processing firms. It is the least expensive of the IBM 360 series and was introduced in 1966. Some of our discussion of Model 20 concepts is applicable to the more expensive Models 30, 40, 50, 65, 75, and 85. The Model 85 in full-blown form rents for approximately $250,000 per month. Other computers are less expensive than the Model 20; for example, IBM System/3 is rapidly growing in popularity for data processing in medium and small businesses. Machines are available from many other manufacturers in all these sizes. We will concentrate here on the Model 20 because it is well suited for the data-processing application and is representative of computers from a major manufacturer.

11.3.1 General Capabilities

When we discuss a specific CPU, such as the 2020 in the Model 20, we realize that it operates with only specific input/output units. Figure 11–1 shows models that might be used in a typical configuration.

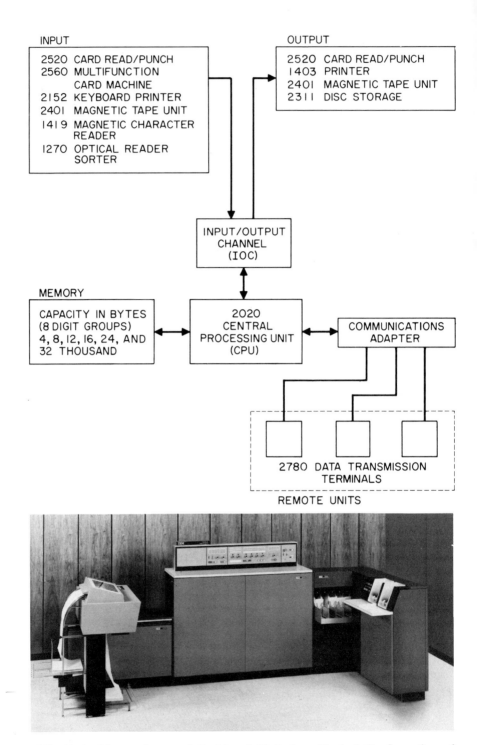

FIG. 11–1   Nomenclature of Peripheral Units in a Typical Configuration of
IBM System/360 Model 20. (Photo Courtesy of IBM)

The *central processing unit* (CPU) of most computers consists of the memory unit, the arithmetic unit, and control circuits for timing information exchange. The CPU of any computer must exchange data with input/output (I/O) units. The term *peripheral units* refers to any one of several pieces of equipment that are used in communication with the computer but are not part of the CPU. The I/O units and auxiliary storage units are peripheral units.

Many other units (some from manufacturers other than IBM) can function as substitute I/O units provided they can communicate with the CPU. The data exchange consists of a stream of electronic pulses that correspond to punch card holes, tape magnetic spots, or keyboard action. The input/output channel (IOC) is the logic circuit for changing the received I/O data to a code understandable by the CPU. The 2020 CPU uses the *e*xtended *b*inary-*c*oded *d*ecimal *i*nterchange *c*ode (EBCDIC), which is an eight-digit code.

Ex. 11–2

The EBCDIC for the letter A is 1100   0001. Suppose that a punched card with the letter A has just advanced under the read head of the Model 2520 card reader. What pulse sequences are involved in transferring this character to the CPU?

The holes in the card are sensed and converted by the wired panel on the reader to the code suitable to this peripheral device. This coded information is sent through an electrical path to the IOC, where it is converted to the pulse sequence in Fig. 11–2.

FIG. 11–2   Pulse Sequence Representing the Letter A.

Any card reader that is acceptable as an alternative to the Model 2520, obviously, must transmit a code that is understandable by the IOC. Wired panels in peripheral units are changeable; thus, nonconforming units can be modified. Input/output units are controlled by the IOC as directed by the CPU to accomplish the data transfer specified by the programmer. The printer, reader, tape, and so on, receive instructions from the IOC. Instructions serve to start, test, and command a read or write. Thus, the peripheral unit must be compatible with these control signals. The IOC of the Model 20 can start and proceed to control the card reader and then later exercise the control over the printer, tape, and so on. Up to eight units can be controlled, one at a time.

The peripheral units shown in Fig. 11–1 are compatible with most IBM computers in the System 360.

The Model 20 is a general-purpose computer that is used in data-processing systems. Exercise 11–3 directs our attention to the practicability of the communications adapter shown in Fig. 11–1.

Ex. 11–3

Can you justify the Model 20 provisions for communication with remote input/output units?

Suppose that the Model 20 forms the data-processing system for a medium-sized bank with branch offices. With a remote terminal, transactions can be entered immediately in the central file by an input terminal at the branch. The customer's account statements can be displayed by a remote printer to verify that funds are available to cover a counter check.

Communications between the CPU and the *remote terminals* are critical and closely scrutinized for transmission errors. The pulse sequences usually are changed in code, form, or interposed with other pulses before they are transmitted over regular or special telephone lines to remote locations. We'll briefly mention two of these hardware units.

The data set (sometimes called a modem) converts the pulses to a signal form in the frequency range of a regular telephone transmission. Pulses of high and low voltage are converted to tones of high and low frequency. The tone is less susceptible to voltage drops due to switching activity in the telephone central office. The telephone company has developed a unit called the DATA-PHONE data communications service shown in Fig. 11–3. They look like a telephone handset with dialing provisions. Once the remote party "answers," interrogation messages pass back and forth to set the stage and make certain that all is ready; then transmission begins. The original pulse sequence enters the device and leaves in a different form through the DATA-PHONE data set. The familiar electrocardiogram is transmitted by the DATA-PHONE unit from the heart patient to a central receiver hospital. At the receiving end, the line signal is converted back to a digital pulse. The Model 20 interfaces with modems complying with Electronic Industry of America requirement RS232B. Examples include the DATA-PHONE data set and IBM 3976 Modem Model 3.

FIG. 11–3   Group of Data-Phone Data Sets. (Courtesy of Bell Telephone Laboratories)

The binary synchronous communications adapter (BSCA) gives the Model 20 the ability to *exchange data with another computer* or an I/O terminal at a remote location. For example, the second computer can be another Model 20 or the Model 25 or 30, each having the appropriate adapter to convert between the transmitted line code and form and the EBCDIC used by the central processor of these computers. The form conversion is accomplished by a modem, generating a high and low tone for transmission over voice-grade telephone lines.

The effectiveness of communication adapters and transmission lines is measured by the *quantity of information* that can be carried. High-quality transmission lines are specially designed to be shielded from various electrical signals along the miles of path. Otherwise, these noise sources would introduce errors by altering the transmitted data. Incidentally, special-service lines are protected from accidental disturbance by craftsmen servicing the network.

High-quality circuits can carry over 1 million binary digits per second at a cost of approximately $40 per month per mile. Regular voice-grade lines can carry up to 2500 binary digits per second at a cost of approximately $2.00 per month per mile. Infrequent users probably would not lease the line and would pay the same rate as a regular telephone call plus the modem. The communications adapter of the Model 20 is capable of rates from 600 to 50,000 binary digits per second. A speed of 4800 digits per second is the normal upper limit without optional features.

For a given quality transmission line, the *effective data rate* can be reduced significantly by nonproductive exchange between the computer and the remote location. The data rate can be diminished by elaborate error-detecting methods or by numerous interrogations between locations. For example, the ultimate error detection is dual transmission, which reduces the rate by at least half. An effective channel is designed to minimize line tie-up caused by back and forth signaling and acknowledgments for starting and ending various message blocks. The Model 20 designers have included provision to help minimize nonproductive exchange over the communication line. The error-detecting method is typical of other computers. Let's discuss these features.

The Model 20 checks for *errors* in each group of 8 binary digits. Before transmission, the pulses from the CPU are changed to either the familiar *parity code or the 4-of-8 character code*. The leftmost digits in a parity coded group are automatically assigned a value of 1 or 0 to make an odd number of ones. As we mentioned in Section 9.4, odd parity checking can detect all single errors and some double errors. There is slight inefficiency in the transmission, because 7 digits are effectively transmitted instead of 8. An alteration in one of the 7 digits would signal the presence of an error. Characters are specially protected by the 4-of-8 code. Each group of 8 digits is structured to have exactly 4 ones. An error would be present if the group contained more or less than 4 ones. At first look it might seem that this code is wasteful because there are 255 combinations of 8 binary digits, but only 64 combinations having 4 ones. The situation really is not that bad, because only 63 different characters are of interest. Examples of characters are the 26 letters of the alphabet and decimal numbers 0 through 9.

The *error condition* commences a routine for the communications adapter. The automatic activity directs processing to a special set of preprogrammed instructions to establish whether the error originated at the sender, in the transmission line, or at the receiver. The faulty record is immediately retransmitted. This information would probably be only a small quantity. Let's assume the sender continues in the run status, indicating that the outgoing information is properly coded. If the error doesn't appear in the retransmission, it is reasonable to assume that a momentary line disturbance caused the error condition. The program continues with the next sequential instruction. However, a malfunction is indicated if the error condition continues in three successive retransmissions. In this situation, the communication adapter terminates the run and appropriately lights the central panel.

The Model 20 designers have considered ways to circumvent lengthy exchanges with the receiver when the sender begins a message that must be handled differently than the preceding messages. The method features an eight-pulse sequence at the *start and end* of each message. These pulses trigger the sender to achieve the desired mode of transmission, and, subsequently, the pulses trigger the receiver. Thus, each message is self-controlling in this respect. Typical sequences in the EBCDIC are 0000   0010 for START OF TEXT and 0000   0011 for END OF TEXT.

The BSCA (binary synchronous communication adapter) is small logic circuits, which we mentioned *interface* the computer with transmission lines to a remote facility. We don't need to delve into further detail on its operation except to explain that it operates in accordance with a set of 13 instructions. Typical instructions are RECEIVE INITIAL (notifies adapter to expect initial pulse sequence from the other adapter) ENABLE BSCA (turns on receiving adapter), and DISABLE BSCA (ceases operation of receiving adapter upon completion of transmission that may be in progress). Other instructions are sometimes inserted into the message requesting that error checks be made at these intermediate points.

We have discussed general features and data transmission with the Model 20. The next section discusses its memory concepts and unique schemes for addressing data in memory. The Model 20, being a data-processing computer, sometimes receives input from a remote facility and usually operates with both long and short data groups.

11.3.2   Internal Memory

The Model 20 stores the information associated with the current program in the internal memory. A portion of this memory is reserved for storing a short system program that controls the operation of the computer. This housekeeping program is conceptually typical of other computers having the usual ability to handle the input/output operations and process instruction in a prescribed order.

The main memory contains the system program and the current program with data and instructions for processing those data. Figure 11–4 shows the general categories of information in the internal memory.

In the Model 20 the binary digits are handled in eight-digit groups

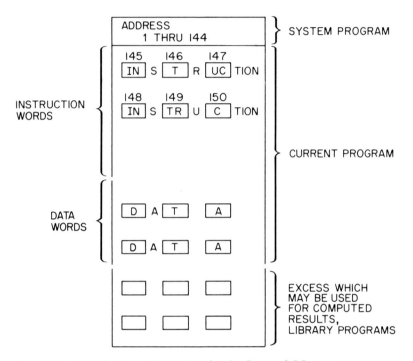

FIG. 11–4   Categories of Information in the Internal Memory.

called *bytes.* Each group has a label called *address,* which identifies its location in memory. For example, Fig. 11–4 shows that the system programs are stored in the first 144 eight-digit groups. Thus, addresses 1 through 144 are reserved. Other computers in the 360 system handle information in bytes. Several bytes can be strung together with, perhaps, four-digit units having significance within some bytes. These long groups are convenient, because data-processing applications involve an unusual variety of information formats, some long and some short. The long groups may occupy several memory addresses, having one for each byte.

Data are stored in the internal memory in 64 by 64 arrays of pinhead-sized ferrite torrids that are magnetized in either of two directions to represent binary 0 or 1. We see in Fig. 11–1 that memory capacity of 4096 bytes is available. As we mentioned in Chapter 8, each magnetic core is threaded with wires to energize the core and detect the direction of magnetism in the core. We said that the wires were connected so that the action of energizing the core in row 6 column 12 of the top 64 by 64 array would conveniently energize all eight cores in the corresponding locations on the lower arrays, as shown in Fig. 11–5. Thus, a byte is the basic unit of information.

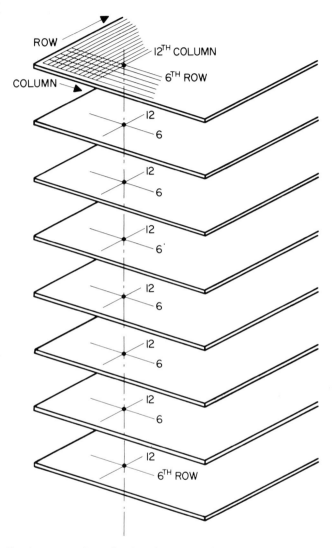

ROW

12TH COLUMN

6TH ROW

COLUMN

12
6

12
6

12
6

12
6

12
6

12
6

12
6TH ROW

FIG. 11–5 Common Organization for Internal Memories.

The Model 20 has eight general-purpose registers. These units are electronic devices that operate at high speeds comparable to the arithmetic and control circuits. Thus, they serve as a buffer between the slower internal memory and the arithmetic units. Registers in the Model 20 can each store 16 digits, which is 2 bytes. High-speed data storage is a usual feature of computers, even though the cost is high. Every arithmetic operation utilizes at least one register for temporarily holding the data moving to and from the arithmetic unit. Two registers are grouped to store the important 32-digit program status word (PSW), which assures that instructions will be executed in the proper sequence. It is continually altered as the program progresses.

In the next section we'll discuss the basic format for representing information in the Model 20. This information is transferred through the internal memory and into the general-purpose registers. We'll see that the format designates the registers or specifies the number of bytes that are handled together.

11.3.3   Formats for Representing Information

Programmers use computer languages, such as FORTRAN or COBOL statements, to specify operation in a program. The computer compiler establishes one or more basic machine instructions for each language statement. This section is concerned with the format of these machine instructions.

Electronic and magnetic devices are designed to have two stable states; hence, binary digits are the only form of information handled by computers. For our discussion of computer activity, it would be unwieldy to fill every sentence with long strings of 0 and 1. Thus, it is conventional to discuss groups of binary digits. The term *computer word* refers to a group of binary digits that are processed as a unit. We mentioned in Section 11.3.2 that the Model 20 handles eight-digit basic groups called bytes. To form larger data units, several bytes are grouped to form data words. Let's discuss the general purpose of computer words and then show specific formats.

In Chapter 10 we described computer operation as a cyclic process involving memory fetches, stores, and control activities. The cycle begins by fetching and interpreting an instruction word during the *instruction cycle*. The logic circuits in the control unit cause the proper signals to be energized in accordance with that interpretation. For example, an instruction word might specify that two numbers be added together to form a sum. The control unit would energize the ADD line to the arithmetic unit. The cycle is completed during the *execution cycle* in which data words are fetched, processed by the arithmetic unit, and stored as specified.

The execution cycle is always preceded by an instruction cycle and followed by the instruction cycle for the next operation. At any time during a run the computer is performing either the instruction or the execution cycle.

The *instruction word* is a binary-coded representation of an operation to be performed and the memory address of the data word involved in the operation. The word has at least two parts, as shown in Fig. 11–6. The term OP code is the abbreviation of the *operation code* specifying exactly what

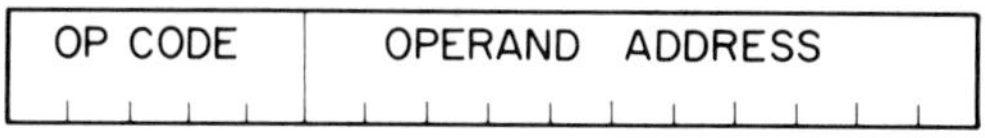

OP CODE	OPERAND ADDRESS

FIG. 11–6 General Format for Single-Address Instruction Word.

is to be performed next. The Model 20 is capable of 36 arithmetic and logical operations; therefore, it has 36 different OP codes. The second part of the basic instruction word gives the memory *address of the operand* (the data word involved in the operation). This single instruction word is used in single-address computers. It is described here in our discussion of the Model 20 as an example of instruction word format. It leads us to the more complex instruction words, shown in Figs. 11–7 through 11–9, that are used in the Model 20.

Arithmetic operations always involve at least two operands. The single-address computer performs arithmetic operations on the specified operand and a storage register called the accumulator. The Model 20 designers have provided more flexibility in the instruction word format. Figure 11–7(a) shows that the first operand can be selected from any one of the *six general-purpose registers*. The instruction word is stored in memory until it is processed. The OP code appears in positions 0 through 7, which have more than adequate binary digits for distinguishing between the 36 individual instructions. In general, the 360 Systems use words having groups of four and eight binary digits. A group of four digits can represent 0000 through 1111, which is only 16 combinations. The binary number for 36 is 100100, which requires at least six storage positions. Thus, the first eight positions in the instruction word are used for the OP code; the four positions, 8 through 11, specify the address of the general register containing the first operand. Of course, three binary digits are sufficient to distinguish between the six registers. Figure 11–7(a) shows that the last four digits in the 16-digit word specify the address of the register containing the second operand. The format in Fig. 11–7(b) is similar, except the second operand is in memory.

Ex. 11–4

What problem might arise if the Model 20 used only the format in Fig. 11–7(a)? In (b)?

Obviously, the computer would be severely limited if it could only process data from six registers, as implied by the format in Fig. 11–7(a). The format in Fig. 11–7(b) is a satisfactory and flexible instruction word. By using both formats, the Model 20 can store frequently used constants in the available registers from which they can be fetched in less time than from memory. For example, in payroll processing the register might con-

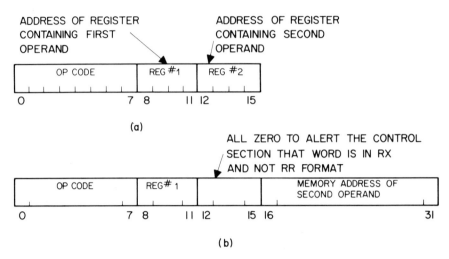

ADDRESS OF REGISTER
CONTAINING FIRST
OPERAND

ADDRESS OF REGISTER
CONTAINING SECOND
OPERAND

(a)

ALL ZERO TO ALERT THE CONTROL
SECTION THAT WORD IS IN RX
AND NOT RR FORMAT

(b)

FIG. 11–7   Model 20 Instruction Word for (a) RR Instruction Format Having Both Operands in Registers; (b) RX Format Having One Operand in a Memory Address and One in a Register.

tain the hourly pay rate of employees. It takes 196 microseconds for the add operation in RR format compared to 231 microseconds in the RX format.

The *variable word length* of the Model 20 is handled by the *SS format.* Figure 11–8 shows positions for the memory address for two operands.

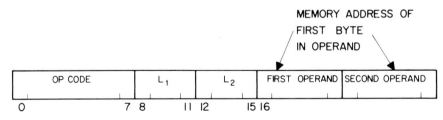

MEMORY ADDRESS OF
FIRST BYTE
IN OPERAND

FIG. 11–8   Two-Address Instruction Words in SS Format.

The binary digits in these positions specify the address of the first byte in each operand.

Operands in data processing may range from long to short or, for example, banks handling accounts process operands that range from cents to millions.

The L_1 position in the SS format specifies the length of the first operand in bytes. The four positions can contain the 16 combinations of binary 000 through 1111. A long number or name would begin in the byte in the specified memory address and continue through adjacent bytes as required up to 16 bytes. The L_2 positions serve a similar purpose in specifying the length of the second operand.

The formats for these *variable-length data words* are shown in Fig. 11–9. The three formats specify a sign and magnitude of the coded number.

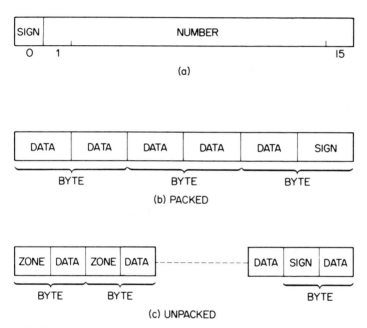

FIG. 11–9   Data Word Formats for Model 20: (a) Fixed Length; (b) Variable Length for Internal Processing; (c) Variable Length for Communication to Peripheral I/O Unit.

Program processing generally begins by compiling the higher-level language program to obtain a sequence of machine instruction. These automatically appear in formats such as RR, RX, or SS. The entire operation of compiling and processing a program is automatic. The computer is designed to commence the processing by fetching an instruction word from a selected memory address. The operator uses switches on a small console to make this address selection. The operation called for in the first instruction is performed. Examples of the arithmetic operation are add and subtract. Upon completion of this processing, the next instruction is fetched. It normally is located in the next memory address in sequence, unless it follows an instruction that called for a branch. In the Model 20, two special-purpose registers are used in the automatic executing of instruction in the desired order. These registers store a 32-digit *program status word* (PSU), which contains the 16-digit address of the next instruction and other digits that are necessary for proper program execution. The PSU contents are tested after each execution. The proper combination of digits in PSU will cause the logic circuits to generate appropriate signals to control the processing sequence.

11.3.4   Controlling the Central Processing Unit and Input/Output

Computer processing is automatic once a program is compiled and stored in memory. However, someone must flip the switches to commence the automatic routine and monitor the activity during the processing. The computer operator uses the switches, keys, and lights on the CPU console to control the system. The console of the IBM 2020 is shown in Fig. 11–10.

From television and newsprint cartoons, we have been presented the notion that flashing *lights* are a fundamental component in computer equipment. The Model 20 console has typical rows of these winking lights. The 16 lights in each row display the 16-digit contents of eight general-purpose registers. For example, all register positions containing binary 1 are displayed by a light that is on in that position in the row of lights. The computer would function without the lights, which is contrary to the television and cartoon impression. The lights aid the operator in commencing a run or checking a malfunction by conveniently showing the binary contents of the registers.

Various keys are available to the *console* operator. Examples are the *start* key, system *reset* key (stops CPU immediately), and program *load* key (starts a card reader). Switches are available to stop the operations when the processing has reached a particular address. By activating the switch called the instruction *step,* the processing goes in slow motion, with one instruction executed each time the switch is pressed. The console has six knobs with dials labeled 0 through 9 and then A through F for a total of 16 characters. These knobs are used by the operator in altering the contents of the internal memory, general register, or the PSU. The two knobs on the left of the console are used to enter the desired alterations. The next two knobs select the register and the next two select the particular memory address involved in the alteration. For example, to enter the binary group 0011, one of the knobs on the left would be set to 3. Using two knobs, a setting of 3F would enter 0011   1111. These knobs are called data switches.

FIG. 11–10   Operator's Console of Central Processing Unit.
(Courtesy of IBM.)

11.4   INTRODUCTION TO UNIVAC 1108

The IBM System 360 Model 20 and UNIVAC 1108 have *many features in common* because both are general-purpose computers that operate from stored programs. They both have high-speed electronic circuits that perform the arithmetic and control operations in the CPU. They both have magnetic-core memories.

The hardware units in the UNIVAC 1108 are shown in Fig. 11–11. The diagram has one CPU and two memory banks each having 65,536 38-digit words including two digits for parity checking. The fixed word length is one basic difference between the 1108 and the Model 20, which can string together up to 16 bytes. Otherwise, the basic configuration of the single processor 1108 is similar in concept to the Model 20. We mentioned several times in Chapters 1 through 10 that most general purpose computers are based on similar concepts.

The UNIVAC 1108 is typical of large general-purpose computers for scientific applications. The Model 20 is a data-processing computer that is well suited for business applications. They are used for different purposes; hence, as we might expect, there are marked differences between these two computers. Figure 11–12 shows that the UNIVAC 1108 fills the room with 5 to 10 times more cabinets, consoles, memory banks, and peripheral units than the Model 20. The memory cycle takes only 0.75 microsecond, which is one tenth the cycle time for the Model 20. It has up to three CPU units that can all function simultaneously.

11.4.1   Capabilities of Computers for Scientific Applications

The UNIVAC 1108 is designed for high-speed processing of scientific problems that may have several million arithmetic operations in the steps to the desired solution. In addition to the multiple processors, the system uses multiple peripheral units and multiple data transfer paths to effectively keep the CPU in nearly continuous activity. The transmission paths are short, because all units are in the immediate vicinity of each other. We remember the Model 20 has provisions for communicating with a remote terminal. In solving lengthy scientific problems, the computer has the objective of getting through each step as rapidly as possible with minimum delay in accessing the memory or peripheral units. These twin objectives are handled by the high-speed devices and multiple-processing features of computers such as the UNIVAC 1108.

The capabilities of the 1108 are expanded by *multiple processors.* Figure 11–13 shows the configuration for a system with two central processor units. In normal multiprocessor operation, three processors are active simultaneously. They share the 262,142-word capacity of four

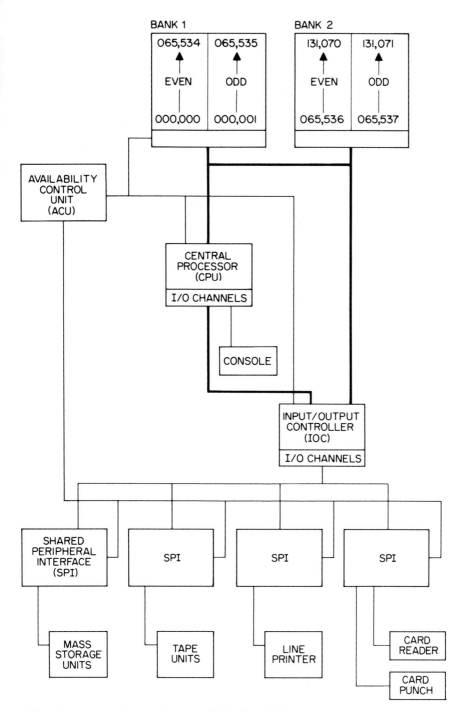

FIG. 11–11   Hardware Units of UNIVAC 1108.

FIG. 11–12   UNIVAC 1108. (Courtesy of UNIVAC.)

memory banks. Three of these banks are shown in Fig. 11–13. The processors share the two input/output controllers (IOC); each IOC is capable
of controlling 16 input/output units.

The processors share the input/output units in four *peripheral subsystems* (drum, mass storage, tape printer, and reader punch). In the
multiple paths between CPU and I/O units, Fig. 11–13 shows two (IOCs)
and a shared peripheral interface (SPI) for each peripheral subsystem. The
IOC and SPI units are basically logic circuits that operate in conjunction
with the availability control unit (ACU). The function of this combination
of equipment is the transfer of data from any one of the three CPUs to
the selected I/O units in an understandable code. The ACU has the main
duty of keeping the CPU informed of which I/O units are available. The
IOC of the 1108 has the same basic function as the IOC of the Model
20. The IOC can control up to 16 I/O units. It turns the units on and off,
decodes the output data, checks the parity digits for errors, and provides
a buffer between the high-speed CPU and lower-speed output units. In a
write operation, the buffering action consists of the IOC gathering a chain
of digits from the CPU and then transferring them at a slower rate to the
printer before gathering the next chain. The SPI functions with an input/
output subsystem and has the basic function of connecting the proper
peripheral unit to the CPU commanding the use of a specific unit.

In multiple-processor systems, we can expect that some units in the

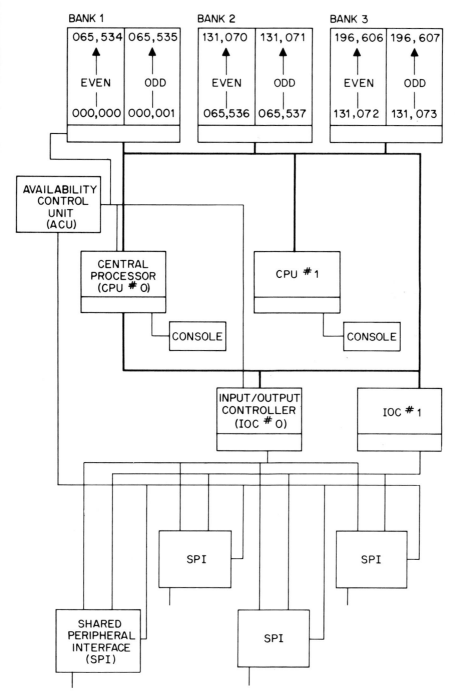

FIG. 11–13   UNIVAC 1108 Multiprocessor System.

195

shared arrangement will be requested by *two CPUs at the same time*. In case of a conflict, the request that arrives first is acted upon, and then all pending requests are handled. In case of a tie, the predetermined priority sequence of CPU 0, CPU 1, and, finally, CPU 2 is used to resolve the matter.

The multiple-processing feature of the 1108 forms a powerful and complex system. In our brief discussion of the system, we can't go into many details. We want to point to basic similarities between the 1108 and other computers and also discuss the features of the 1108 that make it well suited for scientific applications. The next two sections discuss the concepts of the internal memory and the control section.

We should understand the automatically generated format for storing the instructions and data in memory. As a point of interest, we will discuss the concept of memory access in a multiple-processing system. The discussion in this chapter on the control section is a review of the material in Chapter 10, where we discussed the concepts of computer control systems. We used the UNIVAC 1108 control unit as an example. Therefore, our discussion of the 1108 control unit in Section 11.4.3 is a review of the material in Chapter 10.

11.4.2   Internal Memory

All word formats have 36 information digits plus two parity digits for the UNIVAC 1108. The basic storage component is the millions of tiny magnetic cores that are magnetized in one of two directions to store the binary information as 1's and 0's. The memory units and organization into words are similar in concept to other magnetic-core memories. The tiny cores are strung onto two crisscrossing wires that carry electrical currents to magnetize the cores in the desired direction during the cycle of writing information in memory. Other wires sense the direction of the magnetism present in the cores and are used when the CPU requests that information be read from memory. It is standard procedure to have three-dimensional arrangements such as illustrated in Fig. 11–5. The individual core elements are arranged into planer arrays, which are then stacked to fill a cubical column. To perform a write operation, two crisscrossing wires are energized with a current that is one half the level needed to cause the core to become magnetized. All cores in a selected row will receive $I/2$ applied to that row. Similarly, the cores in a column can be energized by $I/2$. One core at the intersection of the selected row and column will be energized with $I/2$ plus $I/2$, which is sufficient to cause that core to be magnetized with the directed polarity. This core may store the first digit in the 38-digit computer words. The 1108 memory is arranged in a manner that is typical in concept with the core memories. It is arranged into 38 stacks of planer array, the corresponding rows and column of arrays threaded with the same wire. Thus, the selection of a core element on the top array will be in unison with the selection of the cores in the corresponding rows and columns of the other 37 arrays to write the 38-digit computer word. The memory cycle time is 0.75 microsecond (750 nanoseconds).

The *instruction word format* for the 1108 is discussed in Chapter 10 and is illustrated in Fig. 10–3. The format has the common parts, such as the OP code and the operand address. The 1108 is a single-address machine, which means that the data word at the operand address is the only word from internal memory that is involved in the immediate operation. It is clear that the instruction word identifies which of the 65,535 memory locations in a memory bank are involved in an operation. The 1108 has 128 registers that can each store 38 digits. Some of these high-speed storage units are involved in almost every operation executed by the computer. The instruction word identifies the register where data will be stored or fetched during an operation. The simple task of the instruction word is to specify the operation to be performed (whether it be add, subtract, read, etc.) and identify the registers and the internal memory address involved in a particular operation.

Let's look briefly at the *instruction word format* in Fig. 10–3. The operation code (OP code) is in positions 30 through 35. These six digits can be arranged in 63 combinations. The 1108 is capable of performing 140 instructions. The portion of the instruction occupying positions 26 through 29 is used primarily as an OP code extension. The 10 digits in the combined field are sufficient to distinguish between the 140 OP codes. Almost every computer operation involves data from internal memory and from the registers. The X and R registers are used sometimes in lieu of the familiar accumulators. There are 16 A, X, and R registers each for a total of 48. The OP code specifies whether the A, X, or R registers are to be used. Positions 22 through 25 identify the particular accumulator, X, or R registers.

It frequently occurs that mathematical solutions contain a sequence of steps that must be repeated several times. The *index registers* that can be specified by the digits in positions 18 through 21 of the instruction word are useful in these applications and others. Mathematicians won't admit it, but sometimes they aren't sure what the exact answer should be, so they write a long series of terms with their sum tending to converge to the exact answer. With the convenient sum series, the sum of the first and second term is closer to the exact answer than the first term alone. By adding the third term and then others, the approach is even closer. In some series, several dozen terms must be included to make a reasonable approximation. Generally, all the terms are very similar, which means the computer is making similar computations in handling each term. This class of problems is one application of the programming technique of looping through several steps a specified number of times. This number is stored where it can be quickly checked every cycle to ascertain whether the repetition processing should be continued for another cycle. Usually the contents of the index register are automatically reduced by one or more counts on each check. Eventually, the count becomes zero, signaling the end of the sequence. The UNIVAC 1108 has 16 index registers that are specified directly by the four digits in positions 18 through 21. There are 16 *executive index registers* that are specified by these same digits and a slightly different OP code. All registers store 36 digits of information and two digits for parity checking.

The most important feature left in our discussion of the instruction word in Fig. 10–3 is the provision for specifying addresses in internal memory. This operand address is specified by the 16 digits at the extreme right end of the word.

Ex. 11–5

The 16 digits in the U field barely are sufficient to distinguish between the 65,535 operand addresses in a single memory bank. Figure 11–13 shows three storage banks but there could be four having a total of 262,142 operand addresses. What schemes would you suggest to handle the addresses in the three higher-numbered banks?

Some ideas, if adopted, might bankrupt the computer business. Other ideas, if originated in this example problem, might make this book a best seller. It is obvious that the operand address must be longer: 17 digits for two storage banks, 18 digits for three, and 19 digits for four. Our first idea might be to make the instruction word longer by 3 digits; however, this means that every magnetic core arrangement would have 41 rather than 38 arrays in each stack. This total is $3 \times 262,142$ or 786,426 extra digits, which is approximately 20,700 words, each having 38 digits.

The conventional scheme is to access memory locations in the higher-numbered banks by *indirect addressing*. This technique uses some of the memory locations in the first bank to store the address of higher-numbered banks. Let's assume that it is desired to fetch data from memory address 127,000. This can't be addressed directly by the scant 16-digits available in the instruction word for the operand address. The compiled program will automatically resort to indirect addressing and may use memory location 50,000 in the operation. The automatically generated instruction word should have a 1 in position 16 to signify indirect addressing, the proper OP code to specify a data fetch, and the binary equivalent of 50,000 as operand address. The logic circuits in the control section will bring digits stored in positions 0 through 21 of address 50,000 into the control registers. If the computer did its job as when the program was in place in memory, initially, the 22 digits should be the binary equivalence of the desired address 127,000 from which data should be fetched immediately.

Data words for the UNIVAC 1108 are shown in Fig. 11–14. They all have the basic structure of 38 digits, which is the same number of digits as the instruction word. The two parity digits are not shown, but they always appear after each group of 18 digits. The format of the instruction word presents the basic information of what to do with the data in specific memory locations. The OP code tells what to do and the operand address tells where the data are stored. Data words are stored in internal memory using magnetic cores that are arranged in and operated in exactly the same manner as the instruction words of the program. In fact, data words of subsequent programs may occupy the same locations in the instruction words as the present program. It is, therefore, reasonable that data words be structured to have 36 information digits. They also have a parity digit after each 18 information digits. A data word occupies a total of 38 memory positions, which is exactly the same as an instruction word.

The 1108 with 36-digit data words may be used in scientific problems. The field of science is immense, dealing with items and numbers that may be very small or very large. For example, the scientist may want computer programs that can solve for distances that may be one millionth of an inch or 1 million miles. We'll see that 36-digit data words are capable of handling either situation.

The *fixed-point data word format* in Fig. 11–14(a) is a simple binary

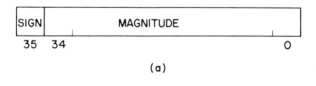

(a)

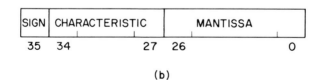

(b)

FIG. 11–14   Data Word Format: (a) Fixed-Point Word; (b) Floating-Point Word.

equivalence of the original decimal number. The format name implies that the radix point is fixed at the right-hand end of both the binary and decimal numbers. Both numbers are integers with no fractional parts.

The *floating-point format* in Fig. 11–14(b) is typical of most computers handling scientific problems. We are familiar with exponential tech-

Ex. 11–6

What is the largest decimal number that can be represented by a 36-digit data word in fixed-point format?

The 1108 has ample capacity for storing the largest integer that is allowable in the FORTRAN IV language. This number is 2,147,483,647, which is 1 less than the binary number that can be stored in a 31-digit data word. The leftmost digit is reserved for sign, with the normal convention that 1 represents minus and 0 represents plus.

The absolute value of an integer must be less than or equal to 34, 359, 738, 367, which is $2^{35} - 1$.

niques for writing numbers that may be large or small. For example, the speed of light propagation is 300 million meters per second, which can be written in shortened form as 300×10^6 or 3×10^8 or 0.3×10^9 meters per second. This value has two parts, the numbers 0.3 and the exponent 9. These correspond to the two parts in a floating-point data word. For this example, the binary equivalent of 0.3 would be stored in positions 0 through 26, which is conventionally called the *mantissa*. The exponent 9 would be stored in positions 27 through 34 along with a sign digit to identify the exponent as positive. Position 35 is used to store the sign of the mantissa, which is positive in this example. In all cases, the *exponent* is the power of 10 that is obtained by shifting the decimal point until the fractional portion of the number is between 1 and 0.1.

Ex. 11–7

How would the number 750 nanoseconds be stored in floating-point format? A nanosecond is 10^{-9} second; thus, our number is 750×10^{-9}. We must shift the decimal point to the left to obtain 0.750×10^{-6}. The mantissa is 0.11000, and the characteristic is negative 110.

The floating-point format uses the 36 available digits to represent numbers in the vast range from 10^{38} to 10^{-38}. However the limited mantissa necessitates all conversion be rounded off to 27 digits, causing a slight sacrifice in accuracy. For greater accuracy, the 1108 has the conventional provision for extending the mantissa into the 36 digits of the data word in the next address. This format is called *double-precision floating point*. It uses two computer words to represent a number.

11.4.3 Control Section (Review of Chapter 10)

The programmer formulates a solution using a program language. The statements and steps in the computer solution may be conceptually similar to those in a manual solution or, at least, they serve the same purpose. The control section in the central processor unit takes charge of the program run once the user language is compiled and a set of machine instructions is obtained. Every instruction for the 1108 will be a member of its 140-instruction repertoire and have an OP code. The instructions are executed in a prescribed sequence that may include conditional branching. The computer designers have formed the control section from logic circuits that have the straightforward objective of generating high or low pulses for a number of terminals upon interpretation of the OP code. These control signals cause data to be fetched or stored in the vast internal memory or in one of the 128 control registers, arithmetic operations to be performed, and the input/output unit to be operated. These basic operations are controlled in the appropriate time frame, and then the address of the next instruction word is made ready. Before the next instruction is fetched, the contents of the *processor state register* (PSR) are set. The PSR of the 1108 serves a purpose similar to the program status word (PSW) in the Model 20. Both the PSR and PSW record the condition of the processing as it may be affected by preceding events. These information digits are considered along with each OP code. The control signals generated by the 1108 correspond to interpreted OP code and PSR.

12 Concepts of Program Compilers

The logic circuits in the control section are permanently wired to execute several basic instructions. For example, the instruction calling for data transfer to memory will cause the logic circuits to send signals to the appropriate terminals in memory to achieve this transfer. The permanently wired instructions are fundamental enough to be a part of almost any numerical operation. By selecting the right instruction and in the proper order, a programmer can cause the computer to function. The compiler automates this task of selecting and ordering instruction by translating the statement from a higher-level language.

Let's depart from the jargon of logic circuits and instruction words to present the concept of computer compilers. The *compiler* translates each statement in a higher-level language into one or more basic instructions. Let's compare this automatic processing with the mental processing that may be done by a *musician* who is translating the written music into instrument sounds. Let's consider the common six-string guitar. The instrument is capable of six fundamental frequencies and other higher frequencies that may be produced by touching the strings with the fingers of the left hand. From one to six strings may be involved in playing a given note. The musician has learned from teaching or experience. This compilation of knowledge is used to translate the notes into music. We don't want to get sidetracked too far with the guitar player. The main point is that a few basic physical moves such as plucking and holding strings at the appropriate time can cause several notes to be played. It would be impractical to design a guitar with a separate string or key for every note or chord that might appear in several songs. It also would be impractical to write music in a form that would show every physical move that is necessary in generating a sound from an instrument. The code would be *lengthy and prone to error* by the writer, but more importantly the music sheet for a guitar could not be used for a piano or other instrument.

Computer codes and music codes have been developed for somewhat the same reasons. These *shorthand notations* lessen the code writer's effort in preparing and checking information.

The higher-level computer languages are designed to handle statements that are similar in structure to the common formula or expressions that may be used in the manual solutions. This similarity makes the computer codes easier to learn and remember. Most languages can be *compiled by several computer* models from several individual manufacturers. By knowing a basic language, the occasional user can solve problems today despite the fact that a new computer system may have been installed last week. This nicety is somewhat analogous to learning the rules for forming a music score and then being able to play the *same song on a piano or guitar.*

We have tried to interest you in computer compilers by showing analogies between computer programs and music scores. There are differences between the two, however. There is probably more creative writing in a song than in a computer program. If you compare music and computer careers, you'll agree that the probability is high that a programmer will work with a $15 million computer whereas the probability is low that a musician will play in a $15 million orchestra.

12.1 PROGRAMMER/COMPILER/COMPUTER INTERFACE

The programmer formulates a general approach to be used in solving a scientific problem or a data-processing problem. The approach is usually outlined by constructing a flow chart to illustrate the branches, loops, and numerous decisions that lead to the solution. Several associates usually participate in the critical formulation stage. They also assist in selecting input data that are representative and output data that are useful. (We'll discuss flow charts in Section 12.2 and the duties of programmers and associates in Chapter 17.)

The language is selected. We'll assume that FORTRAN IV is used for scientific solutions and COBOL is used for data-processing solutions. There are other languages, but the choice is limited. The programmer then writes program statements by rigorously applying the rules of the language. Each statement must contain stereotype information to properly identify it to the compiler. The programmer uses a pencil and a convenient coding sheet to write the program steps. Eventually, punch cards are generated for each horizontal line of coded information. Keypunch operators perform a valuable service in the first step of getting the program into a binary form. Typical programs consist of 100 or more punched cards.

12.1.1   Source Programs and Object Programs

The original language is the *source* language and the desired language is the *object* language. The deck of cards forming the source program usually is closely checked by the programmers before the information is translated by the compiler into the object language. Keypunching and coding errors can sometimes be spotted by looking through the deck. It is easier to proofread a program that has been listed on a printed sheet. Some computer facilities have hardware units that read punched cards and print a listing. Comments are printed at the end of the list concerning obvious errors, such as misuse of the language. After correcting the erroneous cards, the source deck is taken to the computer for the first critical test.

12.1.2   Outputs from Compiler

The compiler is a special program that converts the source language into a form suitable for execution on the computer. Compilers are stored on magnetic discs or magnetic tape. The first few cards in the source program are control cards, and one of them directs that the appropriate compiler be loaded into internal memory. The processing control then switches to the compiler and the programmer's deck is accepted as input. Output is another deck of *punched cards* and a printed *diagnostic* list. Frankly, both outputs are disappointing. The generated object deck is relatively short but practically unreadable because the information is in binary. The diagnostic report makes persons of all intelligence levels feel like idiots, because comments are printed to highlight every mistake in spelling, spacing, and the like.

The overall translation function of the compiler is achieved in three distinct phases. These are *syntactic analysis, storage allocation, and object code generation.* The phases are completed in sequence and all phases are completed before the object deck is punched. Our description of compilers has a linguistic flavor as evidenced by the use of terms such as "language translation" and "syntactic analysis." In grammar, the term syntax is defined to be the arrangement of word forms to show their mutual relations in the sentence. We all have diagrammed sentences by placing the subject, verb, and object on one line and then designating the modifiers.

During the *syntactic analysis phase,* every higher-level statement is compared with permissible statement forms that can be handled by the compiler. Most compilers have a stored table of syntax rules that describes the source language. For example, a section of the table lists the rules for compiling arithmetic statements. The appearance of an arithmetic statement in the source program is identified by the compiler and checked against the rules in the appropriate section of the syntax table. The statement may have addition, subtraction, exponentiation, and so on. Each of these operations is a subset of arithmetic statements. The syntactic information is inserted at points throughout the source program. These inserted flags explicitly identify every statement by type and every operation within that statement. As the syntactic analysis is completed, the modified source program is stored in internal memory or a temporary file. Obviously, the flags contribute to easier generation of the object code in the next phase.

Ex. 12–1

Each operation in an arithmetic statement is identified by type during syntactic analysis. These flags or labels serve the obvious purpose of defining whether the coded instruction should be add, subtract, multiply, or other. In serving a less obvious role, the flags identify which operations should be coded and executed first. The order of execution is important in arithmetic operations, as evidenced by the expression $6 + \frac{3}{4}$. In manual calculation we would divide 3 by 4 to get 0.75 and add to 6 to get 6.75. The flags direct the compiler to generate instruction for division before addition. The complete hierarchy of operations is exponentiation first, followed by division, multiplication, addition, and subtraction. In any expression, all flags are scanned automatically to find the one with highest hierarchy. Instructions for it are generated, and then the next highest is handled.

What answer would be obtained by mistakenly performing the operations in $6 + \frac{3}{4}$ in the order of their appearance? We have 6 plus 3 equals 9 divided by 4 to yield an erroneous answer of 2.25.

Any statement that doesn't follow the pattern of statements in syntax tables will be diagnosed as a *programming error*. Some errors are serious enough to make the statement completely vague and thereby prevent the program from running. The programmer may be a little miffed when greeted with the diagnostic printout, but he or she usually resolves to correct the error and resubmit the source program. Compilers have very limited ability to interpret ambiguous statements. The programmer has no opportunity to mutter, "You know what I mean," in attempting to clarify the nonsense in a computer statement. The diagnostic report is a list of all statement numbers that mistakenly specify operations other than those contained in the syntax table. This straightforward method of automatically detecting programming errors is similar in concept to the manual method of diagramming sentences to detect grammatical errors.

In the second phase of compiler activity, memory addresses are allocated for every data word in the source program. A typical machine instruction specifies arithmetic operations and involves data from one or more registers or memory locations. The compiler generates long lists (commonly called rolls) that contain the data names and the automatically assigned memory addresses. Rolls are generated listing the addresses of arrays, variables, and the like. This tabulated information is available for forming specific codes in the next phase of compiler execution. Instruction words that specify operations on data must contain binary codes for the memory addresses of the data. These addresses are listed on the rolls during allocation. In a few cases, programming errors may prevent the successful completion of the allocation phase. Error messages are issued automatically.

During the code generation phase, the source program (with valid operations flagged) is reprocessed by the compiler. The information between flags is translated into sequences of instruction words. The computer manufacturer supplies compilers to generate instruction codes that are compatible with the instruction repertoire for that computer model. Section 10.2 gives some common machine codes for the UNIVAC 1108.

12.2   PRINCIPLES OF FLOW CHARTS

We sometimes ask others, "What would you do if so-and-so happened?" Often, they avoid the decision and reply, "We'll cross that bridge when we get to it." A roughly synonymous statement might be, "We'll draw that flow chart when the time comes." A *flow chart* is a valuable graphical representation of operations and the sequence in which they are performed. We could draw flow charts to illustrate our activities during a typical day. Fortunately, our daily activities usually aren't confused to the extent that we need flow charts to keep track of them.

12.2.1   Need for Clearly Defined Program Steps

A computer does one operation and then moves on to the next. If the programmer has written source program statements that are out of sequence, the compiler will generate instructions that also are out of sequence. Flow charts are a tool to illustrate the sequence of operations in the source program. Flow charts are sketched in the early stages of formulating computer solutions. They serve programmers at that point in somewhat the same ways as topic outlines serve students in writing a term paper. Flow charts facilitate communications among programmers, engineers, or the business staff. The latter two may not be familiar enough with computer languages to use them to express ideas for problem solution. It is fairly *natural* for all three to use the geometric shape and arrow language of flow charts.

Programmers find that flow charts are an assistance in the *debugging* phases. To save computer-use charges, it is important that the source program be relatively free of mistakes before it is submitted to the computer. Some computer centers have an intermediate debugging step that precedes the compiler. This step is usually performed on a self-service basis by running the source program through a card reader/printer that lists the program on a printed page (as we mentioned in Section 12.1.1) and automatically draws the flow chart. Consider the time saving in polishing the composition of a term paper if we could submit the rough draft to a machine for automatic structuring of the topic outline. This fictional exercise might identify paragraphs or sentences that need restructuring or reorganizing to create a smooth flowing and easily read paper. We might say this editing step serves to debug the term paper. In complex computer programs, manual or machine-generated flow charts are absolutely essential in the debugging process.

12.2.2 Standard Flow-Chart Symbols

Computers process one operation at a time and then move on to the next operation. In the flow-chart technique, operations are represented by drawing the appropriate geometric shape. These flow-chart symbols are connected by arrows to illustrate the sequence of operations. If you are inclined to be individualistic and shun convention, you are free to choose any shape for a given operation. For example, you may choose a rectangle for all operations and simply write inside it what operation is represented by each symbol. You might choose arrows to show the processing sequence. The result would be acceptable, provided the writing didn't clutter the chart.

It is conventional to use symbols of a specific shape for each category of operation. There are about six basic categories; hence, there are only a few symbols to remember. For example, input/output operations are usually represented by a parallelogram, which is one of the basic symbols. Figure 12–1 shows a set of symbols that are sufficient for flow charting many computer solutions. Additional conventions have been developed to make the charts easier to read and draw. Arrowheads are omitted on flow paths directed from left to right and from top to bottom. The first operation in a sequence usually is represented by drawing a symbol at the top of the page. Subsequent operations would be represented by symbols placed lower on the page. Simple charts may be aligned in this manner so that arrowheads are unnecessary.

The symbols in Fig. 12–1 have a practical basis. The rectangle is a natural shape with space within the symbol to write several words describing the operation. The diamond shape is well suited for representing decisions because the left, right, and bottom points are appropriate for the decision outcomes. Nearly all computer decisions are based on comparing

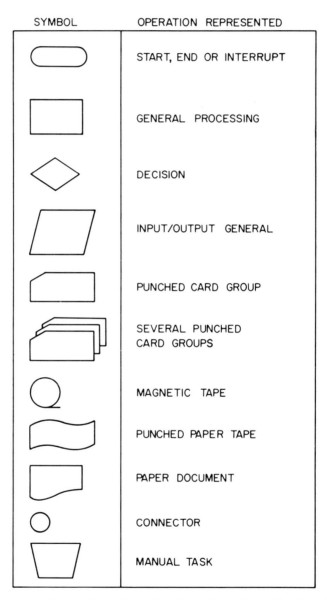

FIG. 12–1   (a) Basic Flow-Chart Symbols; (b) Flow Charting Template. (Courtesy of Bell Telephone Laboratories)

the magnitude of two data words. Of course, one of the words will be less than, greater than, or equal to the other word. The diamond shape is a reminder to provide a flow path for all three possibilities.

FIG. 12-1 (cont.)

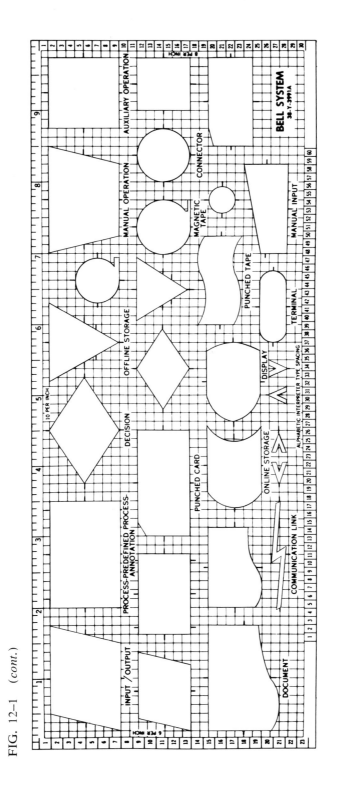

209

Ex. 12–2

Draw a flow chart to show the interrelation of operations in reading *A* and *B* from a punched card and then setting *C* equal to the larger of the two. If $A = B$, make $C = A + B$. Figure 12–2 shows this simple flow chart.

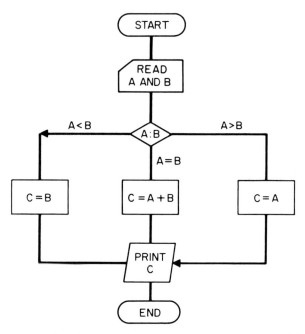

FIG. 12–2   Chart Showing Familiar Shorthand Method of Writing: *A:B* for *A* compared to *B*; *A > B* for *A* is greater than *B*; and *A < B* for *A* is less than *B*.

The parallelogram is the basic symbol for an input/output operation. It is acceptable to write within the symbol the name of the input/output device. For example, the name might be card reader, magnetic tape, or the like. Some flow charts exhibit the more graphic alternative of drawing symbols that are shaped somewhat like the actual input/output device. Figure 12–1 shows some of these symbols. Cards are the most common form of input information. The symbol, obviously card shaped, signifies a group of cards serving a common purpose. In situations where several card groups are read or punched, the flow chart might contain the three-dimensional arrangements of symbols shown in Fig. 12–1. Magnetic tapes store the master file in many data-processing applications. This symbol is a delineation of a circular tape reel with a ribbon of tape unwinding.

12.2.3 Examples of Flow Charts

Careers in the field of computers, office staff, and management have a common nuisance—there's always charts and more charts. An observer in these fields soon learns that all man's drawings are not masterpieces. The basic idea of showing operations in block diagrams is sound, but frequently the message gets obscured in a chart that is difficult to read because it is cluttered or too detailed. We want to show a few examples of the usefulness of flow charts. They have value in outlining and debugging computer programs. Charts aren't people's first love, but a clearly defined chart is well serving in formal and informal communications.

The examples in this section present flow charts for some of the basic data-processing steps. Section 12.2.4 combines these basic steps into an overall flow chart for the typical application of weekly payroll processing.

Most data-processing calculations involve information from both master files and transaction files. In payroll processing, the master *file* contains a data *record* for each employee. Typical data *items* are the employee number, pay rate, overtime status, family dependents, and unused vacation. In general, information blocks are categorized as files, records, or items depending on their size. For our examples on payroll processing, we'll assume that the master files are stored on magnetic tapes and contain all the information bearing on employee earnings. Our records are identified by payroll number, and we'll assume that they are arranged in ascending order according to this number. It is standard practice to separate the records by an interrecord gap (IRG). This blank spot on the tape is approximately 0.6 inch long and serves to identify the end and beginning of records and allows the tape to be accelerated and decelerated without infringing into a record. We'll load the master files onto a magnetic disc during the processing activity. The disc rotates continuously; thus, its IRG is approximately 20 percent of the tape IRG.

We'll read records from the master file in sequence, match with the record from the transaction file, and then proceed to calculate and prepare the paycheck for that employee. Figure 12–3 outlines the steps. Tapes are economical storage media, but aren't well suited for a long series of starts and stops because of the time waste. We'll be transferring the file to a disc from which data can be rapidly fetched. Another alternative is to read a group of master and transaction records into internal memory. When these are processed, several other groups would follow until the file is exhausted.

In Ex. 12–3 we'll draw the flow chart showing the steps in the routine

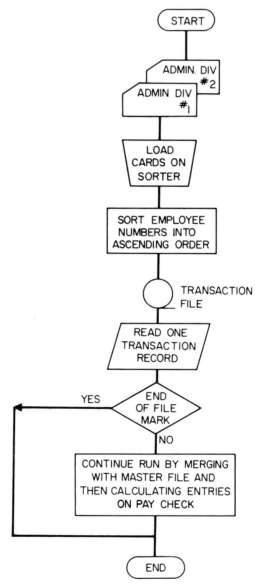

FIG. 12–3 Steps in Entering Data from Transaction Cards.

activity of updating the master file. *File maintenance* keeps the master file current by changing items such as pay rate when raises are posted, adding new employees or deleting employees who retire or otherwise terminate employment, and so on. The maintenance is performed on a periodic basis.

Additions are entered easily because new employees get the next highest payroll number and their records are entered on the end of the file. Deletions are handled by reproducing all the records on the master tape except the desired deletions. In the standard copying process the master file and a blank file are advanced on separate disc or tape units. Each binary digit on the master is read and then duplicated onto the blank tape or disc.

Ex. 12–3

Draw the flow chart for the basic steps in file maintenance. We'll show the flow chart for posting file changes and deletions. These are entered on punched cards in ascending order by employee numbers. In this example the internal memory had adequate capacity to store all changes and deletions. The operations in Fig. 12–4 yield a new master file (File 1), which is a copy of the original master file except that the appropriate records have been changed or deleted. All records are the same length and separated by an IRG. In deleting a record, File 1 is fixed while the master file advances; thus, the record following the deletion becomes adjacent to the IRG of the record preceding the deletion. Changes are posted by simply overwriting the original record.

Files are updated on a periodic basis to be ready for weekly or monthly payroll processing. In Ex. 12–3 all records of changes were stored in internal memory. Few changes will be entered on some pay periods, whereas extensive changes will be necessary for other periods. Many changes in pay rate would be posted after a union contract settlement. Several thousand records would exceed the capacity of internal memory. There are convenient ways of handling this situation. The updating can be done in seperate runs with two or more decks of cards. On the first run, changes and deletions on the first deck would be entered in memory and then posted on File 1, which then would become the master file for the second run. Obviously, extensive changes necessitate a complex file-maintenance procedure.

It is preferred that each record in the master file be kept brief and equal in length to all the other records. Long records cause the situation to become troublesome for several reasons. They require more memory allocation. For example, a 16,000-word memory could accommodate 400 or 500 records giving the basic payroll data. Long records are more likely to be changed, perhaps to update one of the nonbasic items.

As a fringe benefit, some employers provide the employees the convenience of having savings and mortgage payments deducted directly from their paycheck. These special deductions are best handled by a separate file. This approach is better than expanding the records in the master file.

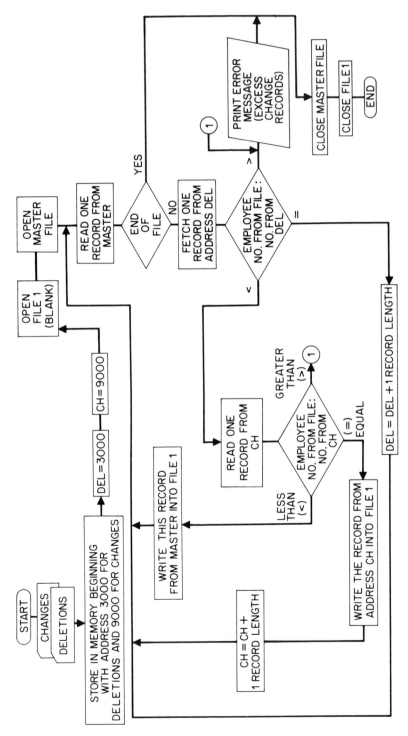

FIG. 12–4 Steps in File Maintenance.

Changes to the special deduction file may be frequent for some employees and, therefore, should be handled separately from the routine master file maintenance. Furthermore, it is desirable that all master records be the same length. Some employees might request a disproportionate number of special deductions. By keeping this nonuniformity separate from the master file, we circumvent the task of allocating memory addresses to variable-length records.

Even though the master file and special files are maintained separately, they are processed simultaneously. Exercise 12–4 shows the flow chart for this operation.

Ex. 12–4

Show the flow chart for merging the master file with the special deduction file. The objective is the formation of combined records for all employees participating in the program. Figure 12–5 serves this purpose.

The flow chart in Fig. 12–5 shows the steps in a scheme for merging the records of two files into memory addresses 7950 to 8050. The payroll computations are based on the combined records when the employee number matches, and on the master records when they mismatch. The employee number on the special record should match the number on the master record that is either currently stored in memory or upcoming. An upcoming match is possible when the special record has a higher number than the master record. Otherwise, an error condition is evidenced. Figure 12–5 shows steps for handling and recording the presence of this error. Flow charts are a convenient reminder of potential trouble. Frequently, errors originate on a decision operation. Since most decisions are based on comparing the magnitude of two data words, it is imperative that the program be designed to handle all three possible outcomes.

12.2.4 Flow Chart for an Example Payroll Problem

The efficiencies of computers in handling repetitious operations have brought data processing to nearly all sizeable payroll departments. They all have the same objective of preparing accurate paychecks and summarizing the cash outflow by accounting categories. It would seem that payrolls throughout the nation would be processed by identical procedures. We haven't made inquiries to sample the current practices, so we can't comment on who has the best procedure and why others aren't using it. Paycheck recipients are tolerant of any reasonable procedure that delivers an accurate check on time. Department managers want a procedure that utilizes equipment and personnel that are available or at least affordable.

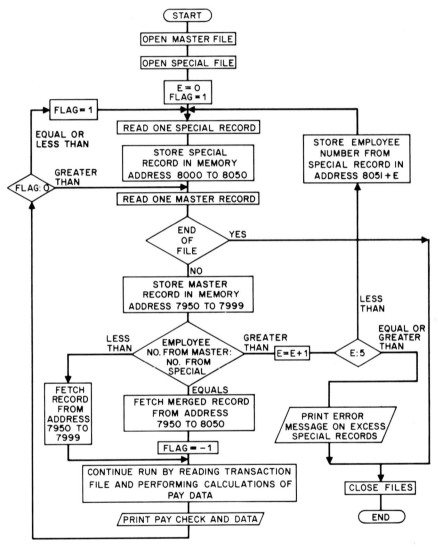

FIG. 12–5 Steps in File Merging.

There is an overall requirement that the procedure be based on files that can be protected from unintentional mistakes or fraudulent manipulation. Within these broad guidelines, there can be many different techniques in payroll processing.

Many employers contact the services of a data-processing consultant, who furnishes a software package for payroll processing. The consultant provides similar packages to all customers; however, differences exist because large employers have special needs that may be different than those of small employers. Sections of the program are tailor-made in accordance with the employer's size and special requests for deductions, file security, and accounting summaries. By file security, we mean the employer is assured that employees working with the program won't tamper with logic in deliberate fraudulent schemes. In most cases the consultant keeps the readable source program under lock and key and sells the nearly unreadable object program. The buyer doesn't want people who understand the object program details to infiltrate the payroll processing department. Usually, consultants stipulate in the contract of sale that their personnel will not accept employment with the software buyer for at least 2 years after the sale.

Ex. 12–5

Draw a flow chart for processing the payroll files to obtain printed paychecks and accounting records. Figure 12–6 shows the detailed steps in this procedure.

The concepts of processing data from files were illustrated by the flow charts in Section 12.2.3. We had examples showing the steps in preparing the transaction file, maintaining the master file, and merging the master file with a special file. This section has shown the overall flow chart for combining these operations into a payroll processing procedure. Exercise 12–5 presents the overall concepts of payroll processing.

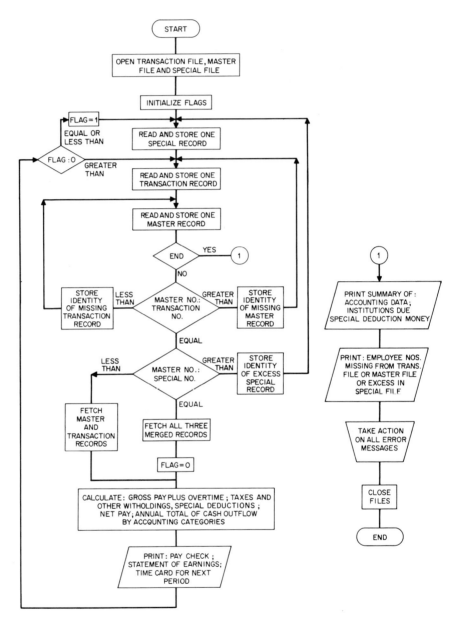

FIG. 12–6   Flow Chart For Payroll Processing.

13 The COBOL Language

Humor is appropriate at times for committees and the things they do or fail to do. Committee members often find the meeting discussions are tangled in a maze of petty arguments that tend to confuse points that should be clear to all. On the other hand, an individual studying the same matter is more likely to pursue a clearer approach in thinking out the solution. We have an opportunity to compare two outstanding higher-level computer languages. One was formulated by an individual from the computer field and the other was produced the hard way in a committee.

John W. Backus of IBM proposed in 1954 that a computer language would save scientists and engineers from the frustrations of using assembly languages. In 1959, the FORTRAN language was used on the IBM 704 by Backus and the group that participated in the development. It still is used today in the basic concepts of FORTRAN IV. The name is an acronym for *for*mula *tran*slation. Chapter 15 presents the concepts of the widely used FORTRAN language.

The Conference on Data System Languages was assigned the task of formulating a computer language that the United States governmental agencies could use to handle commercial and business problems. The new language was to alleviate the wasteful practice of training government employes to program Company X's computer and then Company Y's computer, and so on, as subsequent systems rapidly became available. In 1960, COBOL was unveiled, and with continued revisions it has become the basic language for the vast data-processing field. The name is an acronym for *c*ommon *b*usiness-*o*riented *l*anguage.

13.1   INTRODUCTION

Both FORTRAN and COBOL are outstanding achievements. In discussing the basic concepts of these languages, we will see instances where the languages are a bit tangled. These complications may be a natural by-product of committee projects. The following paragraph is required and illustrates a peculiarity of COBOL.

The following acknowledgment is reprinted from COBOL *Edition 1965* published by the Conference on Data System Languages.

Any organization interested in reproducing the COBOL report and specifications in whole or in part, using ideas taken from this report as the basis for an instruction manual or for any other purpose is free to do so. However, all such organizations are requested to reproduce this section as part of the introduction to the document. Those using a short passage, as in a book review, are requested to mention "COBOL" in acknowledgement of the source, but need not quote this entire section.

COBOL is an industry language and is not the property of any company or group of companies, or of any organization or group of organizations.

No warranty, expressed or implied, is made by any contributor or by the COBOL Committee as to the accuracy and functioning of the programming system and language. Moreover, no responsibility is assumed by any contributor, or by the committee, in connection therewith.

Procedures have been established for the maintenance of COBOL. Inquiries concerning the procedures for proposing changes should be directed to this Executive Committee of the Conference on Data Systems Languages. The authors and copyright holders of the copyright material used herein:

FLOW-MATIC (Trademark of Sperry Rand Corporation), Programming for the UNIVAC I and II, Data Automation Systems copyrighted 1958, 1959, by Sperry Rand Corporation; IBM Commercial Translator Form No. F28–8013, copyrighted 1959 by IBM; FACT, DSI 27A52602760, copyrighted 1960 by Minneapolis-Honeywell, have specifically authorized the use of this material in whole or in part, in the COBOL specifications. Such authorization extends to the reproduction and use of COBOL specifications in programming manuals of similar publications.

Ex. 13–1

The preceding quotation mentions that procedures exist for revising the COBOL language. An alternative is unlimited freedom in language redesign. What are the advantages of restrictions?

An unchanging computer language minimizes the training investment. The user circumvents the vicious retraining cycles that characterize assembly languages or everchanging higher-level language. Many revisions offer only a slight improvement to the user and, therefore, are unnecessary. Nevertheless, computer manufacturers seek alterations that make the basic language more compatible with their machine.

13.1.1 Basic Structure of COBOL Program

In computer solutions to business problems, the data items are collected, grouped into records and files, and eventually submitted to the computer for processing. Data-processing programs are instructions for moving the recorded data from input files to the CPU for computation and then to output files. The programming language makes these steps easier to specify. The language contains statements for data formats and computational procedures. In addition, the COBOL language names the CPU and the input/output units that send and accept every file that is handled in the operation. The basic structure of COBOL is fairly logical. It consists of four divisions, three of which specify the CPU and input/output unit, data format, and computations procedures. These divisions appear in every COBOL program in exactly this order. The other division is the shortest, serving to only identify the program and programmer. This identification division always appears first.

The programmer prepares the appropriate codes for each division and submits the handwritten coded form to the keypunch operator. After the source deck is complete, the compiler is brought into action to generate the object deck. As we said in Chapter 12, the compiler has a contrary nature, and no respect for the programmer's point of view. The program must be written according to the rules or an error message is generated. We'll discuss some of these rules of COBOL programming.

The compiler expects the first card to contain the words IDENTIFI-CATION DIVISION. This heading must be spelled correctly, begin in column 8 on the card, and end with a period. The next few cards name the program and programmer and give other information.

In interpreting the programmer's instructions, the compiler references the syntax table to see what machine instructions are appropriate. The division headings are a signal that directs the compiler to a particular segment of the table.

The compiler expects successive division headings to appear in order. They are ENVIRONMENT DIVISION, DATA DIVISION, and PROCE-DURE DIVISION. Several cards, giving the details of each division, are between headings. Figure 13–1 shows the basic structure of a COBOL source deck. Usually, the procedure division is the longest, and the identification division is the shortest. In Sections 13.2 through 13.5 we discuss the concepts of these four COBOL divisions, respectively.

Information in the COBOL program consists of numbers and words or abbreviations for words. Some statements have the structure of a common sentence with verbs, periods, and filler words for smooth reading. In some divisions, groups of sentences are preceded by appropriate section headings to further guide the compiler in generating instructions.

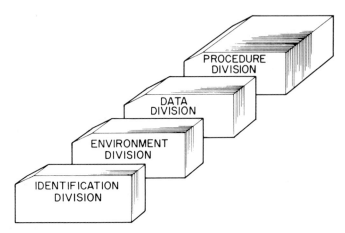

FIG. 13–1   Divisions of COBOL Program.

The COBOL language reads more like English than any other computer language. Programs may never be nominated for a literary prize,
but they are readable to the extent that the general content can be interpreted by members of the laity. For example, the meaning is obvious in the
COBOL sentence WRITE NEW-MASTER-FILE. It is equally obvious
that the style is not a "rhythmical creation of beauty" (Edgar Allan Poe's
definition of poetry).

COBOL words are the basic building blocks of the program. Operations can be specified by certain key words. The compiler recognizes these
words and automatically generates the proper instructions. A key word
must not be used in any other context except to specify that particular
operation. For example, the word MOVE specifies the movement of data
from one region of internal memory to another. Erroneous compiler outputs
would be generated if the programmer used MOVE for any other purpose.
In the next section reserved words are discussed, and a list is given that
includes key words such as MOVE and WRITE and optional words such
as ELSE and FOR.

13.1.2   Some Reserved COBOL Words and Phrases

Warmhearted stories are told of the perils faced by immigrant children
being first exposed to the English language. Some stories assume the language is learned on the streets of New York City. The youngsters have a
dual problem in phrasing their ideas in a new language. One task is utter-
ing the key words that make their thoughts understandable by their play-
mates as well as adults. Another desire of the well-behaved child is not
to be coaxed by his street peers into using the wrong words at inopportune

times. Eventually, young immigrants learn what *words to use* as well as what *words not to use.*

Stories could be told of COBOL programs containing the wrong words, however respectable they may be. The COBOL language is composed of *data names and key words* that specify the operations to be performed on the data. Key words are listed in Table 13–1 in alphabetical order with other reserved COBOL words. *Optional words* are reserved words that may be written to make the COBOL statement read more like an ordinary sentence. *Data names* are reference labels for files and records. The names are composed of alphanumeric characters (letter of the alphabet and decimal numbers) and the hyphen. Names are limited in length to 30 characters. Programmers formulate data names from words that should communicate to program readers the contents of the files or records. This practice makes the program more easily interpreted by associates or replacements for the original programmer.

The programmer and the aforementioned immigrant child face analogous pitfalls in choosing their words. They both must avoid certain words. In COBOL, *reserved words* must not be used for data names or any purpose other than to specify operations associated with that word. Optional words are ignored by the computer; therefore, they are unacceptable for data names.

Table 13–1 lists some of the reserved words. Examples of key words are ADD, DIVIDE, MOVE, division headings and subheadings. Examples of optional words are AN, ARE, and so on. The plural forms of several words in the list are reserved, also. For brevity in the list, only the singular form is given here. Misuse or misspelling of reserved words is detected automatically by the computer and an error message is printed.

TABLE 13–1
Partial List of Reserved COBOL Words

ACCEPT	FROM	PROCEED
ADD	GIVING	PROGRAM-ID
ADDRESS	GO	PROTECT
AFTER	GREATER	QUOTE
ALL	HIGH-VALUE	READ
ALTER	IDENTIFICATION	RECORD
ALTERNATE	IF	RECORDING
AN	IN	REDEFINES
AND	INPUT	REEL
APPLY	INPUT-OUTPUT	REMARKS
ARE	INSTALLATION	RENAMING
AREA	INTO	REPLACING
ASSIGN	I-O-CONTROL	RERUN

TABLE 13–1 (*cont.*)

AT	IS	RESERVE
AUTHOR	JUSTIFIED	REWIND
BLANK	LABEL	RIGHT
BLOCK	LEADING	ROUNDED
BY	LEAVING	RUN
CHARACTER	LEFT	SECTION
CHECK	LESS	SECURITY
CLASS	LIBRARY	SELECT
CLOSE	LOCATION	SENTENCE
COBOL	LOCK	SIGN
COMPUTE	LOW-VALUE	SIGNED
CONFIGURATION	MEMORY	SIZE
CONSTANT	MODE	SOURCE-COMPUTER
CONTAIN	MOVE	SPACE
COPY	MULTIPLY	SPECIAL-NAMES
DATA	NEGATIVE	STANDARD
DATE-COMPILED	NEXT	STATUS
DATE-WRITTEN	NO	STOP
DEPENDING	NOT	SUBTRACT
DIGIT	NOTE	SUPPRESS
DISPLAY	NUMERIC	SYNCHRONIZED
DIVIDE	OBJECT-COMPUTER	TALLY
DIVISION	OBJECT-PROGRAM	THAN
DOLLAR	OCCURS	THEN
ELSE	OF	THROUGH
END	OFF	THRU
ENTER	OMITTED	TIME
ENVIRONMENT	ON	TO
EQUAL	OPEN	UNTIL
ERROR	OPTIONAL	UPON
EVERY	OR	USAGE
EXAMINE	OTHERWISE	VALUE
EXIT	OUTPUT	VARYING
FD	PERFORM	WHEN
FILE	PICTURE	WITH
FILE-CONTROL	PLACE	WORDS
FILLER	POINT	WORKING-STORAGE
FIRST	POSITIVE	WRITE
FLOAT	PROCEDURE	ZERO
FOR		

Ex. 13-2

Suppose that a programmer wanted the printer unit to prepare a list of data with the following literal at the top: FIRST TEN RECORDS FROM PAYROLL FILE. What special problems are presented by this title?

The title isn't too long because literals can be a string of up to 120 characters. However, Table 13–1 shows that some of these words are reserved. The COBOL language has provisions for bending the rules. When placed in quotation marks, reserved words no longer have special significance. By using quotation marks, programmers have greater freedom in word selection.

Phrases appear in many COBOL statements. In grammar, phrases are defined to be a group of two or more related words that express a thought. For our purposes, *phrases* describe operations in a program. The following four groups are examples: SUBTRACT DEDUCTION FROM GROSS-PAY and GIVING NET-PAY, which could be combined to form a sentence, and SELECT NET-PAY and ASSIGN TO PRINTER, which could be another sentence.

Ex. 13-3

COBOL statements usually can be interpreted fairly easily. Let's try our luck on the preceding program sentences.

The first sentence specifies that the net pay would be computed by subtracting the deductions from the gross pay. The second sentence would cause the machine to print the net pay on, perhaps, a paycheck. Keywords are SUBTRACT, GIVING, SELECT, and ASSIGN. Data names are DE-DUCTIONS, GROSS-PAY, and NET-PAY. The other words are optional words, except PRINTER, which is the name of a hardware unit.

13.1.3 Examples of COBOL Statements

Verbs express grammatical action in common sentences. In programs they are the operational center of almost every statement in the procedure division. Most statements are in the form of an imperative sentence. In this structure the verb is the first word in the statement. Table 13–2 gives a few statements using some of the verbs that might appear in a COBOL program.

COBOL programs usually achieve the transfer of data from input files to the CPU for computation. The results are stored in memory or

TABLE 13–2
Examples of COBOL Statements

READ SALES-FILE.
SUBTRACT SALES-THIS-MONTH FROM SALES-LAST-MONTH GIV-
ING GAIN.
IF GAIN LESS THAN ZERO GO TO BOOST-SALES.
ADD RECEIPTS TO QUANTITY-ON-HAND GIVING INVENTORY.

another file, and some are eventually printed as individual or summary reports. The information in Table 13–3 is a brief sequence of statements illustrating the nature of instructions that might appear in payroll processing. The files in this example contain payroll data with a record for each employee. All items on the record are identified and named in the data division.

TABLE 13–3
COBOL Statements in Simple Payroll Processing

Verb	Example Statement	Explanation
ASSIGN	ASSIGN TRANSACTION-FILE TO READER. ASSIGN MASTER-FILE TO READER. ASSIGN PAY-REPORT TO PRINTER.	First step in the sequence of events for entering data into memory. We'll assume that HOURS-WORKED is a transaction item and HOURLY-RATE and DEDUCTIONS are master items.
OPEN	OPEN TRANSACTION-FILE. OPEN MASTER-FILE.	Channel to input unit is opened and made ready in anticipation of data transfer.
READ	READ TRANSACTION-FILE. READ MASTER-FILE.	The data items for an employee are transferred to internal memory. The numerical values for hours worked, hourly rate, and deductions are three of these items.
GO TO	IF END GO TO TERMINATE.	A conditional branch is used to stop input processing after the last record is read.

Verb	*Example Statement*	*Explanation*
		(*cont.*) Otherwise, the next statement in sequence is processed. The word TERMINATE is the name chosen here for a paragraph specifying the sequence of events that terminate the run.
COMPARE	COMPARE EMP-T TO EMP-M. IF NOT EQUAL GO TO MISMATCH.	A verification is made that records from merged files pertain to the same employee. The words EMP-T and EMP-M are the names chosen for employee numbers in the transaction and master records, respectively. The paragraph with the name MISMATCH would specify the action to be taken when merged records don't match.
MULTIPLY	MULTIPLY HOURS-WORKED BY HOURLY-RATE GIVING GROSS-PAY.	The product is stored in the memory address reserved by the computer for GROSS-PAY. Memory digits occupied by this data word must be specified in the data division.
SUBTRACT	SUBTRACT DEDUCTIONS FROM GROSS-PAY GIVING NET-PAY.	The remainder is stored in the memory location reserved for NET-PAY.
PRINT	PRINT PAY-REPORT.	The pay report is prepared. The data items appearing on this report must be specified in the data division. Data for the next employee would be handled by repeating the sequence that begins with READ.

The statements in Table 13–3 sketch the steps involved in computing some of the data for an employee's pay record. The data division would precede these statements in an actual program. Comments appear in Table 13–3 on some of the statements that must be included in the data division.

Ex. 13–4

Draw a flow chart illustrating the programming steps given in Table 13–3. Figure 13–2 summarizes the programming logic of the statements in Table 13–3.

COBOL programs have simplicity in expression, but this advantage is achieved at the expense of conciseness. Wordy statements appear in Table 13–3 such as MULTIPLY HOURS-WORKED BY HOURLY-RATE GIVING GROSS-PAY. In the more concise FORTRAN language, we could write $G = W*R$ to express the same operation. Obviously, lengthy statements absorb more compiler time. The COBOL language is based on the wise precept that catastrophic programming errors are less likely with plain English statements. Spelling errors are a minor consequence because they are detected by the compiler during the debugging phase. Once the program is operational, the binary deck is in service, and the user generally is unconcerned about expenses in originally translating the wordy object deck.

13.1.4 Library Descriptions of Equipment and Files

The remaining sections in this chapter contain detailed statements that might appear in data-processing programs. Of course, all programs are composed of four divisions. The concepts of programming these divisions are presented for the ordinary inventory-control application.

Lest we grow discouraged by the details in the following pages, it is only fair to point out that programmers can save work by using available program codes. *Library descriptions* exist for many sections in common applications, such as inventory control. Programmers refer to a library description by code name appearing in an appropriate statement.

Before compiler runs, the library material is loaded into an auxiliary storage unit to await being called to action. The information usually is in object code. The compiler processes the source deck in normal fashion until a library reference appears. The contents of the library program become part of the object deck at that point in the computer run.

Typical inventory-control programs have several instances when corresponding sections are identical in purpose. Programmers can choose to make these sections identical in content to library descriptions. For ex-

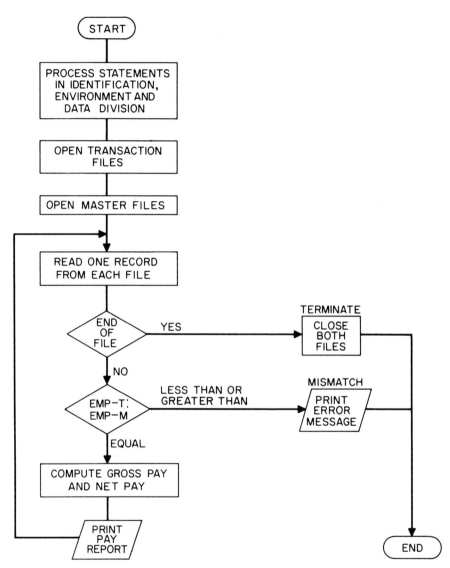

FIG. 13–2   Programming Logic of the Statements in Table 13–3.

ample, the transaction files have records for every part that is received, issued, or otherwise monitored by inventory-control systems. Transactions usually are identified by part number. This label serves the same purpose in making inventories of many types of merchandise. Library codes are convenient in specifying data formats for items in the transaction records. A typical inventory record consists of data entries for part number, code number, quantity on hand, and reorder data. The code number distinguishes between issues and receipts.

Library descriptions are used in the environment division to specify nomenclatures of central processing units and input/output devices. The entire division can be coded and used in programming several solutions. This convenience is one of the *advantages of COBOL programs.* With divisions and sections in a structure, programs have similarity, even though applications may be different.

13.2 IDENTIFICATION DIVISION

Programming skills are acquired with practice and adherence to the rules of the language. The identification division is first in a program. It consists of the heading and only one statement, although other statements can be added to further identify the program. Figure 13–3 has a sketch

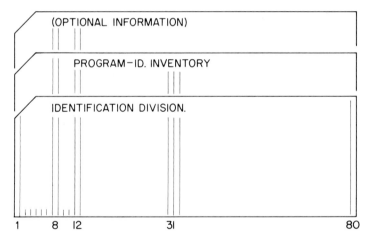

FIG. 13–3   Identification Division.

showing how these statements would appear on punched cards.

The heading IDENTIFICATION DIVISION must commence in column 8 and end with a period. The statement header PROGRAM-ID can begin in either column 8 or 12, but must end with a period and then a space. The program name must be at least six characters. Numbers can be used in the name, but they must not be the first character or the last two. For example, the word INVENTORY is an acceptable program name. Many other words and groups of words also are acceptable.

The option exists for adding other information to this division. Some programs have on separate lines the following headings: AUTHOR (followed by the author's name), DATE-WRITTEN, DATE-COMPILED, and SECURITY. Program listings present this information along with a printed line for all other cards in the source deck. Otherwise, the optional material is ignored by the compiler.

13.3 ENVIRONMENT DIVISION

The computer configuration is specified in the environment division, and library material usually is called upon for this purpose. The *manufacturer's manual* provides the source of information for writing this division. The appropriate COBOL statements are listed in the manual and are available for copying.

Figure 13–4 outlines the contents of the environment division. Com-

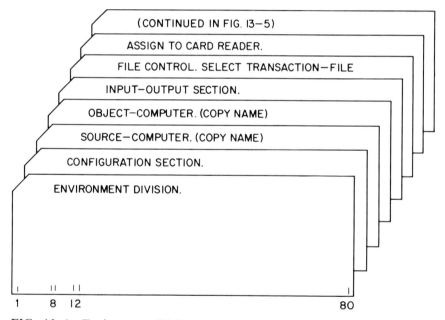

FIG. 13–4 Environment Division.

ments in parentheses show the headings that must be followed by names and nomenclatures copied from a manual.

The *file control* portion of the input/output section assigns the various files to the available input/output devices. For example, Fig. 13–4 has the statement SELECT TRANSACTION-FILE ASSIGN TO CARD READER. The file name is arbitrary, but for our inventory-control application the name is descriptive of a deck of cards for daily issues, receipts, and so forth. Other statements are needed in addition to those in Fig. 13–4. The two master files must be handled, one before and another after the updating run based on today's transaction. In our inventory example, the input/output section must contain the equivalence of at least the statements in Fig. 13–5.

13.4 DATA DIVISION

A magnetic tape has capacity for up to 200 million binary digits, all looking pretty much alike. From a gross assessment, we would find that the digits are stored as magnetic spots having on the average half with clockwise and half with counterclockwise polarity.

The tape may be blank between *records.* Inner-record gaps typically extend along the tape for 0.6 inch, leaving 400 blank character spaces. To increase tape capacity, records are grouped together to form blocks.

The information definitely is in code and not readily interpreted by a machine unless instructions are furnished. The data format specifies the arrangement of recorded information. The binary digits have meaning when a particular number code is specified for records, *blocks,* and elementary items.

13.4.1 File Description Section

Figure 13–6 shows the important headings in the data division. Detailed information is specified on several cards that follow the headings. The abbreviation for file description, FD, is followed by the file name. In the inventory application, we have at least two files being read. One is named TRANSACTION and the other is MASTER. Also, the file TODAYS-MASTER is being written. Several cards describing the data format would appear after these headings.

13.4.1.1 Picture Clause. The *picture clause* is the conventional way of giving the size of data items and whether the characters are numeric, alphabetic, or alphanumeric. A group of four *numeric characters* would be identified by PICTURE 9999 or PICTURE 9(4) for short. These format statements are used by the compiler in interpreting the characters. Picture clauses commence in column 40 in the statement.

Decimal points also can be indicated. The clause PICTURE 9(4)-V99 signifies four digits, a *decimal point,* and then two other digits. The nines are a special symbol for decimal digits. The number −63.7 would be referred to by the clause PICTURE S99V9. The symbol S would be minus in this example, but in general either sign could appear. This picture clause establishes that the characters preceding the first digit must be interpreted as the *sign.* The sign symbol can be omitted from the picture clause for positive values in the file.

GENERAL PURPOSE CODING FORM
(PROGRAMS OR DATA)

PROGRAMMER

JOB NO. EXT.

DATE LOC.

DEPT.

CHARACTER SET: IBM 360 ☐ IBM 7094 ☐ GE 600 ☐ OTHER: ☐

LANGUAGE: FORTRAN ☐ COBOL ☐ PL/I ☐ OTHER: ☐

PUNCHING INSTRUCTIONS

NOTES:

CARD COLOR:

GRAPHIC PUNCH

PAGE ___ OF ___

```
SELECT MASTER-FILE ASSIGN TO TAPE1.
SELECT TRANSACTION-FILE ASSIGN TO READER1.
SELECT ADJUSTMENT-FILE ASSIGN TO READER2.
SELECT GAIN-ADJ-REPORT ASSIGN TO PRINTER1.
SELECT OVERSTOCK-REPORT ASSIGN TO TAPE2.
SELECT OVERDUE-REPORT ASSIGN TO TAPE3.
SELECT TODAYS-MASTER-FILE ASSIGN TO TAPE4.
SELECT ERROR-REPORT ASSIGN TO PRINTER2.
```

FIG. 13–5 File Control Statements in Input/Output Section of Environment Division.

233

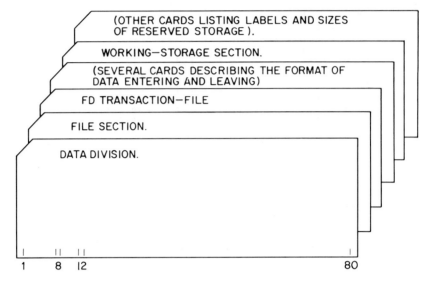

FIG. 13–6   Data Division.

Ex. 13–5

Consider the simple file of 500 cards each having groups of seven decimal digits commencing in columns 1, 11, and 21. Write the proper format statements and assign data names to the groups.

Figure 13–7 has statements to guide the compiler in locating the groups. The name REGION-FILE refers to all 500 cards and SALES-RECORD refers to the three groups of numbers on each card. Also, names are assigned for the groups.

All data are not numbers. In inventory control, data might be reorder dates, parts names, supplier addresses, and so forth. The symbol A represents *alphabetic characters* and X represents the all-inclusive class of *alphanumeric characters*. The clause PICTURE X(6) is the format for a string of six alphanumeric characters. Strings must not exceed 30 characters.

13.4.1.2   Examples of Coded File Descriptions.   The statements appearing in Fig. 13–8 give a fairly logical listing of the data formats in a simple file description. This example is based on records that might appear in an *inventory-control application.*

The format statements in Fig. 13–8 define records and files that are similar in purpose to handwritten records. Manual methods are used in

GENERAL PURPOSE CODING FORM
(PROGRAMS OR DATA)

BTL

PROGRAMMER

JOB NO.   EXT.
DATE   LOC.
DEPT.

CHARACTER SET
IBM 360 ☐   IBM 7094 ☐
GE 600 ☐
OTHER:

LANGUAGE
FORTRAN ☐   COBOL ☐
PL/I ☐
OTHER:

PUNCHING INSTRUCTIONS
NOTES:
CARD COLOR:

GRAPHIC
PUNCH

PAGE   OF

```
FD  REGION-FILE
01  SALES-RECORD.
    02  QUANTITY;        PICTURE  9(7).
    02  FILLER;          PICTURE  X(3).
    02  UNITS;           PICTURE  9(7).
    02  FILLER;          PICTURE  X(3).
    02  PRICE;           PICTURE  9(7).
    02  FILLER;          PICTURE  X(53).
```

FIG. 13–7   Example of File Description.

235

BTL

PROGRAMMER			CHARACTER SET		LANGUAGE		PUNCHING INSTRUCTIONS		GRAPHIC	
JOB NO.	EXT.		IBM 360 ☐ IBM 7094 ☐		FORTRAN ☐ COBOL ☐				PUNCH	
DATE	LOC.		GE 600 ☐		PL/I ☐		NOTES:			
DEPT.			OTHER:		OTHER:		CARD COLOR:		PAGE ____ OF ____	

```
FD  TRANSACTION-FILE
01  ISSUE-RECEIPT-REC.
    02  PART;            PICTURE 9(8).
    02  FILLER;          PICTURE X(1).
    02  PNAME;           PICTURE X(15).
    02  FILLER;          PICTURE X(5).
    02  CODE;            PICTURE X(10).
    02  QUANTITY;        PICTURE S9(4).
    02  FILLER;          PICTURE X(5).
    02  UNIT-PRICE;      PICTURE 9999V99.
    02  FILLER;          PICTURE X(3).
    02  ACTION-DAY;      PICTURE X(8).
    02  FILLER;          PICTURE X(3).
```

FIG. 13–8 File Description of Data Division Inventory Application.

236

GENERAL PURPOSE CODING FORM
(PROGRAMS OR DATA)

BTL

PROGRAMMER
JOB NO.   EXT.
DATE   LOC.
DEPT.

CHARACTER SET
IBM 360 ☐   IBM 7094 ☐
GE 600 ☐
OTHER:

LANGUAGE
FORTRAN ☐   COBOL ☐
PL/I ☐
OTHER:

PUNCHING INSTRUCTIONS   GRAPHIC   PUNCH
NOTES:
CARD COLOR

PAGE   OF

```
FD  ADJUSTMENT-FILE
01  GAIN-ADJ-REC.
    02  PART;          PICTURE 9(8).
    02  FILLER;        PICTURE X(1).
    02  PNAME;         PICTURE X(15).
    02  FILLER;        PICTURE X(5).
    02  QTY-ON-ORDER;  PICTURE 9(4).
    02  FILLER;        PICTURE X(6).
    02  QTY-ON-HAND;   PICTURE 9(5).
    02  FILLER;        PICTURE X(5).
    02  UNIT-PRICE;    PICTURE 9999V99.
    02  FILLER;        PICTURE X(3).
    02  ACTION-DAY;    PICTURE X(8).
    02  FILLER;        PICTURE X(2).
    02  REORDER-PT;    PICTURE 9(4).
    02  FILLER;        PICTURE X(7).
```

237

FIG. 13-8 (cont.)

BTL

GENERAL PURPOSE CODING FORM
(PROGRAMS OR DATA)

PROGRAMMER		CHARACTER SET	LANGUAGE	PUNCHING INSTRUCTIONS	GRAPHIC
JOB NO.	EXT.	IBM 360 ☐ IBM 7094 ☐	FORTRAN ☐ COBOL ☐		PUNCH
DATE	LOC.	GE 600 ☐	PL/I ☐	NOTES:	
DEPT.		OTHER:	OTHER:	CARD COLOR:	PAGE ___ OF ___

```
FD  MASTER-FILE
01  DATE-OF-FILE-REC.
    02  DATE;             PICTURE X(8).
01  INVENTORY-REC.
    02  PART;             PICTURE 9(8).
    02  PNAME;            PICTURE X(15).
    02  QTY-ON-ORDER;     PICTURE 9(4).
    02  QTY-ON-HAND;      PICTURE 9(5).
    02  ACTION-DAY;       PICTURE X(8).
    02  REORDER-PT;       PICTURE 9(4).
    02  UNIT-PRICE;       PICTURE 9999V99.
    02  STOCK-INVEST;     PICTURE 9(6)V99.
    02  INV-SALES-RATIO;  PICTURE 99V999.
FD  TODAYS-MASTER-FILE
01  TODAYS-DATE-REC.
    02  TODAYS-DATE;      PICTURE X(8).
01  TODAYS-INVENTORY-REC  COPY INVENTORY-REC.
```

FIG. 13–8 (cont.)

BTL

PROGRAMMER

JOB NO.	EXT.
DATE	LOC.
DEPT.	

CHARACTER SET: IBM 360 ☐ IBM 7094 ☐ GE 600 ☐ OTHER:

LANGUAGE: FORTRAN ☐ COBOL ☐ PL/I ☐ OTHER:

PUNCHING INSTRUCTIONS: GRAPHIC ___ PUNCH ___

NOTES:

CARD COLOR: PAGE ___ OF ___

```
FD  GAIN-ADJ-REPORT.
01  GAIN-ADJ-REP.
    02  PART;              PICTURE  9(8).
    02  FILLER;            PICTURE  X(4).
    02  PNAME;             PICTURE  X(15).
    02  FILLER;            PICTURE  X(4).
    02  QTY-ON-HAND;       PICTURE  9(5).
    02  FILLER;            PICTURE  X(4).
    02  UNIT-PRICE;        PICTURE  999V99.
    02  FILLER;            PICTURE  X(4).
    02  STOCK-INVEST;      PICTURE  9(6)V99.
    02  FILLER;            PICTURE  X(4).
    02  OLD-STOCK-INVEST;  PICTURE  9(6)V99.
    02  FILLER;            PICTURE  X(4).
    02  ACTION-DAY;        PICTURE  X(8).
    02  FILLER;            PICTURE  X(4).
    02  REORDER-PT;        PICTURE  X(10).
    02  FILLER;            PICTURE  X(21).
```

FIG. 13–8 *(cont.)*

BTL

GENERAL PURPOSE CODING FORM
(PROGRAMS OR DATA)

PROGRAMMER

JOB NO.   EXT.

DATE   LOC.

DEPT.

CHARACTER SET: IBM 360 ☐   IBM 7094 ☐   GE 600 ☐   OTHER:

LANGUAGE: FORTRAN ☐   COBOL ☐   PL/I ☐   OTHER:

PUNCHING INSTRUCTIONS   GRAPHIC   PUNCH

NOTES:

CARD COLOR: PAGE   OF

```
FD  OVERSTOCK-REPORT
01  OVERSTOCK-REC.
    02  PART;             PICTURE 9(8).
    02  FILLER;           PICTURE X(4).
    02  PNAME;            PICTURE X(15).
    02  FILLER;           PICTURE X(4).
    02  QTY-ON-HAND;      PICTURE 9(5).
    02  FILLER;           PICTURE X(4).
    02  REORDER-PT;       PICTURE 9(4).
    02  FILLER;           PICTURE X(4).
    02  ACTION-DAY;       PICTURE X(8).
    02  FILLER;           PICTURE X(4).
    02  STOCK-INVEST;     PICTURE 9(6)V99.
    02  FILLER;           PICTURE X(4).
    02  INV-SALES-RATIO;  PICTURE 99V999.
    02  FILLER;           PICTURE X(41).
```

240

FIG. 13–8 (cont.)

BTL

PROGRAMMER				
JOB NO.		EXT.		CHARACTER SET
DATE		LOC.		IBM 360 ☐ IBM 7094 ☐
DEPT.				GE 600 ☐ OTHER:

LANGUAGE: FORTRAN ☐ COBOL ☐ PL/I ☐ OTHER:

PUNCHING INSTRUCTIONS   GRAPHIC   PUNCH   NOTES: CARD COLOR:

PAGE ____ OF ____

```
FD  OVERDUE-REPORT
01  OVERDUE-REC.
    02  PART;         PICTURE 9(8).
    02  FILLER;       PICTURE X(4).
    02  PNAME;        PICTURE X(15).
    02  FILLER;       PICTURE X(4).
    02  QTY-ON-HAND;  PICTURE 9(5).
    02  FILLER;       PICTURE X(4).
    02  REORDER-PT;   PICTURE 9(4).
    02  FILLER;       PICTURE X(4).
    02  ACTION-DAY;   PICTURE X(8).
    02  FILLER;       PICTURE X(64).

FD  ERROR-REPORT
01  ERROR-A-REC  COPY GAIN-ADJ-REC.
01  ERROR-T-REC  COPY ISSUE-RECEIPT REC.
01  ERROR-M-REC  COPY INVENTORY-REC.
```

241

inventorying small quantities of merchandise. These inventories are made every few months, but in the interim the records are out of date. Current records require daily postings of all merchandise that is issued or received. In addition to being out of date, manual methods have limited capability to manage the inventory because reports of overdue orders or overstocked parts are not issued.

The data files outlined in Fig. 13–8 could be processed daily. Automated inventory control provides *up-to-date files* and *summary reports* for inventory management. Streams of data enter the computer from files and leave in up-to-date files and summary reports. We'll keep the example simple by limiting the program to three files and three reports. Daily *transaction* records are on one *file* and *old and new master* records are on the other two.

Reports are useful outputs in data processing as they summarize the current situation for management's review. Figure 13–8 has statements specifying data records for *summary reports* on some transactions, overstocked parts, and overdue orders. The reports are named GAIN-ADJ-REPORT, OVERSTOCK-REPORT, and OVERDUE-REPORT, respectively.

During a processing run, the data for the reports are recorded on tapes. After the run is completed, the reports are printed from codes on the individual tapes. This option uses three tape units to record the summary data. Other options are discussed in Ex. 13–6.

Ex. 13–6

The nomenclature for each part is on a record in the master file. During processing, several of these records may be selected for display on one or more printed summary records. Discuss equipment configurations that will yield the desired reports.

The choice depends on the report length and hardware items that are available. The *internal memory* is the *first* choice, provided it will hold all the data for the reports. Information stored in separate sections of memory could be transferred to a buffer and then to the printer after the run is completed. These advantages can be attained with the *second* choice, *a magnetic disc,* which has more capacity than internal memory and nearly the same random-access feature. The *third* choice is individual *tapes.* This option requires more nonproductive time in handling and rewinding tapes. The reels must be mounted on the tape unit before the run, rewound after the run, and then read while being copied by the printer.

The statements in Fig. 13–5 relate to the third choice, stipulating that equipment isn't available for the more preferred options.

13.4.2 Working Storage Section

Data from input files may enter into arithmetic computations to produce other data. The working storage section gives the *names and lengths of data words* representing these computed results. The compiler allocates memory addresses for all data words. The format information guides the compiler in allocating sufficient memory digits for each data name. Figure 13–9 shows the appropriate statements for the inventory example. *Initial values* are specified by VALUE IS statements. The statement VALUE IS 5 is an example.

13.4.3 Constant Section

Some data words remain constant throughout the processing run. The constant section gives the name, length, and value of constants. Common examples are interest rate and tax rate. Figure 13–9 has the statement OVERDUE-ALLOWANCE; PICTURE 99; VALUE IS 5. This value is used in the procedure division in computing whether the quantity on hand is below the reorder point and should be posted on the overdue report.

Ex. 13–7

The statement INTEREST-RATE; PICTURE 9V9999; VALUE IS 0.0750 is typical of the information appearing in the constant section of the data division. The data word, INTEREST-RATE, would represent the annual charges for money and could be in several statements throughout the procedure division.

Are there other options for representing constants? If so, why have a constant section?

The constant section isn't absolutely necessary, but it is convenient in case of changes. In our example, the number 0.0750 could be placed in the procedure statements. This option has an advantage because it uses a number that has fewer characters than the data word. Interest rates are constant during a run, but may change after a few weeks. Changes are handled easily in the constant section compared to changing numbers in several procedure statements and, perhaps, missing some. Of course, changes in the source deck require that a new object deck be compiled.

Another option is to enter the constants on cards preceding the transaction file. This special file has only a single record and is read at the start of the run. Changes can be made without altering the source deck.

BTL

GENERAL PURPOSE CODING FORM
(PROGRAMS OR DATA)

PROGRAMMER		CHARACTER SET	LANGUAGE	PUNCHING INSTRUCTIONS	GRAPHIC	
JOB NO.	EXT.	IBM 360 ☐ IBM 7094 ☐	FORTRAN ☐ COBOL ☐		PUNCH	
DATE	LOC.	GE 600 ☐	PL/I ☐	NOTES:		
DEPT.		OTHER:	OTHER:	CARD COLOR:	PAGE ___ OF ___	

```
WORKING-STORAGE SECTION.
    77  OS-REPORT;           PICTURE 9;        VALUE IS ZERO.
    77  OD-REPORT;           PICTURE 9;        VALUE IS ZERO.
    77  SALES;               PICTURE 9(6)V99.
    77  RADJ;                PICTURE 9;        VALUE IS 1.
    77  RTRANS;              PICTURE 9;        VALUE IS 1.
CONSTANT-SECTION.
    77  OVERDUE-ALLOWANCE;   PICTURE 99;       VALUE IS 5.
    77  OVERSTOCK-ALLOWANCE; PICTURE 99V999;   VALUE IS 2.
    77  Z;                   PICTURE 9;        VALUE IS ZERO.
```

FIG. 13–9 Working Storage and Constant Sections of Data Division.

13.5 PROCEDURE DIVISION

The data-processing *objectives are formed* to a large extent by the time programmers finish the first three divisions. The overall plan has been translated into several detailed statements. Specifically, the needed equipment units are available and specified. Also, the input data and output reports have been considered and their formats given.

The procedure division contains statements that cause the processor to accept data from the input files and perform *arithmetic computations and data manipulations*. These operations produce the desired information for the output reports.

Efficiency in the procedure division has potential for saving time and money. The computations are performed quickly, regardless of programming ineptness. However, pitfalls must be avoided in selecting statements for data manipulation. It is desirable to generate all output files and reports on the *first pass* through the input files. The widely used phrase "computers are output limited" refers to situations where the processor is waiting for a printer or other output device. With skill and experience, programmers can reduce the total running time of poorly composed programs by as much as ten to one. The information in this chapter provides a beginner's level of skill. Certainly, more education in data processing is needed before writing major programs.

13.5.1　Flow Chart for Inventory Procedure Division

The situation in the inventory-control example is outlined by the content of the input files and the output reports. There are several options for the intervening steps. As we mentioned in Chapter 12, it is good practice to outline programs by constructing flow charts. Figure 13–10 shows a flow chart for producing the inventory reports.

13.5.2　Example of Coded Procedure Division

Procedure divisions can be as simple as accepting data from a deck of cards and generating a printed sheet for each card. It would be foolish to waste computer time for a simple application. Accounting machines can handle fixed-format files and reports at much lower cost than a general-purpose computer. For example, an accounting machine can accept cards having pay data, perform a few computations, and generate paychecks. These low-cost machines can merge files by working in tandem.

In this section we presented an example that is beyond the capability of accounting machines. The application is straightforward and involves the inputs and outputs outlined in Fig. 13--8. The detailed statements in

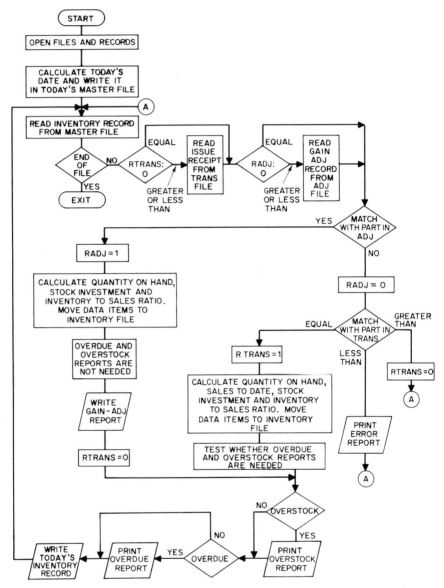

FIG. 13–10   Flow Chart for Generating Inventory Reports and Updating the
Master Files.

the COBOL program are readable to the extent that the concept of the
program is obvious. Figure 13–11 shows the procedure division for generating inventory reports and updating the master file.

BTL

GENERAL PURPOSE CODING FORM
(PROGRAMS OR DATA)

PROGRAMMER

JOB NO.   EXT.
DATE   LOC.
DEPT.

CHARACTER SET: IBM 360 ☐ IBM 7094 ☐ GE 600 ☐ OTHER:

LANGUAGE: FORTRAN ☐ COBOL ☐ PL/I ☐ OTHER:

PUNCHING INSTRUCTIONS   GRAPHIC   PUNCH
NOTES:
CARD COLOR: PAGE ___ OF ___

```
PROCEDURE DIVISION.
FIRST. OPEN INPUT MASTER-FILE, TRANSACTION-FILE, ADJUSTMENT-FILE,
       OPEN OUTPUT TODAYS-MASTER-FILE, GAIN-ADJ-REPORT,
       OVERSTOCK-REPORT, OVERDUE-REPORT.
SECOND. READ DATE-OF-FILE-REC; ADD 1 TO DATE GIVING TODAYS-DATE.
        WRITE TODAYS-DATE-REC.
THIRD. READ INVENTORY-REC; AT END GO TO LAST.
       IF RTRANS IS Z, GO TO FOURTH.. READ ISSUE-RECEIPT-REC.
FOURTH. IF RADJ IS Z, GO TO FIFTH. READ GAIN-ADJ-REC.
```

FIG. 13–11 Procedure Division for Generating Inventory Reports and Updating the Master File.

247

FIG. 13–11 (cont.)

BTL

GENERAL PURPOSE CODING FORM
(PROGRAMS OR DATA)

PROGRAMMER			
JOB NO.	EXT.		
DATE	LOC.		
DEPT.			

CHARACTER SET: IBM 360 ☐ IBM 7094 ☐ GE 600 ☐ OTHER: ☐

LANGUAGE: FORTRAN ☐ COBOL ☐ PL/I ☐ OTHER: ☐

PUNCHING INSTRUCTIONS GRAPHIC PUNCH
NOTES:
CARD COLOR:

PAGE ___ OF ___

```
FIFTH. IF PART IN GAIN-ADJ-REC IS EQUAL TO PART IN INVENTORY-REC,
GO TO MATCH-A. RADJ=Z. IF PART IN ISSUE-RECEIPT-REC IS EQUAL
TO PART IN INVENTORY-REC, GO TO MATCH-T. IF PART IN
ISSUE-RECEIPT-REC IS LESS THAN PART IN INVENTORY-REC,
GO TO ERROR. RTRANS IS EQUAL TO Z. GO TO THIRD.
```

248

FIG. 13–11 (cont.)

BTL

GENERAL PURPOSE CODING FORM
(PROGRAMS OR DATA)

PROGRAMMER			
JOB NO.	EXT.		
DATE	LOC.		
DEPT.			

CHARACTER SET: IBM 360 ☐   IBM 7094 ☐   GE 600 ☐   OTHER: ☐

LANGUAGE: FORTRAN ☐   COBOL ☐   PL/I ☐   OTHER: ☐

PUNCHING INSTRUCTIONS: GRAPHIC | PUNCH

NOTES: **CARD COLOR:**

PAGE ___ **OF** ___

```
MATCH-T.
          IF RTRANS IS EQUAL TO ... IF CODE IS EQUAL TO OR GREATER
          THAN ONE, GO TO CODE-1.
CODE-0.
          IF CODE IS CODE-0.
          ADD QUANTITY TO CODE-1 ... GO TO CODE.
          GO TO SIXTH.
CODE-0.
          SUBTRACT QUANTITY FROM QTY-ON-HAND. IN INVENTORY REC.
          ADD QUANTITY TO SALES.
SIXTH.
          MULTIPLY QUANTITY BY UNIT-PRICE IN INVENTORY-REC.
          ... QTY-ON-HAND IN INVENTORY-REC ...
          IF SALES IS GREATER THAN ... STOCK-INVEST IN INVENTORY-REC
          DIVIDE INV-SALES BY SALES GIVING INV-SALES-RATIO IN
          INVENTORY-REC ... MOVE UNIT PRICE IN
          INVENTORY-REC ... ISSUE-RECEIPT-REC.
```

FIG. 13-11 (cont.)

BTL

GENERAL PURPOSE CODING FORM
(PROGRAMS OR DATA)

PROGRAMMER				CHARACTER SET		LANGUAGE		PUNCHING INSTRUCTIONS	GRAPHIC			
JOB NO.		EXT.		IBM 360 ☐	IBM 7094 ☐	FORTRAN ☐	COBOL ☐		PUNCH			
DATE		LOC.		GE 600 ☐		PL/I ☐		NOTES:				
DEPT.				OTHER:		OTHER:		CARD COLOR:		PAGE ___ OF ___		

```
SEVENTH.
    MOVE ACTION DAY IN ISSUE RECEIPT-REC TO INVENTORY-REC.
    IF SUBTRACT QUANTITY IN REORDER-PT FROM QTY-ON-HAND GIVING QUANTITY.
    IF QUANTITY IS GREATER THAN OVERDUE-ALLOWANCE,
       OVERSTOCK-ALLOWANCE IS GREATER THAN
       INV-SALES-RATIO IS GREATER THAN OD-REPORT
    IF ALLOWANCE IS EQUAL TO - . REPORT IS GO TO EIGHTH.
    MATCH-A. ON-HAND EQUAL TO GAIN-ADJ-REC GO TO
    MULTIPLY QTY-ON-HAND BY UNIT-PRICE GIVING INVENTORY-REC.
       GO TO INVENTORY-REC
    BY SALES GIVING INV-SALES
       INVENTORY-REC GIVING INV-SALES IS SALES IS GREATER THAN
       INVENTORY-REC INVEST IN
    PRINT GAIN-ADJ-REC OD-REPORT REC. DIVIDE INV-SALES-RATIO.
       DIVIDE QTY-ON-HAND
    RTRANS Z. IS REPORT IS
    EQUAL TO Z. EQUAL TO Z. EQUAL TO OS-REPORT IS
```

250

FIG. 13-11 (cont.)

BTL

GENERAL PURPOSE CODING FORM
(PROGRAMS OR DATA)

PROGRAMMER

JOB NO.	EXT.
DATE	LOC.
DEPT.	

CHARACTER SET: IBM 360 ☐ IBM 7094 ☐ GE 600 ☐ OTHER: ☐

LANGUAGE: FORTRAN ☐ COBOL ☐ PL/I ☐ OTHER: ☐

PUNCHING INSTRUCTIONS GRAPHIC PUNCH

NOTES:

CARD COLOR:

PAGE _____ OF _____

```
EIGHTH.  IF OS-REPORT IS EQUAL TO 1, WRITE OVERSTOCK-REC.
         IF OD-REPORT IS EQUAL TO 1, WRITE OVERDUE-REC.
         WRITE TODAYS-INVENTORY-REC.  GO TO THIRD.
ERROR.   PRINT ERROR-A-REC.  PRINT ERROR-T-REC.  PRINT ERROR-M-REC.
         GO TO THIRD.
LAST.    EXIT
```

251

14 Applications of Computers in Business

Computers can handle dozens of business functions. Computer users who are unfamiliar with the details of the business pose severe limitations on the effectiveness of the machine. For example, some familiarity with accounting is needed by persons forming computer programs to handle the accounting function. In this chapter, we'll discuss briefly some hardware devices that have become popular in business applications. Then, we'll look at the concepts of controlling, planning, and making decisions in business operations.

14.1 GENERAL HARDWARE FOR BUSINESS APPLICATIONS

Many of the preceding chapters gave detailed information on the design and capabilities of general-purpose computers. These machines are available for purchase or on a lease basis from IBM, UNIVAC, and others. We want to augment this previous coverage with a brief discussion of alternative hardware devices. Time-sharing systems and minicomputers are used in business applications to the extent that we would be remiss to skip them. These devices are also used in science applications.

Financial statistics show that a vast segment of the computer market is comprised of machines similar in concept to the IBM 360/20 or the UNIVAC 1108, both of which we discussed. Seventy percent of computer users are tied to IBM machines. Annual sales and rentals for IBM machines total about $8 billion. By comparison, the total sales of time-sharing services was about $300 million in 1971. Mini-computers are also a small share of the market.

Businesses have applications that require computer services on an intermittent basis. These users have contributed to the rise of time-sharing systems. By definition, *time sharing* is the simultaneous utilization of a computer processor by users at multiple-access terminals. The terminals in a time-sharing system are tied to a communications controller through a network, usually circuits of the Bell System. A single high-speed processor accepts the user's instructions from the communications controller. Instructions from the multiple terminals appear to be handled simultaneously; however, events actually occur one at a time, as discussed in Chapter 10. The open terminals are queried in a round-robin fashion and appropriate inputs or outputs are transmitted. Two requests for the same processor at the same time presents a conflict that is automatically resolved by a predetermined system of priorities. The user sits at a terminal which resembles a typewriter and enters data by pressing the appropriate keys. The computed results are returned to the terminal and typed on a page or displayed on a cathode-ray tube.

Mini-computers are systems selling for $4000 to $100,000 and performing on a limited scale all the basic functions of arithmetic processing, memory, and input/output control. The cost has made them attractive for jobs that include control of a manufacturing machine to control of inventory records. The basic concepts and logic principles of mini-computers are basically the same as we presented in the preceding chapters. The actual logic circuits and register memories tend to be metal-oxide semiconductors (MOS) on fairly large (close to 1-inch in diameter) pieces of substrate material. These circuits yield a high logic density and tend to be lower in cost. Circuits using MOS design are an ideal package for mini-computers. Also, they are being used in full-scale computer systems.

Mini-peripheral devices are available to complement the mini-computer processor. The theory of assembling peripheral devices and the processor into a system is similar in concept to assembling a stereophonic system from audio components. In fact, one of the mini-peripherals is a digital cassette unit which was derived from the audio-cassette tape. Another mini-peripheral is a small magnetic tape storage unit, which resembles the audio rell-to-reel tape unit. If you like the idea of structuring your home stereo system, you'll enjoy being master of a mini-computer. Our presentation of general hardware concepts is a good basis for understanding the literature on the features of mini-computer systems.

14.2 COMPUTERS IN GENERAL PRODUCTION BUSINESSES

A well-managed production operation is an impressive contrast to the haphazard, uncoordinated situation that might have existed for a few weeks when the firm commenced operation. From some points of view, the disorganized events during the start-up period seem to mysteriously diminish with time. There is some truth in the assessment that events have inertia and that a repeating sequence leads to smooth operations. In a broader sense, events can be managed. Computers are a valuable tool in managing the daily operation of new and mature firms.

Untimely decisions can cause day-to-day disruptions that are small in scale but similar to the confusion at start-up. Managers are responsible for planning, control, and decision making. Changes in conditions are certain to happen. Redirection is recognized in the obvious instance of new facility start-up. The needs for plans and decisions are less obvious in an ongoing operation. As a consequence, timely decisions are not made in many cases. For example, many managers of buggy shops in years past did not recognize immediately that decisions should be made to change their product line. These buggy shops simply postponed the obvious decision until it was too late to save the firm financially.

The need for decisions and plans sometimes do not get the manager's attention until the situation has reached crisis proportions. Many decisions should be based on extensive data; therefore, panicky managers are likely to ignore much relevant information in their last-ditch decisions. It has been said that an idea must grow or die. Most operations are based on ideas and, hence, can be expected to change. Successful firms keep ahead of change by collecting and analyzing pertinent data from their operations.

Manual methods may be adequate for the corner shoeshop but not for firms doing more than $10 million annual sales. Computers have broad capabilities for storing, retrieving, and analyzing data. Information gleaned from the proper data can be useful in day-to-day control, planning, and decision making.

Let's pause a moment to make a distinction between data and information. *Data* can be any structured or unstructured quantity of numbers. *Information* is data that have been refined by further analysis into a form of intelligence. For example, a page of data in haphazard order could become information simply by sorting the data into cohesive groups, such as receipts and shipments. Further intelligence could be added by summing the receipts for the day, week, or other time frame. In this simple case, the historical information could be the basis for evaluating the ongoing schemes for controlling the firm. The data have increased value when analytical techniques are available to project the probability of future events. The past, present, and future are all important in making plans and decisions.

In general, a *business information system* is an organized method for determining the past, present, and future status of the business from continuous collection and analysis of pertinent data. The word "future" in this definition means that historical logs are not sufficient in scope to be classed as an information system. The words "organized" and "continuous" exclude the last-minute scramble for facts from the definition.

In practice, information systems are formed by people and, hence, they reflect some of the traits of the human designers. Unlike standard systems, the structure of an information system vividly reflects the motivations and ambitions of the people who formulate and use the system. The two human traits of reluctance and ambition are discussed in the following paragraphs to illustrate that information systems can be driven to opposite ends of a scale that measures the scope of the project.

Reluctance on the part of the manager tends to yield an information system that is a brief system to serve a single purpose. In some perplexing situations, new courses of direction are difficult to pursue because of entanglements in the situation itself. In short, "you can't get there from here." Firms must overcome this dilemma to form an information system for planning and decision making. A firm that knowingly or unknowingly passes over the opportunity for timely decisions in everyday matters may also postpone decisions to initiate an information system. Ironically, this procrastination or oversight jeopardizes an aid to future decisions. Systems formulated in this environment of reluctance probably will start small, serve a single purpose, and may often lie dormant for days or even weeks. Basically, the system serves special studies in reaction to an imminent crisis in the firm. The staff may be provided on a contract basis and may be temporary.

Ambitious managers of information systems prefer to form organizations with scope large enough to place the manager at the right hand of the firm's chief officer. The organization usually occupy offices in a single location. Elaborate objectives are sketched and far-reaching improvement plans are made in the initial stages of formulating the information system. Efforts are concentrated on staking claims on a vast territory of responsibility and pretentiously applying the newborn information system to current front-office problems.

The mouse-and-lion-like qualities of these managers and their respective information systems are purposefully exaggerated to illustrate two hypothetical examples of unacceptable systems. They have a common flaw because both systems will have inherent difficulty in obtaining a clearly defined and relevent data base. In definition, a *data base* is an integrated file having structure and content sufficient to serve many processing applications. For example, accounting data that serve accountants and other organizations could be part of the data base. On the other hand, a collection of independently prepared files from accounting, inventory, and so on, would not form an acceptable data base. The reluctant manager probably is not continuously committed to the information system to the extent necessary to develop a data base. The grandiose efforts of the ambitious manager may be produced by a staff that is not allied with the daily functioning of potential sources and users of the data base.

Some firms have successfully avoided the pitfalls that obviously exist in such extreme cases. Accounting information systems exist in many firms along with inventory control and other independent information systems. These ongoing schemes use available data and generate information predetermined to be useful. In short, it may not be perfect, but it works. In building on an existing system, some firms have improved the information system with modest fanfare and disruption. Efforts can be concentrated on the tractable answers to the following questions:

> 1. Is the information in the present system adequate for the originating organization? Is the information available and adequately applied by management and allied organizations? For example, is the present accounting information adequate for accounting purposes and is it available and applied by sales personnel?
> 2. What should the data base contain and how should it be structured to serve the information needs at management and operational levels?

New airplanes are added to existing fleets by reorienting the pilots. In an analogous fashion, some firms add new information systems by reorienting the existing system and people. The data base usually requires special attention in order that there be an appropriate flow of data and information between operational organizations. For example, a firm may have an ongoing accounting information system and wish to expand to a business information system by including inventory and sales. The expanded staffing requirements in some firms consist of assigning overall responsibility to a front-office principal and assigning technical responsibility to a small cadre of data-processing professionals. This latter group could interact with inventory and sales to structure a data base and reorient the existing system and personnel. The common objective is the development of an efficient data-processing technique and a useful information system.

In the following sections, we'll look at data-processing needs and methods in individual organizations. These include accounting, marketing and other identifiable groups in most businesses. If firms engaged in product production and having annual sales over $10 million, these groups are all candidates for inclusion in a business information system. For discussion purposes, we will stipulate that two or more of the groups participate in an information system that serves their mutual benefit.

14.2.1 Controlling Business Operations

Many events in an established business unfold little by little in the form of daily transactions. Firms have internal organizations to record and deal with these transactions. These organizations may be an accounting group or have other names. The basic functions are financial control, inventory control, and production control. We'll discuss the purposes of these functions and the concepts of using computers to automate the procedure for controlling business operations.

Let's structure an analogy to illustrate the general objectives of transaction recording and controlling. Consider a water tank with valves on the supply drain that can be adjusted to change the water level in the tank. In the analogy the water outflow corresponds to product sales, and the inflow corresponds to an input of labor, finances, and raw materials. The water level corresponds to an inventory of finished products that are ready for shipment. The manager of the business could be represented in the analogy by a person responsible for manipulating the valves to keep the water at a desired level. An empty tank simulates the undesirable condition of unfilled orders. An overfilled tank means that the firm has overproduced or undersold to the point that too much money is invested in unsold products.

The job of managing a business or controlling the water-flow valves is possible theoretically only for situations in which there exists a *feedback of information*. The word "feedback" is a classical term used in discussing circuits having monitored output levels that are dependent on adjustable inputs. Feedback is the process of transferring information from the monitor back to the input. The level or intensity of the feedback signal becomes a factor in the plans to control the output by adjusting the input. In our simple case, the tank level could be monitored by sight and used as feedback information by a person adjusting the valves. Managers must have schemes to monitor the input and output of their firms and use feedback concepts to make plans and decisions for improving profits. We shall discuss some of these business procedures.

In small firms, the job of keeping the books probably is handled by one person, who may even be the manager. These records become more extensive for larger firms, but they still serve as a basis for controlling the operation. An effective set of records tell "where we are today." They control the daily transactions, for example, by restricting the production level to be approximately the same as anticipated sales. Employees become aware that recorded information is a basis for control when they are told that financial records show that travel budgets have been exhausted, hence no more trips.

Records are a useful administrative tool for controlling events within predetermined bounds. The recorded information is one factor in the process of making plans and decisions. The information can be used for watchdog purposes to monitor the situation induced by previous plans and decisions.

14.2.1.1 Financial Control. *Accounting* is a series of techniques used by most firms to record daily transactions and periodically report summaries, such as a statement of assets and liabilities. These accounting categories relate the financial value of holding and obligated payments to others. In simple cases, both of them can be controlled by fairly general policies from management.

The complexities of accounting surface quickly when we consider the delicate problem of maintaining an acceptable level of cash on hand. In personal financing, spendthrifts find they must borrow or liquidate some assets at the local pawnshop. Business running out of cash must seek credit or, technically, become bankrupt. On the other hand, an unreasonably high cash balance is undesirable because idle money is not a maximum contributor to business profits.

Principal functions of accounting systems include the following:

1. Establishing a credible basis for judging the firm's financial position.
2. Preparing a budget showing the projected incomes and expenses.
3. Aiding the administration of the budget by monitoring variations between the actual and projected financial situations.
4. Monitoring the favorable or unfavorable trends resulting from past decisions by management.
5. Circumventing fraudulent activities in financial dealings by making sure that daily transactions are concurred by at least two people and periodic statements are audited.
6. Generating meaningful summary reports. The balance sheet relates assets and liabilities. The profit and loss statement sums the accounts received and deducts the accounts paid.

There usually is a need for other reports, directed at monitoring specific developments, projects, or products. A new plant is an example of a development that could be reported in a separate accounting summary. A separate budget, balance sheet, and profit and loss statement could be prepared for the new plant.

Accounting was one of the first business jobs to be automated. In adopting to computer methods, firms generally maintained the basic accounting function and took advantage of several new capabilities. Data-processing systems can sort data into various formats and, thus, give considerable flexibility in generating summary reports. The files can be sorted into many subgroups of the identification number or into any cohesive group that has a data name. For example, the data name could be a budget category, project code, shop code, sales district, or shipping cost. Sorting techniques can produce many groupings, such as the profit and loss for a project or shop. Other reports could show totals for the sales districts. The Government Accounting Office performs as watchdog of U.S. government expenditures. Data-processing techniques are used to sort expenditure transactions into groups that reveal spending abuses.

Computers provide a means to augment bookkeeping data with mathematical analyses of the financial position. The theory of ventures and risks can be entered into projections of cash flow. For example, two products, X and Y, could be put into production with a projected net income of $50,000 and $80,000 per year, respectively. There may be a risk that product X will absorb $100,000 extra cash flow to broaden advertising appeal if sales warrant after the first three months. In this simple example, the extra cash flow must come from reserves, borrowing, or sales of other products. Computer methods permit the risk aspects of ventures to be analyzed far beyond the capabilities of manual methods. The objective is to establish how high the projected rate of return should be to warrant undertaking high risk ventures. The analysis can show the magnified risks that result when several high risk ventures are pursued at the same time.

The financial situation must be presented in formats that are useful to others. We have implied the treasurer's interest in balance sheet data and the administrator's interest in profit and loss summaries. Investors must be presented with summaries showing the sources and disbursements of earnings. Lenders want assurances that new ventures are feasible before approving credit for a loan.

We'll use the name *accounting information system* to refer to the ongoing procedure of financial control. In most firms the financial records serve the purpose of the accounting organization more directly than others. They receive data from others. Accounting organizations sometimes are reluctant to freely contribute data to composers of an overall information system because certain financial information should be kept secret from competitors. In this protectorship role, the accounting group usually becomes the keeper of the *overall information system,* whatever its scope. But this does not have to be the case. The potential uses for information systems extend beyond the cost control functions to overall planning and decision making. The data base for an overall information system should include all accounting data that are of general interest and not confidential. This critical determination is best handled by persons with special responsibility for the overall information system.

14.2.1.2 Inventory Control. The inventory in a business is composed of the items or material on hand. It represents an investment and should be scrutinized on a continuous basis to assure that the cost advantages of holding the inventory add up to a fair rate of return for the investment and storage space. An inventory is a hedge against critical shortages and serves as a buffer in situations having fluctuations in demand rates or favorable unit prices for bulk purchases. From these overall advantages, we can infer that a satisfactory inventory avoids the penalties of numerous small orders and the costs of work stoppages due to parts shortages. Retail stores hope that inventory investments will be returned by gaining sales that might have been lost with a lesser selection. Effective warehouse operations have stock available in quantities and, perhaps, near the location where demand is expected. Warehouse inventories may encompass several distribution centers, and the operation may use computer methods to speed orders for shipment.

The cost disadvantages of inventories counterbalance the advantages to some extent. Inventories are a substantial investment in many businesses. Maintenance costs are incurred for cleaning, handling, and record keeping. It is impossible to completely protect against deterioration, obsolescence, damage, and theft.

The job of inventory control is a record-keeping routine that can be governed by a few basic policies. Algebraic expressions can be written to represent the more common policies. (These are shown at the end of this section.) Records and expressions are handled easily by computers. Automatic inventory methods are a worthwhile substitute for almost all manual methods that have been outpaced by expanded stock and higher carrying charges for investment. Computers have been found useful for inventories having as few as 5000 categories of low-volume items.

Manual inventory methods have shortcomings because they generally fail to keep the stock in balance with the demand. For example, there may be some items that are seldom used or obsolete. Other items may be out of stock. Payroll costs are incurred for maintaining the stock, issuing orders, logging replenishments, and keeping the records.

Computer methods can be properly applied to inventory control. A wise designer of an automated inventory system will carefully avoid the pitfalls that can upset the introduction. A manual system may have limitations, but it works to some degree, at least. Computer systems should be introduced as an improvement that is offered to the people running the manual system. After a few days of training, the present stock clerk should be able to code transactions for punched card entry and make the other adjustments involved in transition to the new system.

Ex. 14–1

Suppose that an ongoing inventory system appears to be a candidate for conversion to computer methods. How would you proceed in further research of its feasibility?

There is seldom a single answer to real-life situations; the overall approach should be based on sound business reasoning. It generally is good business to consider the financial and the diplomatic aspects of the situation. There may be other in-house inventories that are already automated. These systems should be studied as a basis for judging the feasibility of the candidate system. It would be unwise to make elaborate announcements to the stockroom or warehouse people at this point because they know that the efficiencies of computer systems lead to personnel transfers. A diplomatic person might agree to help the stockroom by making a catalog list of current inventory items. The catalog could be in ascending order by part number or alphabetically by part name. Each item could be further specified by quantity on hand, quantity on order, unit price, and reorder point. These data form a partial list of the information that, eventually, may be in the records of the master file. This first step produces a useful catalog for the stockroom while providing details for further consideration of project feasibility.

Analytical equations exist that relate the inventory parameters. The independent variables involved are U, unit price; C, cost of issuing an order and receiving a shipment; D, demand for item on an annual basis; and I, interest and all other annual carrying charges on investment and stockroom costs.

An order for 8 electric motors may be good inventory practice but an order for 8 pounds of nails would not be. The order quantity is a critical factor in minimizing inventory costs. The ordering costs per unit are reduced by nearly half by doubling the order quantity. This apparent saving is diminished considerably by the carrying charges for the extra units. These counteracting individual costs can be summed to form a total cost that should reach a minimum. The term *economic order quantity*, abbreviated EOQ, is the best order quantity to minimize total costs.

$$\text{EOQ} = \sqrt{\frac{2CD}{IU}} \qquad\qquad (14\text{--}1)$$

Let's use equation (14–1) to calculate the EOQ for electric motors and nails.

Ex. 14–2

The following data give the costs for ordering and carrying two categories of inventory. For each case, what are the EOQ, annual carrying charges, and ordering costs?

	Electric Motors	*Nails*
U	$25 each	$1 per pound
C	$10 per order	$10 per order
D	16 motors per year	400 pounds per year
I	20 percent	20 percent

Calculations yield:

	Electric Motors	*Nails*
EOQ	$= \sqrt{\dfrac{(2)\ (\$10)\ (16)}{(0.2)\ (\$25)}}$ $= 8$ electric motors per order	$= \sqrt{\dfrac{(2)\ (\$10)\ (400)}{(0.2)\ (\$1)}}$ $= 200$ pounds of nails per order
Ordering costs	$= (2)\ (\$10)$ $= \$20$ per year	$= (2)\ (\$10)$ $= \$20$ per year
Carrying charges	$= (0.20)\ (\$25)\ (8 + 0)/2$ $= \$20$ per year	$(0.20)\ (\$1)\ (200 + 0)/2$ $= \$20$ per year

Carrying charges of the motors, for example, should be based on 8 at the start and none at the end of the period. The average is $(8 + 0)/2 = 4$.

What would be the total costs for alternative schemes of ordering 16 motors and 4 motors?

	4 orders of 4	*1 order of 16*	*2 orders* *EOQ = 8*
Ordering costs	$(4)\ (\$10) = \$40$	$(1)\ (\$10) = \$10$	$\$20$
Carrying charges	$(0.2)\ (\$25)\ (4 + 0)/2$ $= \$10$	$(0.2)\ (\$25)\ (16 + 0)/2$ $= \$40$	$\$20$
Total costs	$\$50$	$\$50$	$\$40$

The alternative schemes lead to $50 total cost, which confirms the fact that the $40 cost at the EOQ is the minimum.

The preceding example illustrated that 8 electric motors should be ordered twice a year. Expressions exist in the inventory field to tell when to order. The *reorder point* is the predetermined level at which the diminishing quantity on hand signals to reorder. The *lead time* is the lapse between order placement and stock receipts. There are various criteria for establishing the reorder point. Some expressions minimize the total cost, but shortages could develop if the demand is unusually high while the item is on order. Other expressions have been derived that base the reorder point on specified shortages.

Let's define the symbols: L = lead time in fractions of a year; R = reorder point. The simple expression

$$R = D \cdot L$$

shows the concept of selecting the reorder point. The more complex expressions involve the probability of having shortages and the costs they incur.

14.2.1.3   Production Control on the Shop Floor.   The computers being manufactured ten years ago were not reliable in the shop environment. Production process control was slow to spread. The presently available mini-computers and mini-peripheral devices can work right beside many shop machines. The capabilities of computers are being applied in increasing numbers, despite reluctance in some instances. Some of the reluctance is logical and some is not. A large production line that functions and returns a profit is usually considered to be fine as it is and best left alone. A changeover to the ideal computer control involves a risk that is beyond the career objectives of most managers.

The opportune time to introduce computer control is during production start-up. Instances include a new line of products or a new plant. Job shops have integrated computers into their operation because they start a new run every few days or weeks.

Let's define some terms. *Computer control* of a production operation means that a special or a general-purpose digital computer

1.   Receives signals on a regular basis from the manufacturing process or machine.
2.   Manipulates the signals in accordance with reprogrammable instructions.
3.   Returns a transmission of control signals.

This definition is more restrictive than absolutely necessary because it excludes analog computers, which are rugged and have been used in the shop for several years. However, we shall feature digital computers in this section, in keeping with the scope of the book.

An *automated factory* usually is an arrangement of conveyors, flow directors, and robotlike machines that repeat a preset cycle of actions. These improvements have been added to many production lines because they can cut cost and time by better than 50 percent compared to manual means. An automated factory can be structured in piecemeal development with little risk of overall catastrophe. In a typical application a robot might replace the function of a half-dozen manual stations. The Vega plant of the Chevrolet Division of General Motors is one instance of automation being applied at start-up in several places along a new line. From our definitions, we see that computer control is a more sophisticated concept than the automated factory.

Numerical control machines are found in all large shops and some shops with as few as five machine operators. These machines resemble a player piano in basic concept. Numerical control machines accept a prepared paper or metal tape and translate the tape code into tool selection and the precision movement of the tool relative to the work stock. Available tools can do drilling, grinding, and milling, among other things. For example, the tape code might specify that six $\frac{1}{4}$-inch holes be drilled with a 1-inch spacing. In rapid sequence, the drill head having that bit would come into position and the work table would automatically traverse to bring each of the six hole sites under the drill.

During the past 10 years numerical control machines have become an indispensible part of precision manufacturing. Compared to manual methods, they save money by producing high volumes of work that can move to the next station with little scrap and, theoretically, without inspection. The machines are operated by logic circuits that accept sets of tape codes and generate corresponding signals to move the stock and tools. These machines have limited capability in comparison with the versatility of computer control. The terms "automated factory" and "numerical control" suggest identity with computer control, but after a closer look, we see that they are more like robots than computers.

Let's discuss applications that are within the category of computer control. These improvements have found their way to some production operations but not to others. The applications have followed certain patterns because there are undeniable constraints on ventures with an ongoing, profitable production operation. For example, the numerical control machines were cautiously accepted as deluxe versions of the machines they replaced. A production line is a formidable golden goose and best left alone.

Several chemical processes are controlled by computer. Pumping stations and regulators along oil pipelines are computer-controlled. Analytical methods are used to activated remote booster pumps and valves to keep the oil moving, despite changes in weather and flow demand. These examples of process control could be tested on a scale-model basis and then applied with confidence on full-scale operations.

Steel rolling mills and paper machines have traditionally been manually controlled. They have become computer controlled within the last few years. These large, complex machines have characteristics that must be expertly adjusted for a high-quality product output. The perplexing interrelations between the output and the adjustments on the input have been found to be beyond manual means. The manual tasks become even more difficult for mills that roll various steel alloys and stock sizes. In making the change to computer control, the designers faced risks but, of course, they could ease the transition by running the manual and computer controllers in parallel for a few days.

Ex. 14–4

Most manufacturing firms operate as a job shop. Unit-price bids are based on production runs of a specified quantity. For example, the firm may bid to mass-produce 50,000 combs at 16 cents each and be finished with the run in six weeks. Computer control is used more in job shops than in sustained mass production firms. What facets of the job shop appear to be candidates for computer control?

Competition motivates innovation in the job shop. Sometimes the bid-winning firm is successful because it knows the capabilities and availability of the production machines. Of course, a machine should not be started on a new run until the present run is finished. The overall *control and scheduling of work flow* on the shop floor is handled in many large shops by computers. Computers are useful in calculating *estimates for price quotations.* They can process programs and data files that mathematically combine the costs of detailed machine operations, labor, overhead, raw materials, and shipping. For two bidders per job, quotes develop into a job only 50 percent of the time on the average. Computers have been used to translate the design of the piece part into configuration-forming *patterns, dies, and molds.* For example, dressmaking firms have machines to translate dress designs into patterns for each size. A shop die or mold is a special alloy metal block with exactly the right dimensions to form copies when the piece-part material is forced into the die. Tool and die making has traditionally been a critical skill in job shops. Computers are relieving this bottleneck by a two-step procedure of (1) calculating the die dimension from an analysis of the forming forces and configuration, and (2) generating the codes to drive a numerical control machine in fabricating the die. The need to be flexible and competitive has led job shops to many of these innovations.

Ex. 14–5

Consider firms engaged in the long-term mass production of products. In the ideal case, the operation repeatedly transforms raw materials and labor into a product of specified quality. What uses do you see for computers in these shops?

Computers are being used to *record measurements of quality* in the products and raw materials. Subsequently, the computer system can retrieve the data for analysis. For example, trends in measured dimensions can signal that a die is nearly worn out. Suppose that a bad batch of raw materials led to unacceptable products that now must be retrieved from shipment. The recorded data could be used to solve this problem. In general, computers *analyze the details* in substained production and analyze flexibilities in job shops.

A large portion of the floor space in most manufacturing shops is filled with parts and subassemblies that require further assembly. In a typical factory, piece parts are being worked only 10 percent of the time. The in-process inventory that results from all this idle time is a prime candidate for computer methods. Floor space is valuable and should be cleared for other uses. The inventory represents an idle investment. Careful analysis would help smooth the flow of work from one process to the next. These improvements can make the inventory manageable with almost no risk to the overall operation.

Computer methods can handle the routing of items in the factory and in other places. Railroad freight cars are loaded and moving only 7 percent of the time. School bus routing in a large regional district is a maze that undoubtedly requires more buses and miles than are necessary.

14.2.2   Planning and Decision Making in Business Operations

The success of efforts on all scales depends on a plan. Many levels of planning are involved in the grand-scale operations of a voyage to the moon or a massive military troop movement. On smaller scales, delivery truck dispatchers form detailed plans for routing the trucks from one destination to others in the same vicinity. By definition, *planning* is a formalized process for clarifying objectives and considering cost tradeoffs of options. Planning is a framework that begins with the overall objectives of an anticipated operation and proceeds to other levels, which have greater detail, until the objectives are finally translated into detailed steps. For example, a plan for writing a book or an article begins with an overall area of interest and proceeds to a broad topic outline, which, subsequently, becomes a detailed outline.

The need for decisions can be identified during the planning operation. A good plan provides a structure and data for making decisions. The steps in some portions of the plan depend upon the laws of nature or the constraints imposed by regulations, competition, or established policy. There are alternative courses of action in many parts of a plan. *Decision making* is the process of assembling and analyzing the data on the contingencies and the alternatives that affect the plan. We see that planning and decision making are interrelated. The plan shows the need for decisions and, in turn, the plan is guided by the decisions.

Market research is a plan for selecting product price and characteristics from an analysis of the demand. In developing the marketing plan, many decisions are needed, which could range from deciding to continue the status quo to deciding to market a whole new product. In other cases, an analysis of the demand might reveal that sales of the present product could be improved by changing the advertising scope or appeal.

The stakes are high in planning a new product or advertising campaign. Profitable fads can be created for new products. Existing products can be popularized by redirecting the advertising appeal.

Computers are used to analyze characteristics of the demand and the product. Many makers of consumer products consult experts to do market research. Special techniques are used in market research to gather data and define cohesive groups in the demand. The research might reveal a gap in the market by defining groups that would buy a new product.

Data gathering is often in the form of a questionnaire that is filled out by an interviewer who visits or phones potential customers. The types of questions asked would be: "What would cause you to become a bigger buyer of our product?" "What new product would you buy?" With long questionnaires, the interviewer can pose more options and cross-check the answers. Computers are used to sort and analyze the data to ascertain the overall size of groups that appear to be buyers.

Several mathematical techniques have been applied in computer analysis of plans and decisions. *Simulation* is an analysis method that we have all used in our everyday planning. As a child we might have said: "Let's suppose I buy a whistle and a comic book, do I have enough money for both?" Our analysis at that age might have consisted of simulating the expenditures by counting our change and observing the end result of the plan. *Simulation analysis* by computer is based on the concept of rapidly sequencing from step to step through plans. The plan may contain hundreds of interrelated steps and in span several hours or months of real time. Simulation is a straightforward way of establishing the consequences of proposed plans, whether it is a child's plan to buy a whistle or a corporation's plan to expand its product line. Simulation techniques are programmed in steps that follow the steps in the plan on nearly a 1:1 basis. This advantage makes the data for plans directly usable in the analysis. Changes are easily entered and computed results can be interpreted by people familiar with the plan.

Other mathematical techniques have proved useful in planning and decision making. These range in complexity from a simple tabulation of sorted data to complex optimization of the cost benefits of every step in a plan. Neither of these extreme methods are accepted readily by management. A simple table of survey data makes no attempt to explain the interaction of events. The complex optimization is too abstract to be useful. *Factor analysis* is a fairly simple technique for identifying cohesive groups of data. In mathematics, we know that a factor clearly contributes to the value of the overall expression. The quotient of all factors yields the overall expression. Factor analysis of data from a market survey might reveal groups that like or dislike certain aspects of the planned products.

Regression analysis is a statistical method of measuring the intensity of coupling between different factors. For example, market survey data for carpets could be concerned with the regression of new carpet expenditure on annual incomes. In the range of, say, $15,000 to $20,000, the data would show a distribution for expenditures. The regression of carpet expenditures on income is the mean value of this distribution. The technique relates the demand for carpet to income level. Other data, showing the number of people having incomes in each level, would be used in estimating the overall demand for carpet.

15 The FORTRAN IV Language

Engineers and scientists were the first users of computers. They discovered new fields of science and wanted to analyze the nature of their discoveries. Engineers develop and use mathematical models to relate actions and reactions that effect structures, active processes, or forms of motion. These models are a set of formulas that have been derived from experiments or theoretical considerations.

Simple *models* may consist of a single formula such as the relation between the force applied to the center of a bridge beam and the deflection. The applied force and the calculated deflection both may be at the center of the beam or elsewhere, at the same or separate locations. The effect of this loading can be calculated by manual methods.

The scope of the analysis begins to increase when the situation dictates that many off-center loads also are present. Furthermore, it may be desirable to know the magnitude of the deflection at many points along the beam and for many loading distributions. For example, it may be informative to know the bridge deflection at 10 points for a 60-ton load at the center. Other distribution of the 60-ton load could be 6 tons at each of the 10 points.

The parameters in bridge design are loading, structure configuration, deflection, and breaking strength of the members. *Parametric studies* are routines to calculate the situation for a set of values and then repeat several times for other sets of values. To optimize the bridge structure and cost, the design process is based on parametric studies. Bridge structures are composed of beams, plates, and cables. These members interact to share the total load. Formulas are available for analyzing the response of composite structures; however, they may be based on iterative techniques. For example, a bridge beam may share the load with a suspension cable. The *iteration* process begins with an assumption that the beam carries a certain fraction of the load. It then is calculated whether the cable will deflect the right distance to carry the remaining fraction. If not, it is assumed that the beam carries more or less, and the sequence is repeated until compatible deflections are obtained.

Many engineering studies are based on fairly simple formulas; however, manual methods are uneconomical for extensive analysis. The total number of calculations may be several thousand for all the iterations in a detailed parametric study.

The original objective in developing the first computer was to automate the manual task of calculating trajectory charts for artillery rounds. Charts were needed for many elevation angles, ranges, wind, and weather conditions (see Section 1.1). The work force just wasn't large enough to keep pace with the proliferation of weapon models. Formulas were available, but manual methods were not practical.

In the early 1950s it was estimated that less than 10 computers would serve the country for the forseeable future. These special-purpose machines were to be located at a few universities and research laboratories where the expertise was available to reprogram the system. The first users of computers were scientists, who by nature are inclined to work with formulas. They had to know the details of the machines and the formulas. It seems logical that the first widely used compiler would be for translating formulas into machine language. FORTRAN (acronym for *formula translation*) was the first language to make computer solutions available to nonexperts in programming. The language was introduced in 1959. The advantages of FORTRAN programming opened the field to thousands and eventually millions of new users.

Arithmetic operations are expressed in the FORTRAN language by *assignment statements* that are similar in structure to the original formulas. For example, the formula $A = B(D + E)$ is written as A=B*(D+E) and punched as such on a Hollerith card. The symbol * signifies multiplication.

Data files are handled by *format statements* that specify the data types and their location on punched cards. Programs contain input/output statements that cause transmission paths to momentarily be opened to the input/output device. Data inputs and outputs in scientific applications usually enter from one magnetic tape and leave on one. These tapes contain input information that has been copied from several punched cards and output information that typically is transferred to a printer.

Other FORTRAN statements are used by the programmer. Branches in the processing sequence are specified with GO TO, and IF statements. These convenient *decision statements* are described in Section 15.2. The DO statement specifies the number of times that a set of statements is to be repeated. These statements appear in most FORTRAN programs and are discussed in Section 15.3.

Some analytical solutions are based on the technique of matrix manipulation. A matrix is an array of quantities that are arranged in rows and columns. Each element in the array has a numerical value and is assigned to a particular row and column. For example, the statements A(1, 1) = 6, A(1, 2) = 4, A(2, 1) = 3, A(2, 2) = 2.8 assign the values shown in the 2 by 2 matrix in Fig. 15–1. In general, the quantities $A(I, J)$ relate to

$$A(I,J) = \begin{vmatrix} 6 & 4 \\ 3 & 2.8 \end{vmatrix}$$

FIG. 15–1   Two by Two Matrix.

the effect at the Ith point caused by a load, force, voltage, or the like, that is applied at the Jth point. For example, A(1, 2) might be the current flow at one point in an electrical circuit caused by a voltage at a second point. FORTRAN statements are available to easily specify the contents and *dimensions of arrays*. It is not unusual to have over 100 rows and columns. It is necessary to specify their dimensions in terms of memory addresses occupied. Array and DIMENSION statements are discussed in Section 15.4.

Section 15.5 has examples of *input/output statements*. Section 15.6 introduces the concept of *subprogram statements*. Similar analytical methods are used in many engineering problems and often a method is used several times in the solution of a particular problem. The common information can be written as a subprogram and referenced at the appropriate places in the program by a SUBROUTINE statement.

15.1   ARITHMETIC STATEMENTS

The hardware units in Chapters 6 through 10 are designed for fetching data from memory, generating sums, products, and so on, and then storing the results in memory. Arithmetic statements specify the data names and the operations for computing the desired results.

15.1.1   Fixed-Point and Floating-Point Data Names

The compiler allocates memory addresses for all data words. In Chapter 11 we discussed the two methods for storing data in the memory of the UNIVAC 1108. One of these, the *fixed-point* method, stores the binary equivalent of only integers (no fractional parts). There are *no round-off errors* involved in converting decimal integers to binary. For example, the number 6 can be compared with a data word defined to be 4 and the difference will be exactly 2. With the other alternative, floating point, the difference would be 2, but with a small round-off error. As we mentioned in Section 11.4.2, a *floating-point* number is converted to a *fractional* part and an *exponential* part and stored in a memory address also having two parts. Round-off errors are present in converting all fractional numbers to binary.

Ex. 15–1

Suppose that a bridge structure is 50 feet long and has 800-pound loads applied at 5 points that are 4 feet apart. Furthermore it is loaded with 1500-pound loads at 2 points that are 10 feet apart (see Fig. 15–2).

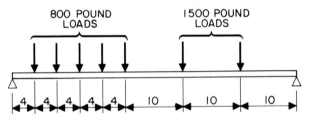

FIG. 15–2   Load Distribution of 50-Foot Bridge.

The data values are 50, 800, 5, 4, 1500, 2, and 10. They all could be stored as floating-point numbers, but there are advantages to storing 5 and 2 as fixed point. Why?

Indexes are keys used to designate information in a set or sequence. In this example the set consists of 7 points, which are separated by given distances. Loads are applied at these points. Usually, programmers handle sets of this sort by assigning an index to represent each point. Decision statements would check each index to determine the appropriate loading and separation. Once the check establishes that an index is exactly 4, 5, 6, and so on, unique loadings and separations can be assigned.

The FORTRAN compiler checks the first letter of all data names. The letters I, J, K, L, M, and N are used to denote *integers*. In the statement I=6, for example, the binary equivalence of 6 would be stored in a fixed-point memory address. Any acceptable name that *begins with the letters* I, J, K, L, M, or N will be handled as *fixed-point data*. Any number that is written with a decimal point is a FORTRAN real number as opposed to a FORTRAN integer. FORTRAN variables are allocated memory addresses and are fetched or stored when these are involved in an assignment statement.

If you followed a person's tracks in the snowy woods, you might deduce after a few hundred meters whether the person was lost or on a steady course. An imprinted trail that wanders to the right and then to the left would be a good sign that the hiker was confused.

Compilers don't roam through the snow, but instead they analyze programmer's statements, alias tracks. Statements assigning *floating-point data to a fixed-point address* indicate that the programmer is confused. The computer issues *error messages* instructing the programmer to correct the apparent mistake. Exercise 15–2 discusses the consequences of mixing the two types of data words in the same statement.

Ex. 15–2

The following sequences of statements assign data to memory addresses for I and F. What would be stored in each case and is it correct?

$$I = 2.6$$
$$F = 18.9$$

The fractional part is omitted when 2.6 is assigned to I because memory addresses allocated for integers cannot handle fractions. The number 2 erroneously is assigned to I and 0.189×10^2 is assigned to F. Consider a second sequence:

$$JF = 2$$
$$LOSS = 13$$
$$I = 6 * (3 * JF + LOSS)$$
$$F - I + 8$$

Correct values of 114 and 0.122×10^3 are assigned to I and F, respectively.

Consider a third sequence:

$$JF = 4.8$$
$$LOSS = 2.0$$
$$I = 6.2 * (3 * JF + LOSS)$$
$$F = LOSS + 4.7$$

Manual methods yield $I = 101.68$ and $F = 6.7$. The computer would assign 0.67×10^1 to F and erroneously assign 86 to I, because $I = 6.2 * (3 * 4 + 2) = 86.8$.

15.1.2 Constants and Variables

All data words appearing in a program are allocated a memory address. *Variables* are data words having names. Their memory allocations depend on the first letter in that name. The contents of these addresses can be expected to change one or more times during a processing run. Names must begin with a letter of the alphabet and not exceed a total of six letters and digits. In Section 15.1.1 we said that first letters I, J, K, L, M, and N denoted integers. The numerical value for a variable must either be input information or assigned by an arithmetic statement. These inputs or assignments must be made in a statement before the variable is used in computation. The compiler issues an error message for statements having an undefined variable on the right-hand side of an arithmetic statement. For example, the variable LOSS was defined in Ex. 15–2 and then used in computing I.

Constants are data words that are similar in concept to variables, except they don't have a data name and don't change during a processing run. In manual computations, the lone expression $A = B + 6.3$ would draw the reaction, "What is the value of B?" It wouldn't occur to us to ask, "Where is the value of 6.3 located?" In machine computation, the contents of the address assigned to B is added to the contents of address assigned to 6.3 and the sum is stored in the address assigned to A.

Clearly, memory addresses must be assigned for constants as well as variables. The memory allocations are *fixed point* for *constant integers* and *floating point* for numbers having a *fractional* or an *exponential part*. Figure 15–3 shows examples of memory allocations for constants and variables.

ARITHMETIC STATEMENT	MEMORY ALLOCATIONS		ERRORS
	FIXED-POINT	FLOATING-POINT	
$I = 3*(J+6)$	ALL	NONE	NONE
$AN72 = 2.6*(SUM+3.0)$	NONE	ALL	NONE
$I = 3.0*(J+6)$	I,J,6,	3.0	MIXED DATA WORDS
$I \div 3 = J + 6$	J,6	NONE	ILLEGAL CHARACTER IN DATA NAME, $I \div 3$
$SUMTOTAL = A + 3$	A	3	DATA NAME, SUMTOTAL EXEEDS LIMIT OF 6 CHARACTERS

FIG. 15–3   Examples of Common Errors in Using Constants and Variables.

15.1.3 Basic Operations

FORTRAN handles formulas by using the basic arithmetic operation codes shown in Fig. 15–4. The codes are familiar except for * and **. The conveniences of these new symbols are illustrated by Ex. 15–3.

OPERATION	CODE SYMBOL	ORDER IN EXECUTION
EXPONENTIATION	**	FIRST
DIVISION	/	SECOND
MULTIPLICATION	*	THIRD
SUBTRACTION	—	FOURTH
ADDITION	+	FIFTH

FIG. 15–4 Summary of FORTRAN Arithmetic Operations Codes and Hierarchy.

Ex. 15–3

Suppose that a certain city has a population of 3 million. How would this data be represented in a FORTRAN statement?

The statement POP = 3.0 * 10 ** 6 is suitable.

In a formula, we might write POP = 3.0 × 10^6 using the familiar × for times and placing 6 in the superscript position. All characters must be uppercase and on the same line in a FORTRAN statement, making the superscript impractical. The multiplication symbol * is preferred to ×, which would be mistaken for a data name.

With a little practice, it is fairly straightforward to compose FORTRAN statements from mathematical formulas. Common mistakes can be circumvented by remembering the permissible symbols and the order in which operations are executed. Programmers occasionally forget that addition is performed after division. They might mistakenly write A/B + C instead of A/(B + C) for A divided by the quantity B + C. Figure 15–4 shows the rules of hierarchy. Operations having the same level in the hierarchy are executed in order from left to right.

The formulas in Fig. 15–5 are examples of FORTRAN statements for a few formulas. Data names in these statements resemble the symbols in the original formula. This practice is preferred because the user probably

FORMULA	FORTRAN STATEMENT
$P = \dfrac{RT}{V}$	$P = R * T / V$
$P_2 = P_0 \left(\dfrac{V}{V+v} \right)$	$P2 = PO * V / (V + VS)$
$F = G \left[\dfrac{a_1 a_2}{d^2} \right]$	$F = G * A1 * A2 / D ** 2$
$F = 6\pi\eta a v$	$PI = 3.14$ $F = 6 * PI * ETA * A * V$
$\Delta H = C_v (T_2 - T_1) + \dfrac{\Delta W}{J}$	$DELH = CV * (T2 - T1) + DELW/J$

FIG. 15–5   FORTRAN Statements for Typical Formulas from Physics.

is familiar with the formula and hence can easily spot mistakes in the similar FORTRAN version.

The formula $V = IR$ is fundamental in studying the flow of electrical current, I, through a resistor, R. The resulting voltage drop is V. The statement, V = I * R, might be written after a first glance. However, it is *not a suitable expression,* because the variable I will be handled as an integer. The first letter must be different from I, J, K, L, M, or N. We'll *remedy the situation* by choosing the symbol X and writing V = XI * R.

15.1.4   Expressions in Parentheses

Formulas can include several terms and have groups that are arithmetically related to groups of other terms. For example, the formula

$$\beta = \frac{(h_t - h_0)}{(H + h_0)t}$$

has groups $(h_t - h_0)$ and $(H + h_0)$.

Parentheses are used in FORTRAN statements to enclose groups of variables. During computation, the data words for these variables are fetched and the *total value of the group is computed.* It is held in temporary storage until other groups are computed. Then the overall expression is evaluated. This practice is similar to the common manual methods.

The expression BETA = (HT − H0)/((H + H0) * T) is a suitable FORTRAN expression for the preceding formula. We notice that

$(H + H0)$ is *nested* in another set of parentheses enclosing all the terms in the denominator.

Ex. 15–4

Write a FORTRAN statement for the formula

$$\beta = U \left\{ \frac{I_1 P_0}{U P_1} \left[\frac{(f_e + D_n)}{(f_e D_n)} \right] \right\}$$

Brackets and braces are convenient, but they are not permitted in FORTRAN. The entire statement must be written on the same line or a continuation. Nested parentheses must serve to separate groups. The expression BETA = U * ((XI1 * P0)/(U * P1)) * (FE + DN)/ (FE * DN) is suitable. There are five pairs of parentheses.

It is common to make mistakes in using parentheses. The compiler is designed to scan the statement and check whether *parentheses are used in pairs*. There should be the same number of parentheses facing to the right as to the left. To avoid errors, it is recommended to manually count the number that face each way to ascertain that they are used in pairs. Figure 15–6 shows three examples of parentheses in FORTRAN statements. Are any of these wrong?

FORMULA	FORTRAN STATEMENT
$t = \frac{1}{2}(m + \frac{1}{2})\lambda$	T = XLAMDA *(XM + 1/2)/2
$R = \dfrac{1}{\lambda(1/n_2^2 - 1/n_1^2)}$	R = 1/(XLAMDA *(1/XN2 **2 − 1/XN1**2))
$v = \dfrac{2\pi^2 M e^4}{h^3}\left(\dfrac{1}{n_2^2} - \dfrac{1}{n_1^2}\right)$	V = 2.0 *(PI**2)*XM *(E **4)*(1/XN **2 − 1/XN1 **2)/(H**3)

FIG. 15–6 Examples of Parentheses in FORTRAN Statements.

15.1.5 Assignment Statements

It is common practice to use a separate punched card for every arithmetic statement. Positions 1 through 5 are reserved for *statement numbers*. Position 6 is either blank or contains a nonzero character to signify that a *statement* is being *continued* from the preceding card.

Comment statements begin in position 1 and can continue to position 72. These always begin with the letter C to alert the compiler that the statement is not to be processed. All other statements begin in column 7 and must end before column 72 or be continued to the next card.

Arithmetic operations are specified by assignment statement. Figures 15–5 and 15–6 show several of these being used to represent formulas. The left-hand side of the equal sign is a single data name and the right-hand side is one or more data names and corresponding arithmetic symbols. The statement $A = B$ means that the data in the memory address allocated to data name B must be assigned to the address allocated to data name A. Of course, the data in B remains.

Assignment statements are sometimes mistakenly called equations. The expression $X + Y = Z + 1$ is an equation; however, it is nonsense as a FORTRAN statement, because there is more than one term on the left-hand side. The equivalent expression $X = Z + 1 - Y$ is a suitable assignment statement.

15.2   TRANSFER STATEMENTS

Statements in any program language are processed in their order of appearance until a transfer statement is encountered. *Transfer statements* are the programmer's tool for causing the computer to *make decisions* about the processing sequence. After a transfer, the next statement that is processed must be labeled with a *statement number*. These labels are optional on other statements.

The processing sequence is defined uniquely in cases where a transfer is specified to a particular number and

1. A statement is labeled with that number in columns 1 through 5.
2. No other statement has that same number.

The compiler checks that these conditions are satisfied, and, if not, it issues an error message.

15.2.1   GO TO Statement

The address of the next instruction is always stored in the instruction counter. The contents of the counter usually are one plus the address of the instruction being processed (see Section 10.5).

Unconditional branches are specified by the machine codes in a regular two-part instruction word. The first part, the operation code, has the proper combination of binary digits to specify the branch. The second part contains binary digits giving the address of the next instruction. The net result of processing the *branch instruction* is to *load this address into the instruction counter.*

The GO TO statement is translated by the compiler into the machine codes for an *unconditional branch.* The resulting machine instruction word bears a one-to-one resemblance in purpose and form to the FORTRAN statement. This simple interpretation is unusual, because the compiler translates most statements into several instruction words.

The GO TO is an easy statement for the programmer as well as the compiler. The form is

GO TO 99

The 9's are symbols for digits in the next statement number. The statement must begin in column 7 on a punched card. For example, the expression GO TO 376 would transfer control to the statment number 376.

15.2.2   IF Statement

The arithmetic IF statement provides the FORTRAN language with a powerful *decision* feature. The next statement is selected from *three possible* numbers while the program is running. In the Goldilocks nursery rhyme, she tested the bears' beds; one was too hard; one was too soft; and then one was found to be just right. The IF statement is used to test the value of an expression. Computers are tireless and have no feel for beds, but they can determine whether the expression is *negative, zero,* or *positive.*

Machines are permanently wired to execute several instructions upon command. One of these is a branch when the accumulator is *minus* (or positive or zero). Section 10.5 has the details of the *branch on minus.*

Arithmetic IF statements have the form

IF(AAA) 9,99,999

The 9's and A's are general symbols for decimal digits and variables in an arithmetic expression. The number groups can have up to four digits and the expression can be any length.

The value of the expression within the parentheses is computed to establish the transfer. Let's use the symbolic numbers 9,99 and 999 to explain the details of the computer decision. The next statement will be 9 if the expression is *negative,* 99 if *zero,* and 999 if *positive.* Figure 15–7 shows an IF statement in a sequence of a typical program. The variables *A, B,* and *C* are computed elsewhere in the program but before the IF statement.

```
        IF(A+(B/C)**2−3*A*C)621,74,8
  621   I = −1
        GO TO 12
   74   I = 0
        GO TO 12
    8   I = 1
   12   CONTINUE
```

FIG. 15–7 Application of an IF Statement.

Ex. 15–5

What value is assigned to *I* in Fig. 15–7 when $A = 3$, $B = 1$, and $C = 2$?

The expression in parentheses is minus 14.75. Control is directed to statement 621, where *I* is assigned minus 1 and a jump is made to statement 12. Thus, $I = −1$.

Ex. 15–6

A coil spring is used to suspend a heavy load composed of three individual weights. There is a design requirement that the stretch in the spring must not be greater than 3 inches. Write a short program segment for selecting either a heavy-duty spring (150 pounds per inch) or a regular spring (100 pounds per inch).

Figure 15–8 shows the steps in a decision process for selecting the spring size.

```
        (W1, W2 AND W3 ARE WEIGHTS THAT ARE
        COMPUTED ELSEWHERE)

        X LOAD = W1 + W2 + W3
        IF (3 − XLOAD / 100) 12, 20, 20
   12   IF (3 − XLOAD / 150) 5, 7, 7
    5   PRINT (6, 25)
    7   SPRING = 150.0
        GO TO 21
   20   SPRING = 100.0
   21   CONTINUE
```

FIG. 15–8 Application of IF Statement in Designing a Suspension Spring.

15.2.3 Computed GO TO Statement

The computed GO TO can be used in some applications that are beyond the three-point branch of the IF statement. It can transfer control to *one of several* statements. The form is

$$\text{GO TO } (9,99,999,9999), \text{ I}$$

The symbol I represents the data name for an integer and the 9's represent statement numbers. The computed GO TO causes a *branch to one of the numbers* enclosed in parentheses. The selection from this sequence depends on the value of the integer following the parentheses. The *first* number is selected if I = 1, the *second* if I = 2, the *third* if I = 3, and so on. The value of the integer variable may be computed elsewhere in the program.

There is a potential *source of trouble* in programs when the integer is negative or too large. The processing sequence is predictable only when I is positive and less than or equal to the number of entries inside the parentheses. For example, the outcome would be unpredictable for JOE = 5 and GO TO (38,6,8), JOE, because it is impossible to select the fifth item from a sequence of three.

15.2.4 CONTINUE Statement

The next few sections present rules on permissible sequences for statements. Some statements must be preceded by others. We'll see that the group controlled by a DO statement cannot end with an arithmetic IF statement.

The attractive feature of the CONTINUE statement is *freedom from* these *rules*. Any statement can be a CONTINUE, regardless of the sequence. The DO group must end with a numbered statement, but it cannot be IF. We can't write a number and leave the statement blank, so we fill it with CONTINUE. It *doesn't enter* the computational process.

15.2.5 Logical Transfer Statements

The arithmetic IF statement and the computed GO TO statement direct the processing to one of several next statements. In many cases, the branch is made to an assignment statement. The logical transfer statement combines the assignment and decision statements. For example, the spring selection in Fig. 15–8 caused the variable, SPRING, to be assigned the

value 100 if XLOAD/100 is less than or equal to 3. The following single
statement handles this programming operation:

$$IF(LOAD.LE.3) \ SPRING = 100$$

The term .LE. means less than or equal to. The other items of the
logical transfer statement are apparent now that we know their purpose.
Figure 15–9 shows other decision options.

LOGICAL OPERATOR	EXPLANATION
.LE .	LESS THAN OR EQUAL TO
.LT .	LESS THAN
.EQ .	EQUAL
.GT .	GREATER THAN
.GE .	GREATER THAN OR EQUAL TO
.NE .	NOT EQUAL TO

FIG. 15–9   Operators for Logical Transfer Statement.

15.3   ITERATION STATEMENTS

Groups of statements can be processed repeatedly in an extremely
short period. Statements in the source deck are labeled for *repetitive processing* by placing the DO statement at the beginning of the group.

15.3.1   Concepts of Iteration Solutions

The convenience of programming with the DO statement has speeded
the development of several iteration techniques. Most of these solutions
are based on approximations to situations having actual actions and reactions.

The expression $V = XI * R$ is an example of an exact solution. It
represents electrical current flow through a resistor. Approximate solutions
become necessary for complex electrical networks. The current flow might
be apportioned between hundreds of resistors that each pass their share and
capacitors that absorb part of current increases.

An iteration solution for capacitor–resistor networks is obtainable.
The solution begins at time = 0 by apportioning the current according to
the values of resistors and capacitors. The programmer writes a group of
FORTRAN statements to define the circuit. During each millisecond, the

capacitors store more current. At time $= 0+$ (a fraction of a millisecond), the unstored current is reapportioned to the network components. The procedure in this second iteration is repeated perhaps 1000 cycles until all capacitors have stored their limit.

In an efficient program, repetitive processing of statements is handled by a DO statement. The FORTRAN statements defining the electrical circuit should be preceded by a DO statement giving the desired number of iterations.

Index registers store integer data words, and very often their contents are set by information from DO statements. The *number of repetitions* is an integer that the compiler codes for loading into *an index register.* The computer circuit is designed to *decrease* the integer value *by one* upon command. The index register will contain zero after a certain number of cycles. The *presence of zero* initiates a command that automatically causes a *branch* to *next statement.* These built-in circuits are specially designed for efficient iteration solutions with the DO statement.

15.3.2 DO Statements and Loops

The form of DO statement is

$$\text{DO } 999 \text{ I } = 9,99$$

The symbol I represents the data name for an integer. It is called the index. The 9's represent positive integers.

The DO statement is placed at the beginning of a group of statements. The last statement in this group must be labeled with a statement number. The CONTINUE statement is used often to terminate the group. The digits 999 represent the number of this *last statement.* The digits 9 and 99 are integers representing the *initial and final values* of I, respectively. Together they define the number of repetitions.

The term DO loop is a descriptive name for the group of statements controlled by a DO statement.

15.3.2.1 Single DO Loop. The statement DO 42 MORE $= 1,100$ defines a DO loop that ends with statement number 42. The index, MORE, has an initial value of 1 and a final value of 100. The index is changed by one unit on each repetition. Hence, the DO loop will be repeated 100 times before a branch is made to the statement following number 42.

It is important that the programmer adhere to the *formal rules* for the DO. Of course, the statement begins in column 7 and can be labeled with a number. Referring to the general form, there must be a space after DO and after 999. A comma is needed between 9 and 99.

The DO statement can be extended to

$$\text{DO } 999 \text{ I } = 9,99,9$$

where the integer on the right defines the *increment for the index*. For example, DO 127 IN $=$ 100,200,5 would commence with IN $=$ 100. On the second pass through the loop we would have IN $=$ 105, then 110, and so on. Finally, IN would be 200 and a branch would be made out of the loop. In this example, there would be 20 repetitions. The increment is always 1 unless specified to be otherwise. The statement DO 127 IN $=$ 100,200 would cause 100 repetitions with IN increased by 1 each cycle.

15.3.2.2   Nested DO Loops.   DO statements can be small groups of statements within a larger group being controlled by an outer DO loop. The rule specifies that the *inner* DO loop must be contained entirely within the *outer* DO loop.

It is *wasteful* of functional units and generally nonsense to skip around leaving *uncompleted loops*. During machine operation, an index register is set by the DO statement and incremented by each cycle through the loop. There are several built-in index registers; thus, several DO loops can be handled. Registers remain set and thus *unavailable* for other purposes until the loop is *legally completed*. The compiler checks that DO loops are properly nested before assigning an index register to control the loop.

15.3.2.3   Restrictions on Using DO.   It is good practice to encircle DO loops on flow charts and check that the following rules are not violated. The *restrictions* are

1.   Nested DO loops can end with the same statement, but an inner DO cannot extend beyond the outer loop.

2.   The last statement in a DO loop must have the proper statement number and should be CONTINUE.

3.   The last statement must not be arithmetic IF, GO TO, DO, STOP or any other statement that alters the processing sequence.

4.   The statement immediately after DO must not be DIMENSION, FORMAT, or another nonexecutable statement.

5.   The DO index must not be reassigned in value within the loop.

6.   Branching into and out of a DO loop is prohibited.

It is important to remember that the *index* within a DO loop is *unassigned* until the DO statement is processed. An illegal branch into a loop controlled by DO K $=$ 1,4 would be presented nonsense by the simple statement I $=$ K $+$ 1 because K is undefined.

15.4 ARRAYS AND DIMENSION STATEMENTS

Thousands of parameters are important to some physical processes. It is common practice in mathematics to represent vast numbers of parameters by a *shorthand notation* called matrix representation. A matrix is an array of information that can be written with individual quantities in rows and columns. With this techniques, thousands of numbers can be presented on a written or printed page by a single symbol. It is a convenient technique for summarizing information before attempting to communicate ideas to other persons.

15.4.1 Subscripts and Variables

In computer applications, all data words must be assigned a name. It would be a difficult job to creat individual names for 1000 data words. Also, shortcuts are needed to enter the numbers as input into the program.

The *simple name* A(M,N) can become *1000 names* by using $M = 1$ to 100 and $N = 1$ to 10. The integers M and N are index numbers.

The term *subscripted variable* is a carryover to programming from mathematics. Variables in rows and columns of an array are represented by a_{11}, a_{12}, and so on, with actual subscripts for the index numbers. An index in FORTRAN cannot be written below the line; hence, the necessity for parentheses.

The *general forms* for subscripts in a one-, two-, and three-dimensional array are

$$A(I)$$
$$A(I,J)$$
$$A(I,J,K)$$

The symbol A represents the *subscripted data name,* and I, J, and K are *index numbers.*

The computer will issue an error statement if a subscripted name is used for a nonsubscripted variable. For example, a program cannot have names A and A(I).

15.4.2 DIMENSION Statements

Memory addresses are automatically allocated for every data name and subscripted variable. It is easy for the compiler to count the number of regular data names. They always appear as variables on the left-hand side of assignment statements.

The programmer must give *explicit instructions* on the number of data words associated with a subscripted variable. The single term

A(I,J,K) would exceed the 270,000-word capacity of internal memory if the programmer, using the UNIVAC, chose each index number to be 100 because $100 \times 100 \times 100 = 1$ million.

The DIMENSION statement guides the compiler in allocating memory addresses for subscripted variables. It must appear in every program having subscripts. The DIMENSION statement must appear before any statement containing a variable. Most programmers follow the good habit of placing the DIMENSION statement at the very *beginning of the program*. The *general form* is

DIMENSION A(50,20),AA(10,5),AAA(30)

The compiler will allocate 1,000 addresses for A, 50 for AA, and 30 for AAA. The programmer must be careful that the index numbers never become larger than the limits set by the DIMENSION statement.

Ex. 15–7

A programming error is present in the statement in Fig. 15–10. What is it and what will be the consequence?

```
      DIMENSION TON (30), XTON (50)
      DO 28 I = 1,50
      TON (I) = I
28    CONTINUE
      DO 32 J = 1,50
      XTON(J) = TON(J) + 4 / TON(J)
32    CONTINUE
```

FIG. 15–10   Example of Subscripted Variables That Overextends the Limits.

Obviously, memory addresses are not available for TON(31) through TON(50); thus, XTON(31) through XTON(50) will be assigned nonsense values.

15.5   INPUT AND OUTPUT STATEMENTS

Suppose that an input card had a six-digit decimal integer punched in columns 1 through 6. The number could be read as input and assigned the name K by the following FORTRAN statements:

READ(5,38) K
38 FORMAT (I6)

The words READ and FORMAT, as well as WRITE, PUNCH, and PRINT, are reserved words that guide the compiler in generating instructions for controlling input/output units. The numbers in parentheses after READ and FORMAT specify

1. Input channel 5 is to be opened.
2. Card columns 1 through 6 contain decimal digits that are to be converted to binary.
3. Assignment to a fixed-point memory address.

The letter I is always used in FORMAT statements that refer to *integers*.

In this example, the number 5 designates the *input/output* unit, 38 is the *statement number* of the appropriate FORMAT for the read, and 6 specifies the *size* of the data field.

All columns on an input data card contain either decimal digits or blanks. The compiler assigns zeros to all banks in fields that are read. Integers must end exactly on the right-hand side of the field. The number 4237 followed by a blank in a five-digit field is interpreted as 42370. There is more latitude in placing nonintegers within the data field, because a decimal point causes the extra zeroes to be harmless. For example, the number 38.91 would be interpreted corectly in an eight-digit field as 0038.9100. It is *good practice to* place both integers and nonintegers to *end at the right-hand side* of the data field.

In our examples, we'll use input channel number 5 and output channel number 6. The numbers identify the tape units that are used to buffer the data entering from cards or leaving for a printer. Other channels also would be tapes but have a different binary number code. The programmer should check the input/output numbers that are appropriate for a particular computer center.

Fractional *decimal numbers* can be read from columns 1 through 6 on a card by

READ(5,19)A
19 FORMAT(F6.2)

The letter F is the special symbol that identifies the input as a decimal number with a *fractional part*. The number is to be converted to a floating-point binary number. In our example, the number 2 specifies the *decimal digits* after the radix and 4 plus 2 is the *size* of the data field.

It is practical to use the *exponential notation* on input cards to represent large decimal numbers. The velocity of light-wave propagation is 3.0×10^8 meters per second. This decimal number could be entered in columns 1 through 6 on a punched card and converted to a floating-point binary number by the following statement:

READ(5,36)A
36 FORMAT(E6.2)

The special symbol E specifies input data is in the exponential notation. In this example, the number 6 is the *size* of the data field and 2 is the number of *decimal digits* after the decimal point, not counting the exponent. The input card would be punched with 3.00 E8 in columns 1 through 6.

The rules for reading input data apear at this point to be easy. We might choose to place the heading FORTRAN IS EASY at the top of a printed page. The statement

WRITE (6,71)
71 FORMAT (16H1FORTRAN IS EASY)

is an example of *Hollerith field specification*. The special letter H alerts the computer that Hollerith characters are to be printed. The digit 1 after the H is a code that controls carriage return and line feed on the printer. Other *printer control numbers* are shown in Fig. 15–11. There are 16 characters and spaces after H.

PRINTER CONTROL CHARACTERS	PURPOSE	EXAMPLE
1	START PRINTING AT TOP OF NEW PAGE	FORMAT (I4H1NOW HEAR THIS)
O	ADVANCE LINE FEED TWO SPACES BEFORE PRINTING	FORMAT (I4HOTHE FOLLOWING)
BLANK	ADVANCE LINE FEED ONE SPACE BEFORE PRINTING	FORMAT (2IH SECTIONS ARE COMPLEX)

FIG. 15–11   Printer Control Codes in Hollerith Field Specifications.

These basic concepts of specifying data fields with FORMAT statements are used by programmers of all skill levels. To this point we have discussed reading one data item from cards using one READ and one FORMAT statement. Obviously, we have more to discuss on input/output statements.

15.5.1 READ and WRITE Statements

Input statements cause a name and a memory address to be assigned to input data. Fields are specified for input data by FORMAT statements. The statement READ (5,83) A, AA, AAA assigns the name A to the data in the first field, AA to the second, and AAA to the third. Cards are scanned from left to right; thus, the first field is on the left.

Input cards must be in exact order and have data in the exact format to be interpreted by successive READ statements. Data on the first card in the input deck are assigned the data names specified by the first READ statement in the program. Many cards can be entered by repeated processing of a single READ statement. On each cycle the data on the next card are assigned the same set of names.

15.5.2 FORMAT Statements

Several data fields usually appear on each card. The comma is used to designate fields on the same card. For example, FORMAT (I4,I8,E8.2) specifies *three fields on the same card*.

Data fields on *two adjacent cards* can be specified with the statement FORMAT (I6/F8.3). The slash symbol causes the read operation to switch to the next card. Of course, this example statement specifies that the first card has a decimal integer and the second has a fractional decimal number.

In many cases the *same-sized field* is used for several data words on a card. The statement FORMAT (6I12) apportions the first 72 columns on the card into 6 fields of 12. For two adjacent cards we could use FORMAT (8I9/7F6.3).

15.5.2.1 Concepts of Nonexecutable Statements. Most FORTRAN statements cause machine instructions to be generated. These sets of machine codes are entered into the object program in precisely the same sequence as the source statements. This tidy procedure is not followed in executing a few statements.

Programmers are free to place FORMAT statements at most any point in the program sequence. Of course, they must not be the next statement after a DO loop.

It is *good practice to group* all FORMAT statements together *toward the end* of the program. The group can be easily scanned for errors during the manual debugging phase.

Programmers often use comment statements to add clarity to the program. The letter C is entered in column 1 to alert the compiler that the statement is nonexecutable.

15.5.2.2   Examples of FORMAT Statements.   Several options for
FORMAT statements are shown in Fig. 15–12. We see statements of the

STATEMENT	DECIMAL DATA	BINARY DATA	DATA FIELDS	CARDS
FORMAT (4I10)	INTEGER	FIXED–POINT	4 FIELDS OF 10	ONE
FORMAT (6I8, 3E7.2)	INTEGER, EXPONENTIAL	FIXED–POINT FLOATING–POINT	6 FIELDS OF 8 AND 3 FIELDS OF 7	ONE
FORMAT (2(4E6.2, 3F5.2))	EXPONENTIAL, FRACTIONAL	FLOATING–POINT	2 SETS HAVING 4 FIELDS OF 6 AND 3 FIELDS OF 5	ONE
FORMAT (3(8EI0.2/FI0.2, 7EI0.2))	EXPONENTIAL, FRACTIONAL, EXPONENTIAL	FLOATING–POINT	3 SETS HAVING 8 FIELDS OF 10, 1 FIELD OF 10 AND 7 FIELDS OF 10	SIX

FIG. 15–12   FORMAT Statements for Multiple Fields and Sets.

type FORMAT (2(I4,I6)). This example specifies that a 4-column field
and a 6-column field can be repeated in that order. In sequence from the
left of the card, the field would be 4,6 and then another 4,6.

15.5.3   Input and Output of Arrays

Efficient programs take advantage of built-in features of the computer
circuits and compiler. Considerable time can be saved in handling input
and output of arrays. Large groups of numbers should be represented by
subscripted variables in arrays. Vast quantities of data from array AA
can be entered by a single statement having the general form of a DO
statement.

$$\text{READ } (5,67)(AA(M), M = 9, 999)$$
$$67 \text{ FORMAT } (7E10.4)$$

The subscript index is identified by the symbol M. It runs from 9 to
999 in increments of 1. All 7 fields of 10 of each data card are scanned.
There are numerous succeeding cards.

The statement READ (5,67)(AAA(N), N = 1,99,3) assigns data to every third array element. The statement READ (5,67)AAA assigns data to every element in the one-dimensional AAA array, starting with AAA(1), AAA(2), and so on.

Efficient handling of two- and three-dimensional arrays yields even greater savings in processing time. The statements DIMENSION A(15,-20,10) and READ (5,103)A would cause 3000 numbers to be assigned to A(I,J,K,). The *order* is established by the relative limits in the DIMENSION statement for I, J, and K. The *smallest index* is scanned first and then *larger ones.* In this example, K is smallest and then I and J. The order of assignment would be A(1,1,1) to A(1,1,10), A(2,1,1) to A(2,1,10), A(3,1,1) to A(3,1,10), and so on.

Of course, the regular DO statement could be used in transferring array data. This option is slower by a slight amount.

15.6 SUBPROGRAM STATEMENTS

The *trigonometric functions* of sine, cosine, tangent, and others are basic expressions in mathematics. In a manual solution, the sine 57° would be obtained from a table of values or a slide rule. In computer solutions, several common functions are generated by a special group of instructions in the program library.

15.6.1 Arithmetic Functions

The FORTRAN programmer calls for library functions by using one of the special names that identify subprograms. Figure 15–13 shows these reserved names.

FUNCTION	VALUE GENERATED	
SIN (A)	SINE OF A	ANGLES IN RADIANS
COS (A)	COSINE OF A	ANGLES IN RADIANS
TANH (A)	TANGENT OF A	ANGLES IN RADIANS
ATAN (A)	ARCTANGENT OF A	ANGLES IN RADIANS
SQRT (A)	SQUARE ROOT OF A	
ALOG (A)	NATURAL LOGARITHM OF A	
ABS (A)	ABSOLUTE VALUE (A IS POSITIVE REGARDLESS OF ACTUAL SIGN)	
EXP (A)	EXPONENTIATION OF NATURAL LOGARITHM BASE e = 2.781 TO THE A^{TH} POWER TO GIVE e^A	

FIG. 15–13 FORTRAN Functions.

In a manual solution, we might write $X =$ sine $(A + B) -$ cos
D. The equivalent FORTRAN statement has a similar form, for example,
$X = $ SIN $(A + B) - $ COS (D), where A, B, and D are variables
representing the angles. The subprogram is based on the angles having the
units of radians. The *general form* for all functions is one of the reserved
names followed by one or more terms in parentheses.

15.6.2   Subroutines

Function statements are short binary-coded subprograms that have
general application and are automatically available in internal memory.
They can be used several times in the main program. The intermediate-level
programmer will write his own special-purpose subprograms. This option is
convenient in cases where two or more segments of the main program are
identical except for the data names.

The subroutine is a limited-application subprogram containing several
FORTRAN statements and designed for a particular purpose. It can be
compiled and checked independently of the main program. The subprogram
has its own DIMENSION statements and data names. It computes *one or
more values* that are useful in the main program.

The subroutine begins with a statement having the word SUB-
ROUTINE followed by its name and then the set of data names, called
arguments. The next statement is DIMENSION in subroutines having
arrays. Figure 15–14 shows statements of the form that always appear at
the beginning and end of a subroutine.

SUBROUTINE HELP (A, AA, I, AAA, J)

DIMENSION AAA (30,40)

(SEVERAL STATEMENTS LEADING TO
THE CALCULATION OF AAA FROM
THE OTHER PARAMETERS)

RETURN

END

FIG. 15–14   General Outline of a Subroutine.

The purpose and content of a subroutine are fairly straightforward.
They may be called several times during a processing run.

The argument names in the segment of the main program where the
subroutine is called may not be (A,AA,I,AAA,J). For example, we may

want to calculate the array X using Y, Z, K, and L. The subroutine in Fig. 15–14 calculated the array AAA using A, AA, I, and J. When the subroutine is called into action, it applies exactly the same procedure to calculating X. This result normally is used in the main program.

The subroutine is called by a single statement in the main program. CALL HELP (Y,Z,K,X,L). The arguments in parentheses must correspond exactly with the arrangement in parentheses after the SUBROUTINE. In this example, the value of Y is used in all subroutine statements containing A; Z replaces AA; K replaces I; X replaces AAA; and L replaces J. Of course, the main program must have DIMENSION statements for all of the arrays, including the array X.

After the subroutine is completed, control is returned to the main program and the next statement after CALL is processed. The new values in the X array are available for use.

As a further example, the statement CALL HELP (B,BB,3,BBB, N+1) would cause BBB to be calculated using B, BB, 3, and N+1. There is considerable flexibility in choosing argument names. The subroutine is a convenient method for programming similar segments in the main program.

16 Applications of Computers in Science

We have discussed two higher-level languages for smoothing the interface between the machine codes and the computer user. Obviously, the computer has potential value for those who understand these rules and are able to write programs that generate a desired output. Many computer users do not take full advantage of this potential because they do not recognize problems that need analysis. Computer programs are useful that deal with relevant problems.

Scientific applications for computers normally originate in engineering studies. Engineers have an idea of the general problem to be solved and presumably can express their approach for a solution in terms that are understandable by their colleagues. In many cases, the solution is based on existing formulas or on numerical methods. The scope of this book cannot accommodate a coverage of these formulas or numerical techniques beyond the introductory level. Further study and experience are necessary for persons to become proficient in programming scientific information. This chapter presents an introduction to the concepts of mathematics that should be useful in composing scientific programs. There exists a certain amount of communications "wax" between those who formulate the solution in mathematical terms and those who formulate program solutions. By understanding each other's methods of expression, programmers and engineers can save time in cooperative developments. In a few instances, general discussions are given in this chapter of means for handling situations at this troublesome interface.

Three distinct language translations are made before eventually obtaining pulse sequences to control functional units in the computer. In Chapter 10 we discussed the interpretation of machine codes in generating control signals. In Chapters 12, 13, and 15, we discussed the advantages of using compilers to interpret higher-level languages and generate the machine codes. In this chapter, we have the concepts of the sometimes overlooked translation from the special language of engineers and scientists to a language familiar to programmers.

16.1 SOLUTIONS IN MATHEMATICS

On a broad basis, mathematical expressions are an abstract representation of a physical process. They may be simple formulas or a group of rules, axioms, or theorems. For example, the basic mathematics of Boolean algebra are expressed by the 18 theorems in Section 4.4. Mathematical expressions are a reasonable representation of the relation between cause and effect in a process. In many situations the equations, formulas, and so forth, are accurate for only a certain range of process inputs or outputs. For example, the equation $P = RT$, expressing the effect of temperature, T, on gas pressure may be limited to a certain range of temperatures or another range of pressures. In all cases, mathematics are at best an educated guess of the way that natural forces affect the process over a range which is sometimes specified. New fields of study are characterized by nearly as many guesses as there are guessers. For this reason, many mathematical techniques are in widespread use.

The broad categories of mathematical solutions are

1. *Closed-form solutions*, which uniquely relate the parameters affecting the situation in one or more formulas. Section 16.1.1 discusses closed-form solutions.

2. *Approximate solutions*, which are formulas that are not closed form because the right-hand side is open ended with many groups of terms in series form. The series can be finite with a specified number of terms. It is more common to have infinite series. Section 16.1.2 discusses approximate solutions.

3. *Numerical solutions*, which have the unique capability of combining numerous parameters into practical engineering studies. Typical solutions are formed by numerous individual steps with as many parameters as desired brought into consideration on each step or on selected steps. Section 16.1.3 discusses the concepts of numerical analysis.

16.1.1 Closed-Form Solutions

Engineering and scientific researchers prefer the closed-form solution because it is a concise form for reporting their findings. Formulas can be verified by other researchers and extended or restricted in range where appropriate. Once the solution is obtained and the range is established, the researcher probably will move to other areas of interest, and engineers will use the formulas for analysis and design purposes.

Computer methods have applications in closed-form solutions. Engineers prefer closed-form solutions because they give the relative significance of each parameter. The formulas can be easily combined with economic information to give a basis for minimizing the cost of a design.

In electrical circuits and other analogous systems, the basic formula for potential drop across a resistance is simple. The familiar equation is $I = E/R$, or current = potential drop/resistance. The situation becomes more complex when the current flows through several resistors with splits in the flow path at network junctions along the way. For example, a current I_{11} could enter a junction and split to I_{12} and I_{13}. The magnitude of the three currents must balance to give a net flow of zero. This gives $I_{11} - I_{12} - I_{13} = 0$.

Other junctions are present in even the basic networks. The current I_{12} could enter a second junction and leave as I_{22} and I_{23}. Figure 16–1 shows these currents and in addition shows that I_{13} enters a third junction and leaves as I_{32} and I_{33}.

The three-junction network in Fig. 16–1 is described by three linear equations. For all resistors equal to 1 ohm and a battery potential of 14 volts, the equations are

$$3E_1 - E_2 - E_3 = 14$$
$$-E_1 + 3E_2 = 0$$
$$-E_1 + 3E_3 = 0$$

The linear equations are commonly solved by a simple method that uses a *matrix* of the coefficients for E_1, E_2, and E_3. The coefficients are 3, -1, and -1 in the first equation. These numbers appear in the first row of the following matrix along with other coefficients for the equation set.

$$\begin{bmatrix} 3 & -1 & -1 \\ -1 & 3 & 0 \\ -1 & 0 & 3 \end{bmatrix}$$

The three linear equations can be solved to give values for the three nodal voltages as $E_1 = 6$, $E_2 = 2$, and $E_3 = 2$ for the 14-volt battery. Equations that must be solved as a set are termed *simultaneous equations*. All equations in the set must be satisfied by the same values of the variables.

Library programs have been developed that quickly solve simultaneous equations. The set of equations is specified by the values of the coefficients. The situation is straightforward and not particularly prone to programming errors.

From a physical view of the electrical circuit, we see that there are exactly the *same number of equations* in the set *as there are nodal voltages*. In fact, each equation is based on the current flow from a respective node.

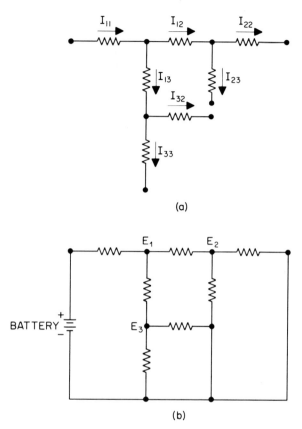

FIG. 16–1   Electrical Network: (a) Direction of Current Flows; (b) Potential E_1, E_2, and E_3.

It is mathematically possible to solve for any number of voltages provided that enough equations are available.

There are *restrictions* on the type of equations that are permissible. Each *equation must be independent* of all other equations in the set. The equation $-E_1 + 3E_2 = 0$ is independent of $-E_1 + 3E_3 = 0$. However, $6E_1 - 18E_3 = 0$ is dependent on $-E_1 + 3E_3 = 0$ and differs from it only by the multiplying factor of minus 6. Of course, it isn't intentional to fabricate an equation in this way and sneak it into the set just to fill out the number required. It is more likely that the dependent equations are introduced by oversight.

It is common to *mathematically test* the matrix of coefficients in order to identify dependent equations. The *determinant* of a matrix has the same number of rows as columns and a single value. A few determinants are evaluated in Ex. 16–1. The *rank of a matrix* is the number of rows in the largest nonzero determinant in the matrix. The rank is reduced by 1 if a row or column is identical to another row or column. Of course, the rank is exactly the same as the number of independent equations. There are no dependent equations in a matrix in which the rank remains unchanged when

> 1. A row or column is multiplied or divided by a nonzero number; or
> 2. A row or column is added to a multiple of another row or column.

Ex. 16–1

The value of a 2 by 2 determinant

$$\begin{vmatrix} a_{11} & a_{12} \\ a_{21} & a_{22} \end{vmatrix}$$

in
general form, is $a_{11} \times a_{22} - a_{12} \times a_{21}$. Find the value of

$$\begin{vmatrix} 6 & 3 \\ 4 & 7 \end{vmatrix} \qquad \text{and} \qquad \begin{vmatrix} 58 & 10.2 \\ 11 & 4 \end{vmatrix}$$

The answers are $42 - 12 = 30$ and $232 - 112.2 = 119.8$.
The value of a 3 by 3 determinant is

$$\begin{vmatrix} a_{11} & a_{12} & a_{13} \\ a_{21} & a_{22} & a_{23} \\ a_{31} & a_{32} & a_{33} \end{vmatrix}$$

$$a_{11} \times \begin{vmatrix} a_{22} & a_{23} \\ a_{32} & a_{33} \end{vmatrix} - a_{21} \times \begin{vmatrix} a_{12} & a_{13} \\ a_{32} & a_{33} \end{vmatrix} + a_{31} \times \begin{vmatrix} a_{12} & a_{13} \\ a_{22} & a_{23} \end{vmatrix}$$

where the individual 2 by 2 determinants are called *cofactors* of the larger determinant.

Find the value of the determinant from the preceding three-node circuit. We had

$$\begin{vmatrix} 3 & -1 & -1 \\ -1 & 3 & 0 \\ -1 & 0 & 3 \end{vmatrix}$$

which gives

$$3 \times \begin{vmatrix} 3 & 0 \\ 0 & 3 \end{vmatrix} - (-1) \times \begin{vmatrix} -1 & -1 \\ 0 & 3 \end{vmatrix} + (-1) \times \begin{vmatrix} -1 & -1 \\ 3 & 0 \end{vmatrix}$$

for an answer of $27 - 3 - 3 = 21$.

Ex. 16–2

Find the rank of the matrix

$$\begin{bmatrix} 12 & 3 & 6 \\ 2 & 1 & 7 \\ 4 & 1 & 2 \end{bmatrix}$$

At first glance, the rank appears to be 3, because there are 3 rows in the matrix. However, it remains to prove this. It must first be shown that the determinant is *nonzero*. The computation yields a value

$$12(2 - 7) - 2(6-6) + 4(21 - 6) = 0$$

which is a sure sign that the original equations were not independent and solvable. In fact, the first and last row in the matrix are identical except for a multiplying factor of 3. The rank of the matrix is, therefore, only 2.

16.1.2   Concepts of Approximate Solutions

The linear equation $Y = C_1 X + C_2$ is the general form for all straight lines in the XY plane. Figure 16–2 shows that the line pass through the origin of the coordinate axis for $C_2 = 0$. The slope of these lines is steeper for higher values of C_1. A positive value of C_2 causes the line to intersect the axis above the origin, and below the origin for negative C_2. The values of the *undetermined coefficients* are selected to make the plot appropriate for the situation. For example, information may be available on the magnitude of X and Y at two points through which the line passes. In other situations the slope of the line may be known.

Many engineering applications cannot be formulated by methods that lead to an exact solution. In all cases, there exists a limited amount of information from which an approximate solution can be derived. The procedure begins by *selecting a general form* for the solution that has several undetermined coefficients. The general form for the straight-line plots had C_1 and C_2. The next step is to use the available information about the problem to *evaluate the cofficients*. For example, the value of the parameters might be known at a physical boundary, or the initial value of the parameter might be known in situations that change with time. These classical situations are called *boundary-value problems* and *initial-value problems*. A third type is *final-value problems*.

The techniques of approximate solutions are effective for series that have an acceptable general form. One criterion for selecting the general form is that the solution have enough coefficients to accommodate a range

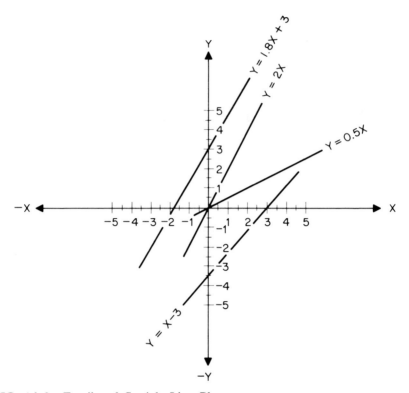

FIG. 16–2   Family of Straight-Line Plots.

of situations. Most classical approximations have an infinite series of terms, with the coefficients for the first few terms calculated from the conditions of the situation. The other coefficients are evaluated from a recurring pattern established by the first few values.

A series is useless that diverges by getting bigger with each successive term and shows no tendency for reaching a finite final value. To be useful, the *series must converge,* and for hand calculations it is convenient when the final value is reached after a few terms.

The *Fourier series* is popular for studying the distribution of potential in a two-dimensional member.

$$\phi = \sum_{m=0}^{\infty} \sum_{n=1}^{\infty} A_{m,n}(\cos m\pi x)(\sin n\pi y)$$

The series converges rapidly, which is a characteristic of series having the trigometric sine and cosine, because they both are always in narrow range from -1 to $+1$.

Infinite series are common in mathematics, and even the *basic functions* are defined in series form:

$$\sin X = \frac{X}{1!} - \frac{X^3}{3!} + \frac{X^5}{5!} - \frac{X^7}{7!} + \dots$$

The natural logrithm base has a value of

$$e = 1 + \frac{1}{1!} + \frac{1}{2!} + \frac{1}{3!} + \frac{1}{4!} + \dots$$

The denominators of the terms in these series are *factorials* where

$$
\begin{aligned}
1! &= 1 \\
2! &= 1 \times 2 \\
3! &= 1 \times 2 \times 3 \\
4! &= 1 \times 2 \times 3 \times 4
\end{aligned}
$$

and so on. The series form of the trigometric functions are used in computer solutions. For example, the appearance of $Y = \text{SIN}(0.61)$ in a FORTRAN statement automatically causes the series

$$Y = \sum_{n=1,3,5,\dots} (-1)^{(n-1)/2} \frac{(0.61)^n}{n!}$$

to be computed.

The *binomial series* is a practical method for calculating the square root and other powers of a two-term expression. The general form is

$$(1 + X)^a = 1 + aX + \frac{a(a-1)(a-2)X^3}{2!} + \frac{a(a-1)X^2}{3!} + \dots$$

The binomial series converges for X between -1 and $+1$ and diverges for all other values.

The concept of converging to a total sum is illustrated by the classical *power series*

$$\text{sum} = 1 + X + X^2 + X^3 + \dots$$

The range of convergence is limited to X values between -1 and $+1$.

The power series for $X = \frac{1}{2}$ has terms that are successively divided by 2.

$$\text{sum} = 1 + \tfrac{1}{2} + \tfrac{1}{4} + \tfrac{1}{8} + \dots$$

This series converges to a total sum of 2. For X between -1 and 0, the terms in the power series are alternately positive and negative. For $X = -\frac{1}{2}$, the *alternating power series* converges to $\frac{2}{3}$.

$$\text{sum} = 1 - \tfrac{1}{2} + \tfrac{1}{4} - \tfrac{1}{8} + \dots$$

Computer methods for infinite series are capable of combining hundreds of terms in a short time. Additional terms makes the computed sum closer to the total series sum. Programmers enter statements that cause the processing to terminate at a preselected level of accuracy. These statements usually test the sum before and after the inclusion of a term. If the difference is unimportant, relative to overall accuracy desired, the series evaluation is considered to be complete.

16.1.3 Concepts of Numerical Analysis

Many situations in applied mathematics are based on the theory of differential and integral equations. Equations of motion have velocities and accelerations represented as derivatives with respect to time. For a steady motion, it is reasonable to compute the velocity from large distances and long time intervals.

$$\text{constant velocity} = \frac{\text{distance traveled}}{\text{time elapsed}}$$

$$= \frac{50 \text{ miles}}{1 \text{ hour}}$$

$$= 50 \text{ miles per hour}$$

In many applications the parameters are changing so rapidly that it is ridiculous to base the velocities on large distances or time.

$$\text{instantaneous velocity} = \frac{\text{increment of distance}}{\text{increment of time}}$$

$$= \frac{\Delta x}{\Delta t}$$

In the limit, the ratio of the increments yields the *classical derivatives*.

$$\text{instantaneous velocity} = \lim_{\Delta t \to 0} \frac{\Delta x}{\Delta t}$$

$$= \frac{dx}{dt}$$

The *diffusion* of one substance into another or the *dissipation* of a potential are two classical applications of *partial derivatives*. In concept, the term $\partial \varphi / \partial x$ specifies that other parameters are kept constant except x and the aspect of φ that are influenced by x.

Let's consider a *diffusion* process that is easily visualized. Suppose that a pail of water is slowly poured into a briefly existing puddle on the sand. The function, φ, could be a measure of the dampness and x could be a coordinate axis that is oriented vertically into the sand. In an experiment to ascertain the value of the term $\partial \varphi / \partial x$, it is established by the definition of the partial derivative that the measurements be made along a specified vertical line or plane. In this way, data for points 3 feet to the side of the puddle are excluded from a study of the dampness at closer points. Partial derivatives serve a useful purpose because they categorize the actual situation into a form that can be handled mathematically. The concept of measuring the partial derivatives of the dampness function restricted the data to virtual partitions in the sand. The situation can then be described in a concise manner, which is preferred to a vague reference to a "damp place in the sand."

Differential equations exist for many physical situations. Some express the rates of change with respect to one variable. An example is rate of change of temperature along the x axis of a heated rod:

$$\frac{dt}{dx} = q/kA$$

where k is the thermal conduction, q is the heat transfer rate, and A is the cross-sectional area of the rod in which the heat diffuses. The equations can be second order, meaning the rate of change of the derivative is present. The term $\frac{\partial^2 \varphi}{\partial x^2}$ means $\frac{\partial}{\partial x}\left(\frac{\partial \varphi}{\partial x^2}\right)$, which specifies that a second partial derivative has been taken with respect to the first. A classical second-order differential equation is

$$\frac{\partial^2 u}{\partial x^2} + \frac{\partial^2 v}{\partial y^2} = 0$$

where u and v are velocity components in the direction of the x and y axis, respectively. The equation, having the classical form of the Laplace equation, is called the *continuity equation* of fluid flow, and in mathematical notations states that the sum of the mass of fluid entering a region from the direction of the x or y axis must leave along the negative x and y axis.

Most differential equations that have engineering applications can be categorized as being one of 12 or so basic types. The form of the differential equation is known from the early phases of a typical analysis. The *form of the equation* can be found with a modest level of mathematical skill. The difficult task is concerned with *finding a solution* to the equation. For example, the equation is known for thermal diffusion through a flat sheet of metal. The solution could be elusive for irregular boundaries or cutouts in the sheet. There could be three or four different metals in various regions of the sheet. Portions of the sheet could be heated, water cooled, or mated with a massive block. These complicating features for the sheet are called *boundary conditions*. Of course, an acceptable solution must satisfy the differential equation and the boundary conditions.

Mathematical methods are limited in their ability to handle even the classical analysis of dissipation and diffusion in applications having complex boundary conditions. Considerable difficulty is introduced by numerous sources and sinks or exchanges between several members in an intertwined structure. These configurations are present in too many engineering designs for the matter to be dismissed as simply unsolvable.

Numerical methods are techniques that generally use the computer in solving the classical differential and integral equation for practical engineering applications. Many of the methods were developed long before the computer. In general, the solution is composed of hundreds or thousands of steps that characterize the geometry of the structure or span the time of interest. Computer solutions are well suited to methods that require repetitive processing of a sequence of steps.

From a practical standpoint, the techniques of numerical analysis are in a class above the classical mathematical methods. There are *shortcomings,* however, because the unadorned output is a few discrete values that may be important to the application but unimportant to a colleague analyzing a somewhat different application. On the other hand, the classical methods yielded solutions that might attract a general community of scientific interest. For example, there would be few bridge designers who would take note of an elaborate numerical analysis that established that $1\frac{1}{2}$-inch suspension cables are the optimum size for a particular bridge span. There would be general interest in a mathematical analysis that derived a formula for computing the cable size based on other parameters in the bridge design. It takes a conscientious effort to present data from a numerical analysis in a form that is useful to others.

Consider the differential equation for velocity

$$\frac{dx}{dt} = v$$

and the Taylor series

$$f(a) = f(t) + (a - t) \frac{df(t)}{dt} + (a - t)^2 \frac{d^2f(t)}{dt^2} + \cdots$$

with time functions $f(t)$ and $f(a)$. The initial velocity could be $f(t)$ with derivatives $df(t)/dt$; $d^2f(t)/dt^2$, and others.

The values of the derivative at time, t, are used to predict the function at a short time later. These predictions define the function, $f(a)$. The series is based on the theory that continuous functions do not change radically from point to point. Velocity functions are continuous.

The *Taylor series* is useful in numerical methods because it forms a basis for *changing differential equations* into a form that can be handled by the computer. Addition and subtraction are handled easily in computer solutions. It is common practice to argue that $f(a)$ is defined by the first two terms in the Taylor series and the higher-order terms are insignificant. This assumption leaves

$$f(a) = f(t) + (a - t)\frac{df(t)}{dt}$$

which can be solved for the differential.

$$\frac{df(t)}{dt} = \frac{f(a) - f(t)}{a - t}$$

The time interval between $a - t$ is assumed to be short, such that $a - t = \triangle t$ or $a = t + \triangle t$. This substitution gives

$$\frac{df(t)}{dt} = \frac{f(t + \triangle t) - f(t)}{\triangle t}$$

The *differential has been replaced by a single difference* in the value of the function at two successive times.

The solution consists of using the value of the function at t to predict the value at $t + \triangle t$. The sequence of computations in Ex. 16–3 simulates the typical steps in computer solution of differential equations with numerical methods.

Ex. 16–3

Consider the *differential equation*

$$\frac{df(t)}{dt} = \frac{1}{t^2 + 4}$$

with an initial value of 6 at $t = 0$. Find the value of $f(t)$ at $t = 2$ using time increments of $\triangle t = 0.5$.

The general form of the *difference equation* is

$$f(t + \triangle t) = f(t) + \triangle t \frac{1}{t^2 + 4}$$

First time increment:

$$f(0.5) = 6 + 0.5 \frac{1}{0 + 4} = 6.125$$

Second time increment:

$$f(1.0) = 6.125 + 0.5 \frac{1}{(0.5)^2 + 4} = 6.243$$

Third time increment:

$$f(1.5) = 6.243 + 0.5 \frac{1}{(1.0)^2 + 4} = 6.343$$

Fourth time increment:

$$f(2.0) = 6.343 + 0.5 \frac{1}{(1.5)^2 + 4} = 6.423$$

The numerical answer is 6.423 and the exact answer is 6.393.

Second-order differential equations also can be converted to difference equations for easy computer solutions. The general form is

$$\frac{d^2f(t)}{dt} = \frac{f(t + \Delta t) - 2f(t) + f(t - \Delta t)}{(\Delta t)^2}$$

16.2 CONCEPTS OF OPTIMUM DESIGN

Experimental and analytical studies should be managed in a way that they complement each other and contribute to the design effort. Both methods serve to keep design projects on schedule and prove the feasibility of design concepts at the conclusion and at critical stages in their development. Analytical studies can be performed effectively by computer methods. The experimental effort can be reduced in scope for situations where a high degree of confidence can be placed in the analytical results. Design concepts are often changed as a result of new evidence evolving from analytical and experimental studies. These changes lead to modifications or termination of computer programs that are being developed. The vacillations in an ongoing situation can cause programmers to become frustrated. In this section we'll discuss the usual stages in analytical studies to optimize designs. It is hoped that an understanding of the situation will help us cope with the inherent perplexities.

A modest design project may have 5 to 10 engineers assigned to it. In more extensive projects, there may be 100 or more. Design concepts must be studied and tested to circumvent schedule slippages and cost overruns. These efforts are undertaken at three or so *stages* in the project and use analytical models that are formulated in *phases* of, perhaps, preliminary, intermediate, and final. The overall objective of design analysis is to select configurations and properties of components that satisfy the specification and have reasonable costs. During all stages of a project it is important that information be available to management for their use in assessing the situation and allocating manpower and funds to develop design concepts that are feasible and within the schedule and cost constraints.

Preliminary models are sometimes hand calculations made by engineers and their assistants, using an idealized assessment of the actual situation. These studies can be completed quickly but don't include all the factors that affect the problem. The *intermediate* phase may consist of a computer solution, and should concentrate on areas of the study that are critical to the feasibility or schedule. The less significant factors are entered by lumping them in a way that their overall effect can be represented. A fraction of the studies originated will reach a *final* phase in which a wide range of factors can become inputs to the analysis. In some situations the final model is the original intermediate model, except that some of the lumped factors have been given a detailed study.

Projects originate with a group of people, usually only a small fraction of the final force, who perform the *project definition stage* of the design. A solution is conceived in general terms and technical specifications are established. An estimate is made of the work force, schedule, and economic feasibility of pursuing further development. The analytical models that are applied during the definition stage probably are preliminary or intermediate. Economic aspects of the design are studied closely. Experience and judgment are applied to establish feasibility to the extent that an initial level of funds and people can be committed to study the concepts further.

The second stage in the design involves more people. They *investigate* a dozen or so facets of the initial concept that appear important. This effort serves to keep the critical items of concern in focus and in proper perspective with respect to sideline items. By circumventing the ever-tempting "wild-goose chase," the manager has a better chance of keeping the resources concentrated on the real problems. Analytical methods are effective during the investigation stage. They can be used to probe into the design and identify areas that may be critical. It is equally important that nonconsequential items be dismissed with a minimum of expenditure. There will be one or more major redesigns of the initial concepts.

In the *final phase,* most of the design details have been established. It is useful to know that the individual components will function together as a system. This overall analysis is fairly complete and includes all the major aspects that interact in the design. Experimental data from the investigation stage can be incorporated into the final overall analysis.

Some components form independent subsystems and can be tested completely before the final experimental studies. Final testing is performed on a functioning system that usually is called the *prototype.* The outcome of the prototype tests form the basis for decisions on manufacturing the device.

It is good practice to commence analytical studies with a *first-trial* model. Numerical methods are well suited to this approach, because they quickly produce solutions and can accommodate various degrees of mathematical sophistication. Once the important parameters are identified, the solution can be expanded to give more accurate results. An experienced programmer will understand that an engineer who outlines a straightforward solution and asks for computed data in 3 weeks is pursuing a first-trial solution. Some programmers can't adapt to this scheme and develop the impression that engineers skim the surface of an investigation. Other engineers are more pleasant to work with because they formulate an elaborate analytical solution and leave the programmer to compose a program that is complete in every detail. When the grand effort finally is completed, the programmer and others on the project may be disappointed by design changes or project redirection. In many cases, funds are wasted, because the study concerns an area that early proved to be unimportant to the overall project. It is also disheartening for a colleague to present a thumbnail analysis that leads to the same conclusion that took several months in a grand-effort scheme. The use of first-trial models helps reduce the possibility of these undesirable happenings.

17   Careers in the Computer Fields

Some students will follow this introductory course on computer concepts with further training in programming, computer science, data processing, mathematics, or business administration. In the past few years there have been plenty of jobs available in many of the computer fields. The usefulness of the machines has been proved and for that reason the employment opportunities look good, particularly for persons who are properly trained and make a special effort on the job to solve practical problems. With proper guidance, it is possible to select formal training to match the career choice. Performance on the job is enhanced by a willingness to work, to communicate with others, and to keep abreast of a rapidly changing technology.

This chapter presents a summary of the duties in the various positions in a typical computer organization. Approximate salaries are given, based on data for the early 1970s. Some of the initial assignments are obvious stepping stones to higher positions. Further training usually is needed to advance in many careers, and particularly with computers. The technology and equipment change rapidly, and a determined effort is needed to keep one's experience current. A general outline is sketched of the formal training that is needed to enter each position and the additional training that is expected of persons hoping to advance in their careers. By entering a selected occupation with a full measure of formal preparation, the new employee has more potential for promotion than the person who enters marginally qualified. Of course, performance on the job is an undeniable merit for advancement. In Section 17.2 we discuss the concepts of performing in a manner that gets the work done, earns recognition, and tends to help promotional chances.

17.1 POSITIONS AND DUTIES

In an assembly line, jobs are structured and the work sequenced to yield a finished manufacturing product. People are assigned to the job and continue to perform day after day because it earns a livelihood and, perhaps, it appeals to their psychological makeup to engage in meaningful work having a stable routine. The positions in computer operations also are structured in a manner such that the machines and people are effectively combined to yield an effective output. The jobs are a necessary part of the whole operation, and all must be done with proficiency for overall efficiency.

Some positions involve work of a routine nature but certainly are important to the overall effectiveness of computer methods. They require a skill that may be learned in a few days or weeks. Daily functioning in these repetitive jobs calls for special personal talents to maintain enthusiasm and proficiency. The duties of keypunch operators and junior computer operators can be entered with a minimum education, which usually is a high school diploma.

The *keypunch operator* earns slightly over $100 per week and performs a sit-down, light-duty job that is very much like typing. The output is a deck of correctly prepared punched cards that have been transcribed from a handwritten coding form. The cards usually represent the source program. In small organizations the keypunch operator may sit in a small sound-proofed room, because the machine makes slightly more noise than a typewriter. In larger organizations, the keypunch machines are in a larger room and lined up like a typing pool.

The *computer operator* must have a high school education and often has several months to 2 years of formal education in data processing. This assignment normally is preceded by a 2- or 3-month apprenticeship as a *junior computer operator*. In the junior grade, the duties include fetching tapes from the library and returning them after a run; loading cards in the reader; and generally performing tasks that the computer operator judges to be within the capability of an apprentice grade. The computer operator works from the control console, but also walks around a great deal to make ready and observe the functioning of the peripheral units. The operator follows a set of instructions that specify the sequence for loading tapes and cards and opening and closing communication channels between the central processor and the peripheral units. The control console is used to start and stop processing and enter data into selected registers. Control switches are available to select memory addresses from which processing must begin. Lights on the console alert the operator of stoppages. These are handled routinely or immediately brought to the attention of the operations supervisor. It is important that the operator be dedicated to following a procedure and refrain from panic in urgent situations. Of course, a disciplined operator will avoid the common mistakes of having the wrong forms in the printer, having the wrong peripheral channels open, mutilating the input cards, or harming the file tape. Operators are paid $140 to $170 per week depending on their classification.

Programmers perform the basic function that makes computers valuable. All persons who choose careers in computers should learn programming in the language or languages used by the organization. Chapters 13 and 15 give the details that must be mastered for a beginning level of programming skill. The educational requirement is from 6 months to 2 years of formal training in computer operations, programming, and basics in college mathematics. Some programmers enter data-processing jobs with a college degree in accounting or business administration. These may have some programming skills, but generally use on-the-job training to become proficient in business computer applications. A college degree in mathematics coupled with skill in scientific programming is excellent training for careers in scientific computer applications. The promotional potential is higher for persons with college degrees that are applicable to the nature of the work. With advancement, programmers can assume the duties and positions of senior programmers and then computer analysts. The pay for senior programmer is approximately $220 per week. In most situations the output is a working source program that usually is written in a higher-level language. There is a good deal of satisfaction in using a specialized knowledge to harness the capabilities of the machine and find a worthwhile solution to a problem. Engineers, accountants, and others originate the projects. The general programmer is an intermediary between these originators and the analysts and system programmers who formulate the procedures and the operating systems for the language. Through the years there has been a tendency for the programming job to become less complex. Engineers become fairly proficient in doing their own programming. As the actual coding operation becomes easier, the specialized programming knowledge becomes less important. For these reasons, it is wise to be trained in concepts of engineering, accounting, and other fields from which applications originate.

System programming is performed by companies that design computers and operating procedures. This career position affords an excellent opportunity to be a part of the trend for more elaborate operating systems. The system programmer must understand the detailed capabilities and peculiarities of the machine in order to contribute in the complex work of writing programs to interpret operator commands, control operation of the compiler, provide service for error messages, coordinate activity in a time-sharing system, and allocate tasks in a multiprocessing system. Future spread of computer services to schools, homes, and shops would be enhanced by breakthroughs in operating systems. The present work is a direct application of a special knowledge that is needed to overcome the puzzling situations which arise in writing programs for new operating systems. Persons in these positions are senior programmers with a minimum of 2 year's experience in programming. The pay reaches up to nearly $250 per week.

The *systems analyst* serves in a data-processing center to define the program solution from the general outline of problems originating in a user department. For example, the analyst or perhaps a team might be payroll applications experts that would become familiar with the payroll operation and confer with department heads to establish the overall requirements for data origins, file updating, and summary reports. Alternative methods are studied and decisions are reached on methods that are economical and compatible with the user's needs, the machine's capabilities, and schedules. The analyst is joined by one or more programmers as the user requirement becomes defined and formulated in programmable form. The position usually is filled by a college graduate majoring in business administration or accounting. The pay is approximately $270 per week. Programmers without college degrees can become analysts through experience. Training in mathematics is helpful.

Some data-processing centers operate as a *closed shop* in which the machines can be used only by employees of the center. The user department of accounting, payroll, and others must submit their data-processing requirement through an analyst. Most scientific computer centers are *open shop,* which means that programs will be accepted from all departments who have structured their budget to accept their share of machine charges. Engineers do some of their own programming. They are not expert programmers and choose the do-it-yourself method because they usually feel it would take too long to explain the situation to a programmer. Engineers who misuse themselves as programmers and even keypunch operators are victims of the communication gap between themselves and computer workers. Programmers who strive to overcome this problem are more productive and have better changes for promotion.

Management in a computer center has administrative duties that are common to most supervisory positions. They also must be as competent in the technical skills as their subordinates. For example, the operations supervisor must be skilled in the duties of the computer operator because they are immediately notified of nonroutine trouble. The supervisor either corrects the difficulty on the spot or notifies programming or maintenance personnel. The basic tasks of operations supervisor and most other managers is to direct and coordinate ongoing activities, train personnel, and participate in decisions concerning new activities, policies, or schedule.

The educational requirements for computer management are at least the same level as the subordinates, and preferably it should include additional formal training. Their experience should include 2 to 3 years in the skill practiced by members of the group. The special characteristics of a manager consist of the ability to handle situations involving other people, quickly process the routine administrative matters, interpret the current situation and developing trends, and keep abreast of new technology. The pay for the *manager of all data processing* is from $400 to $500 per week, followed by the *manager of analysis or programming* at $300 to $400 per week. The *operation supervisor* makes from $200 to $300 per week. Of course, the range in pay for these managers corresponds to the range in installation sizes.

17.2 PERFORMANCE, RECOGNITION, AND PROMOTION

Persons in computer careers or any other field of employment can choose to set and achieve lofty, modest, or no goals for their advancement. They can concentrate on hard work, which usually is recognized, or pursue the approach of the opportunist, which occasionally is effective. These choices are made on a personal basis and even may be partially reversed or combined after a few years.

Most people would accept an option that got the work done, earned recognition, and tended to help promotional chances. In this section we'll discuss the concepts of this approach; however, the overall psychological factors that enhance or impede career advancement are beyond the scope of this book. The objective of this discussion is to make it clear that there is

1. A time to work hard.
2. A time for more training.
3. A time to assess the work situation and new technology.
4. A time to tell others about your progress, plans, and products.

Let's compare the ability of programmers and salesmen to time their activities in a way that earns recognition for the programs or products. Programmers may be somewhat indifferent to items 3 and 4 in this list. Salesmen are trained and have a natural tendency to concentrate on these items. Of course, salesmen work hard, but for their own good they don't let the details of the work situation overshadow their main objective of gaining recognition for their products and themselves. On the other hand, programmers become involved in flow charts and program coding. As a result, they tend to forget that colleagues and management are interested in the concepts and progress of the work.

Few people will have an *initial interest* in a salesman's specification sheet or in a programmer's detailed codes. There is a better chance that a *summary* of these details will be considered and understood. Programmer's should find that it is worth the modest extra work to maintain a summary of progress and plans. Our recommendation is that a continuing effort be made to keep the details of a complex task summarized and ready for a logical presentation to others. The presentation need not be formal with elaborate exhibits, but there should always be a condensed version of the situation.

It has been said, "The world steps aside for the man who knows where he is going." This quote is applicable for programmers, because their *performance should improve* after a few months of keeping an overview of their progress and plans. They will focus their attention on critical areas once these have been identified. Unimportant aspects should become apparent from an overall plan, and work on them can be terminated. A perspective of the circumstances may reveal the advantages of consulting with colleagues or management. It is obvious that a well-understood course of action should lead to improved performance by reducing the time wasted on unimportant areas. Programmers are often reluctant to help each other, but they should be more willing to contribute their time and expertise to a colleague who appears to be in control of the situation.

A summarized plan should serve the programmer in *gaining the support of management*. Sometimes progress is impeded by lack of equipment or liaison with other departments. A clear presentation of the difficulty and the consequences will give management a basis for action to correct the situation.

Opportunities to *gain recognition* will arise sometimes in an off-hand manner. The greeting, "How are things going?" probably is not intended to draw a lengthy response. Certainly a manager, offering this salutation, is not going to wait around while a programmer tells about all the boxes in a current flow chart. It is reasonable to expect that a superior would be interested in a two- or three-sentence reply on individual progress and its implications on the overall project. The *programmer* might answer, "I estimate that my inventory-control program can be processed in 8 minutes for normal outputs, but runs 4 minutes longer to produce next month's reorder estimates. I'm working with Department XYZ to find the number of businesses wanting this special provision." For comparison, it would be expected that an *eager salesman* might answer such an off-hand greeting from his superior with, "My sales this month are up 15%, which took some extra work on my part because deliveries were delayed by bad weather." Salesmen maintain a summary of their situation with the expectation that they will have the opportunity to reveal their progress. For the same reasons, programmers, analysts, and computer managers at all levels should be prepared to present brief summaries.

Prior to attending meetings, it is good practice to review the latest job accomplishments and difficulties. Recognition is sometimes gained in *meetings* by persons who are aware of the concepts and features of new equipment and software. These informal, prepared synopses are particularly effective when they are structured in a form that is compatible with the theme or purpose of the meeting. Several articles and a few books have been written on opportunities that are available to attendees at meetings. These writings make interesting reading, and some of the concepts apply to workers in the computer field.

For our discussion here, it is judged that *recognition at meetings* will be gained by persons who

1. Spend a few minutes preparing information that will be pertinent to the scope of the meeting.
2. Offer ideas but refrain from criticizing ideas of others.
3. Be willing to accept commitments for further study of worthwhile ideas that arise during the meeting.
4. Spend a few minutes after the meeting reconsidering the discussions that took place.

Knowledge of specific areas in rapidly changing fields of work can become obsolete in a few months. It is extremely important to *keep abreast of the concepts* in new developments. These advancements might be applicable to the current assignment, in which case the details can be studied immediately. The new information, in other instances, may be useful on an upcoming project. Most people have a limited capability to remember all the details of the many new items of equipment and software. The task can be made tractable by persons who are willing to spend a little extra time in filing the details for future reference and composing a brief summary for convenient reference.

The information in this section alludes to the tendency for employees in fields such as programming to be passed over for recognition and promotion because they become overly engrossed in the step-by-step details of the job. By making a deliberate effort to gain a perspective of the assignment, they should be better prepared to take advantage of opportunities that arise. Productivity should also improve for persons who engage in meaningful activities with both feet firmly on the ground.

Problems and Questions

CHAPTER 1

1. The transmission channels in digital computers carry
    a) sequences of long and short pulses in Morse code form.
    b) binary numbers.
    c) sequences of electrical pulses.
    d) symbolic characters.

2. A decimal digit is one of the characters 0 to 9 forming the base ten number system. A binary digit is one of the two characters (usually 0 and 1) in the number with base two. A binary number is
    a) a sequence of binary digits that are arranged in rank order of positional value.
    b) the numerical value of a binary digit.
    c) synonymous with the term binary digit.
    d) a printed representation of a binary digit.

3. Devices for storing binary digits have only two stable states. Compared to devices having more than two stable states, binary devices
    a) are considered obsolete and were replaced by more practical devices in most computers manufactured since 1970.
    b) share the market with several alternative devices having the same function.
    c) tend to produce errors because the two states are nearly identical.
    d) have the advantages of high speed and reliability that have made them dominate in computer design.

4. The decimal number 0 through 16 can be stored in the form of binary numbers. How many bistable devices are required?
    a) One device is needed for positions of sixteens, eights, fours, twos, and units giving a total of 5.
    b) One device is needed for positions of tens and units giving a total of 2.
    c) One device is needed for each number giving a total of 16.
    d) One device is needed for every two decimal numbers giving a total of 8.

5. Name four distinguishing characteristics of modern digital computers.

6. Analog computers can be used alone but they often are combined with digital computers when extensive data computations are being performed. Digital computers are better for these computations because

- a) analog computers use electrical signals of voltage, current, and frequency to represent measured levels of magnitude of process parameters but analog computers cannot do any computations.
- b) digital computers are faster and less prone to errors caused by signal distortion or electrical interference.
- c) voltage signals cannot be mixed with frequency or current; hence practical analog computations are limited in scope.
- d) analog computers can do limited computations but the analog signals cannot be displayed as useful printed output.

7. In this chapter, we discussed a few number systems for representing information in binary form. One number system was developed for business applications that generally have short computations compared with the time for data input and output. Another number system has the fewest binary digits and, for economics in memory cost and processing time, it has become the standard. In respective order, these number systems are:

- a) binary-coded decimal and hexidecimal.
- b) octal and binary number systems.
- c) binary-coded decimal and binary number systems.
- d) excess-3 and octal.

CHAPTER 3

1. The clock in the computer generates pulses that serve to keep events in order. Computers that are timed by the clock (locked to the clock) are called

- a) asynchronous computers.
- b) hybrid computers.
- c) ring counters.
- d) synchronous computers.

2. In Fig. 3-10, the two stable states for output voltage are high or 1 and low or 0. The 0-state at C corresponds to ground potential at A or B terminals. What feature of the diodes limits the minimum output voltage to a practical level that is slightly above ground potential?

- a) The diodes have a small resistance to the flow of current from C to A or from C to B. The corresponding voltage drop makes the minimum value of C slightly higher than ground potential.
- b) The truth table for diode AND gates is based on 0 and 1 for voltage levels of ON and OFF.
- c) The output can't be lowered all the way to ground potential because there is a resistor between the output and +V.
- d) The minimum limit for the 0-state depends on the voltage +V which could be raised to drive the 0-state practically to ground potential.

3. An electronic amplifier is a device in which
   a) a steady input signal is formed into a sequence of high pulses.
   b) small changes in the input signal level affects large changes in the output signal level.
   c) low-level input signals are stored in a capacitor which can then be discharged to achieve a high output level.
   d) the output frequency is greater than the input frequency.

4. An amplifier (refer to the transistor circuit in Fig. 3-15) is an electronic switch that can be opened by
   a) lowering the frequency of the input signal.
   b) inverting the output voltage pulse.
   c) distorting the input signal.
   d) lowering the current flow to the input terminal.

CHAPTER 4

1. The variables A, B, and C appear in the Boolean algebra expression $A + B = C$. This is the logical OR function. What do these variables represent?
   a) analog signals.
   b) sequences of electrical pulses.
   c) electronic gates.
   d) switches.

2. Which of the following choices is *not* appropriate for the function of A AND B?
   a) $A \cap B = C$
   b) $A' \cdot (A + B) = C$
   c) $(A' + B')' = C$
   d) The truth table has a 1 in the output column for $A = 1$ and $B = 1$ and 0 elsewhere.

3. What is the logical product of I, a pulse sequence having all high pulses and Ø, a pulse sequence having all low pulses?

4. Referring to the theorems in Table 4–2, we can change the left-hand side of the expression by replacing pluses with dots and, if either I or Ø is present, replacing I with Ø (or vice versa) to form
   a) a simplified expression.
   b) the mathematical dual.
   c) De Morgan's theorems
   d) a proof by perfect deduction.

5. Which one of the following expressions is incorrect?
   a) $(A \cdot B) + (A \cdot B) = A \cdot B$
   b) $(A' \cdot B')' \cdot (A + B) = A + B$
   c) $(A' + B')' + (A + A \cdot B) = A$
   d) $(A + B) \cdot (A + B)' = A$

CHAPTER 5

1. Truth tables can be constructed from a word description of logic problems. The next step in the process for deriving the lowest-cost circuits is to consider the 1's and 0's in the output column and
    a) form the Boolean expression as a product-of-sums based on the 1's.
    b) apply the Boolean algebra theorems.
    c) form the Boolean expressions as a sum-of-products based on the 1's.
    d) structure a logic circuit having these outputs.

2. The expression $(W + X' \cdot Y) \cdot (W' + X) + W' \cdot X \cdot Y = Z$ has three variables W, X, and Y and can be implemented with
    a) two AND gates.
    b) two-level logic circuit having 3 NAND gates.
    c) three OR gates.
    d) three-level logic circuit having 2 NAND gates.

3. The Karnaugh map is based on the theorem $X + X' = I$ and is a classroom aid for simplifying Boolean algebra expressions. If one of the cells in the map contains a 1 that can be grouped with other cells into either a two-cell subcube or into a three-cell subcube, the simplified Boolean expression should contain product terms based on
    a) the three-cell subcube and a one-cell subcube.
    b) the two-cell subcube and the three-cell subcube.
    c) the two-cell subcube and other subcubes that might be formed having one cell or multiples of two cells.
    d) the three-cell subcube.

4. Many homes have at least one electrical light that can be controlled from either of two switches. Assume the light is off when both switches are in the down position. The light can be turned on and then off from either switch. Draw the truth table and the circuit for interconnecting these double-pole switches using a three-wire cable. The truth table corresponds to the
    a) EXCLUSIVE OR function.
    b) NOR function.
    c) EXCLUSIVE NOR function.
    d) NAND function.

5. The simple two-level logic circuits in this chapter were considered to operate from a set of input pulses that
    a) were held in temporary storage devices.
    b) traveled on parallel paths leading to each input terminal with a separate sequence for each terminal.
    c) arrived in sequences with the first pulse going to the first input terminal and the second pulse going to the second input terminal and so on.
    d) were compared with the output to detect the presence of data errors.

6. Draw a NAND gate logic circuit having input variables W, X, and Y and output Z where $Z = Y$ when $W \cdot X = 0$ and $Z = Y'$ when $W \cdot X = 1$.

7. Draw a AND, OR, NOT gate circuit having input X, Y and output Z_1, Z_2 such that binary numbers represented by the input are encoded to the Gray

code at the output. For example, $X = 1$, $Y = 0$ encodes to $Z_1 = 1$, $Z_2 = 1$ and so forth.

CHAPTER 6

1. The accumulator is part of the arithmetic unit and is used in the handling of most arithmetic operations. This basis computer unit is
   a) a counter with output that corresponds to the cumulative elapsed time for the arithmetic operation being handled.
   b) the fundamental building block in a full adder.
   c) a register that accumulates a group of binary digits and then uses them in handling look-ahead carry by groups.
   d) a register that usually stores one of the operands and, upon completion of the operation, stores the binary answer.

2. A half adder can handle two binary digits and form the sum of one column in a binary number. A full adder can
   a) form the sum and carry for three binary digits.
   b) handle all columns contained in a binary number.
   c) form intermediate values for sum and carry and can handle the carry ripple.
   d) form the logical sum of the outputs from two half adders.

3. Consider that a 36-digit data word is stored in the accumulator. Which one of the following statements correctly relates the capability of a functional adder forming the sum of this data word and a word from another register?
   a) A parallel functional adder accepts all 36 digits at the same time from both the accumulator and a shift register.
   b) A parallel functional adder processes the digits in a manner that is parallel exactly to the manual method of considering each column in turn.
   c) A serial functional adder performs 36 consecutive operations of adding the serially presented digits from two shift registers along with the carry.
   d) A serial functional adder accepts all 36 digits from the accumulator at the same time and then accepts one digit at a time from a B-register.

4. The final sum and carry of a serial functional adder handling the binary numbers of 01 plus 11 is
   a) 10 for sum and 0 for carry.
   b) 00 for sum and 1 for carry with both available after twice the time it takes to shift and add.
   c) 00 for sum and 1 for carry with both available after one shift and add.
   d) none of the above answers.

5. The carry ripple is the time delay for a carry to propagate through each higher-order position and finally become the left most digit in the answer. Techniques for reducing this delay are most important to designers of
   a) low-cost binary decimal adders.
   b) parallel-functional adders.
   c) serial-functional adders.

d) full adders.

6. Draw the logic circuit for a functional adder handling the 4 columns of binary digits in the addition of 2 binary coded decimal digits. Remember that a carry to the next column is appropriate when the sum exceeds 1001 and higher sums are not permissible.

CHAPTER 7

1. Flip-flops can store one binary digit as exhibited by the logic circuits in Figs. 7-4 and 7-5. If the stored digit is binary 1, further changes in SET or CLEAR will give the same output as
    a) an AND gate with inputs SET and the inverse of CLEAR.
    b) the inverse of CLEAR.
    c) a NOR gate handling SET and CLEAR.
    d) a NAND gate handling the inverse of both SET and CLEAR.
2. Referring to the preceding question, find the appropriate answer for a flip-flop storing binary 0.
3. Electrical power failures are an occasional inconvenience in our home circuits. What would be the consequences of restarting operation after an unprotected power failure on the flip-flop circuit in Fig. 7-6?
    a) The contents are erased and replaced with binary 0.
    b) The only major problem is in preventing the voltage, +V, from overloading the transistors during the power surge phase of the restart.
    c) The momentary loss of +V in this simple circuit leads to an indeterminate situation because the state of some restarting flip-flops may be unchanged and others may be changed from 1 to 0 or vice versa.
    d) No real harm has been done because the SET and CLEAR terminals don't require constant electrical energizing.
4. Draw a logic circuit that accepts the binary sequence 00, 01, 10, 11 and generates the Gray code sequence 00, 01, 11, 10.
5. Draw a trigger flip-flop circuit for a two-stage counter that generates the Gray code sequence.
6. Consider a computer operation that normally is completed in less than 7 μs and sends a status signal to a counter. Draw the circuit for a three-stage trigger flip-flop counter that will accept a 1 megahertz timing pulse and normally restart to 000 when the status signal is energized. Include provisions for lighting an alarm light if the time lapse for the operation reaches 7 μs. Refer to Fig. 7-16.
7. Telephone customers are connected to their central switching office by a pair of wires that can cost the telephone company from $150 to $500. Since all customers don't use their wires at the same time, there are economic reasons to concentrate several customers onto a lesser number of wires. One pair of wires could be saved in the simple situation where the lines from 3 customers are served by a nearby logic circuit and 2 pair of wires making the long run back to the central office. Consider a logic package that accepts a three-digit binary signal and controls the energizing

of 6 relays. We'll assume digits 001 energizes relay A1 that places a call from customer A on line 1 and digits 011 through 111 energizes B1, C1, A2, B2, and C2, respectively. Starting with a 3-position register, draw the logic circuit for this simple line concentrator.

CHAPTER 8

1. In Section 8.1 we defined memory and storage in terms that show the differences between these computer units. We mentioned that magnetic tapes and discs usually are used for storage. However, the name *virtual memory* is consistent with these definitions even though the vast virtual memory capacity is mainly on magnetic discs. Computers with the virtual memory provision have
   a) special disc units with approximately the same access time as the internal memory.
   b) no internal memory.
   c) an elaborate interface between the internal memory and the disc units to move information for upcoming operations into the internal memory.
   d) magnetic drum memories in the interface between the internal memory and the disc storage.

2. Computer programs usually originate as punched cards, paper tape, or keyboard input. What other memory or storage units are used in transferring these initial forms into a high-speed internal memory?

3. The magnetic core memory is
   a) the only medium-capacity memory having the random access feature.
   b) much faster than magnetic tape in random access but slightly slower than tape in sequential access.
   c) lower cost than a medium-capacity MOS memory.
   d) a widely used internal memory having reasonable cost, capacity, and access time compared to other memory and storage units.

4. During the read operation, the contents of fully-selected cores in magnetic core memories are destroyed by
   a) the I/2 current applied to the X and Y drivers of fully-selected cores.
   b) energizing the cores slightly beyond the threshold current limit.
   c) the current induced in the sense wire.
   d) the I/2 current applied to the inhibit wire.

5. Describe the rewrite operation that follows a destructive read of magnetic core memories.

6. The normal module in magnetic core memories is a stack of 64x64 element arrays. Compared to larger or smaller arrays, the 64x64 array is a reasonable limit for the three-dimensional configuration because
   a) most computer words don't exceed the 64-digit capacity of the array.
   b) larger arrays would be prone to miscount errors in assembly.
   c) larger arrays are slower because they have longer sense wires and correspondingly longer propagation times.
   d) larger arrays require more reliable logic control circuits.

7. The read/write head in a typical magnetic recording unit is made of

high-permeability material with a gap of 0.001 inches. Usually, these heads have two gaps

a) for recording on tapes with one gap doing the recording and the other gap reading the recording to immediately detect errors.

b) for recording on magnetic discs with one gap handling the inside tracks and the other handling the outside tracks.

c) for recording on high-speed drums in a two-step saturation process because the drum is under the head too briefly for one gap to saturate the magnetic layer.

d) with one for reading and the other for writing binary information on tapes, discs and drums.

CHAPTER 10

1. Logic circuits accept input signals and are designed to have a predictable output depending on the input. The circuit that accepts the binary coded form of program instructions and gives the interpretation by energizing the appropriate signal lines is called

a) the program status circuit.
b) the digital-to-analog convertor.
c) the input/output controller.
d) the control section.

2. Every compiled statement in computer programs is decomposed and the parts classified as either instruction words or data words. An instruction word contains

a) the format and address of the instruction.
b) the code name for the operation (OP code) and the address of the next instruction.
c) the OP code and operand address.
d) the mantessia and characteristics.

3. Single-address instruction words are

a) well suited for the short and repetitive calculations in data-processing applications.
b) generally obsolete in concept.
c) a compact format for high-speed computers having the basic function of fetching data words and then arithmetically combining them with data in the accumulator or other registers.
d) severely limited in handling the complex instructions generated from a higher-level language.

4. Use the symbolic codes in Table 10-1 to form a sequence of instructions that will form the sum of operands in addresses 121 and 122. Processing then stops if the sum is zero by adding the operands in addresses 123 and 124. The sequence, starting in address 51, is

a) LA 121, AA 122, JNZ 56, AA 123, AA 124, HKJ.
b) LA 121, AA 122, JNZ HKJ, AA 123, AA 124, HKJ.
c) LA 121, AA 122, JZ 51, AA 123, AA 124, HKJ.
d) LA 121, AA 122, TNZ, AA 123, AA 124, HKJ.

5. Table 10-3 gives the detailed sequence of signals that are energized in executing the addition operation (symbolic code AA on the UNIVAC

1108). Table 10-4 does likewise for the operation of storing a data word (SA). Construct two corresponding sequences for the LA and TZ codes in Table 10-1.

CHAPTER 11

1. Name 3 or 4 general application categories that are broad enough to encompass most of the practical computer applications. What are 3 general categories of impractical applications?

2. Computer methods now handle the voluminous data associated with many jobs. Some of these jobs existed in the early 1950's and were handled manually. We might rationalize that workers of those years were overwhelmed by the immensity of their collective tasks and that computer relief would give them more time to gain a perspective of how to apply the computed results. The new tool was applied in the intervening years by computer specialists and, ironically, they have replaced their predecessor's questions with other questions of equal perplexity. For example, they might now ask, "What events are practical to analyze and what results are useful?" Discuss ways that you could plan a computer career that is practical and, thereby, circumvent this irony.

3. The general capabilities of IBM 360 Model 20 show the computer is useful for medium-volume data processing and is fairly economical. In considering the design of this computer and comparable computers from other manufacturers, give justifications for the following capabilities:
   a) an IOC that handles the standard EBCDIC;
   b) a communications adapter that interfaces with standard modems;
   c) a parity code error detecting method;
   d) a binary synchronous communication adapter;
   e) multiple formats for the instruction words;
   f) variable length data words; and
   g) a few general-purpose registers.

4. Referring to the control console in Fig. 11-10, the two knobs on the left might be set on B and 5. What information has been entered by these settings along with 8 and A on the two right knobs?
   a) The binary number 1000 1010 is entered in memory address 1011 0101.
   b) The binary number 5 is entered in the B-register and 8 is entered in accumulator or A-register.
   c) The binary number 1011 0101 is entered in memory address 1000 1010.
   d) The B-register is set at 1000 1010.

5. The UNIVAC 1108 computer is similar in basic concept to the IBM 360 Model 20 and many other general purpose computers. We discussed a version of the UNIVAC 1108 that is designed for scientific applications. Consider the following list of computer features. For each item in this list, ascertain whether it is a feature of the UNIVAC 1108 and then discuss the contribution of the feature to the overall capability of the machine in scientific applications.

a) multiple processors.
b) shared peripheral modem interface.
c) sixteen index registers.
d) indirect addressing of internal memory.
e) floating-point format as one option for storing data words.
f) approximately 260,000 operand addresses in internal memory.

6. The IBM 360 Model 20 has several format options for data and instruction words and functions with an instruction repertoire of 36 OP codes. By contrast, the UNIVAC 1108 has a single format for instruction words but uses a vast instruction repertoire of 140 OP codes. The UNIVAC 1108 has more OP codes because

a) the computer has a large number of functional units and the operational speed of each unit is maximized by using an OP code that is specifically designed for the operation.
b) two OP codes in single-address instructions are needed to handle operations that can be handled with one multiple-address instruction.
c) the basic computer is designed such that many of the OP codes are initially unused but are available for functioning in expanded versions of the basic computer.
d) many of the OP codes compensate for this inflexibility of the single-address instruction word.

CHAPTER 12

1. In normal definition, the word *compile* means to compose out of materials from other documents. We said that a COBOL compiler, for example, translates COBOL statements into basic machine instructions. This definition implies that the term COBOL *translator* might be more appropriate than the conventional term COBOL *compiler.* To clarify the terminology, we ask, what is compiled by a program compiler?

a) A list of diagnostic comments is compiled.
b) A list of machine codes is compiled in proper sequence and format for loading directly into internal memory.
c) An object program and a diagnostic list are compiled.
d) A source program and diagnostic list are compiled.

2. What phase of program compiling is similar in concept to the grammar course exercise of diagramming sentences?

a) syntactic analysis phase.
b) roll generation phase.
c) object code generation phase.
d) diagnostic phase.

3. What are the three basic phases in compiling a source program? How many passes are made through the source program or its modified form before the compiler activity is completed?

4. A flow chart is

a) a computer program in a shorthand form that can be used as a substitute for punched cards.

b) a graphical illustration of the program options that are available to the computer.

c) a graphical representation of operations and the sequence in which they are performed.

d) a graphical representation of the steps in planning a computer program.

5. Computer programs can be processed without using flow charts; however, they are recommended for writers of medium-complex programs. Give three reasons that tend to justify the apparent extra work in constructing a flow chart.

6. Referring to Fig. 12-3, suppose that the administration division starts with the names Adams, Baldwin, and Boone. The second division starts with Arnold, Bean, and Blum. If the first transaction record contains information for Adams, the next records to be read are

a) the transaction with the next higher employee number.

b) the next higher employee number.

c) Arnold and then Baldwin.

d) Baldwin and then Boone.

7. What alterations in Fig. 12-4 might be necessary if the time interval for file maintenance were doubled? Pick the best answer from the following choices.

a) There would be many alterations throughout the flow chart and program to accommodate this substantial modification in the normal routine.

b) Deletions and changes might be entered on separate data processing runs.

c) The records would be twice as long as normal.

d) Changes might be stored in memory address beginning with address 15000 and the statement CH = 9000 would be rewritten as CH = 15000.

8. Provisions are made for error messages in both Figs. 12-4 and 12-5. Which of these flow charts illustrates the more efficient method for printing error messages? Why?

9. In Fig. 12-5, the master file is merged with the special file. Suppose that Mr. X has signed his first authorization for a data item to be posted in his special file. The length of his new master record is

a) increased but the entry can't be made until the next processing run because a new master record is needed.

b) the sum of the length of master plus special record.

c) the sum of the length of master record plus the new data item.

d) unchanged.

10. Critics of data processing systems sometimes say that we have become numbers in a computer world. We invited this sort of criticism by using employee numbers in our payroll processing example. As a critic-pleasing alternative we could have used employee names and compared the files by sorting the records according to alphabetical order. Refer to Fig. 12-6 and comment on the impracticality of using employee names.

CHAPTER 13

1. COBOL programs serve to read and write data-processing files, select records by their identity from those files, perform computations on data items within the records, and write summary reports. There are unbending rules that must be adhered to in composing COBOL programs. We must use certain words in statements and headings. Correct spelling is important. The statements are longer and more verbose than absolutely necessary. The word environment contained in the heading, ENVIRONMENT DIVISION, is likely to be misspelled by a large fraction of the U.S. population. Our first reaction might be to suggest the abbreviation ED. Give three reasons why the COBOL language designers wisely choose wordy statements and long headings.

2. Consider the statement WRITE UPDATED-MASTER-FILE. These words are categorized as
   a) all data names.
   b) all reserved words.
   c) a mixture of key words and optional words.
   d) all filler words.

3. The IDENTIFICATION DIVISION and ENVIRONMENT DIVISION are the first two of four divisions in any COBOL program. Why is the PROCEDURE DIVISION left until last even though it contains statements specifying the computations to be performed by the computer?
   a) Some programs don't involve computations, which makes the omission of the fourth division an easy task for the programmer and compiler.
   b) The compiler checks that all data items used in the computations are defined in either the DATA DIVISION or prior to the computation.
   c) The DATA DIVISION, which specifies the reading and writing of files, should be handled first during a programming run to decrease the likelihood that a subsequent malfunction will destroy the file contents.
   d) Computations are an insignificant part of data-processing programs.

4. Hourly-paid employees receive extra pay for overtime work. Salaried employees usually are directed by their salary agreement to forego overtime pay except in certain instances. Monthly payroll processing for most salaried employees is based on the annual salary divided by 12. Where would you suggest that these data items be specified? We'll use the data name ANNUAL-SALARY.
   a) ANNUAL-SALARY is specified in the TRANSACTION-FILE and the number 12 is set on an internal register.
   b) ANNUAL-SALARY is specified in the MASTER-FILE and the number 12 is specified in the CONSTANT-SECTION.
   c) Both ANNUAL-SALARY and the number 12 are specified in the FILE-SECTION.
   d) The pay is based on a new master data item for the ratio of ANNUAL-SALARY divided by 12.

5. The clause, PICTURE 999, specifies that the data item is
   a) a decimal number with value less than one thousand.

    b) a group of decimal numbers filling 999 punched cards.
    c) a group of three numeric characters.
    d) a binary-coded decimal number.

6. The clause PICTURE X(3) specifies that the data item is
    a) a group of three alphabetic characters.
    b) a group of three extra decimal digits.
    c) an XS-3 coded number.
    d) a group of three alphanumeric characters.

7. In a typical data-processing run, reports are generated to summarize the findings. The report may be a statement of pay or a summary list such as back orders, overtime, overdue or overstocked. The data items in these reports are computed or identified from existing records. After the data items are defined, how are they handled?
    a) They are stored on a tape or disc until processing is complete and then printed.
    b) They are stored in the peripheral interface until it is filled and then printed.
    c) They are stored in internal memory until processing is complete and then printed.
    d) Each data item is printed as soon as it is defined.

8. The transactions during the processing interval are entered to update the master file. This activity leaves an old master file which should be
    a) removed from the vicinity to avoid misidentity with the new master file.
    b) merged with the new master file during the next processing run.
    c) used to immediately check the new master file.
    d) kept with the transaction file in a secure place until the new master file is verified and replaced during the next processing run.

CHAPTER 14

1. Mini-computers have earned a share of the overall computer market and
    a) may soon be acceptable substitutes for full-scale computers.
    b) account for 3 to 5 percent of computer sales.
    c) have developed interest in MOS circuits for this special application.
    d) have led to the development of mini-peripheral devices for use on full-scale computers.

2. Management forces in organizations with more than $10 million annual sales can improve their effectiveness by using
    a) a business information system.
    b) an accounting information system and many other separate information systems.
    c) data and information.
    d) a cadre of information specialists to expedite pending decisions by emergency searching for data from all available sources.

3. Computer methods are fairly easily applied in
    a) business operations in which existing personnel can be transferred elsewhere and replaced by advocates of computer methods.

   b) established business ventures.

   c) business operations having a standard procedure such as a standard accounting procedure.

   d) business organizations having no operational complexities such as feedback of information.

4. We would rarely find two business information systems with exactly the same data collecting procedure, purpose or scope. Some systems are distorted in purpose to the extent that they are a misnomer, according to the definition in Section 14.2. Suppose you are studying the feasibility of a business information system that would lead to an organized and continuous collection and analysis of pertinent data from several departments within the business. What would be your recommendations for standardizing the information exchange between departments?

   a) Assign overall responsibility for the system to the accounting department.

   b) Improve the organization, availability, and general relevance of data in existing information systems by assigning responsibility to a manager and a cadre of data-processing experts. They would provide technical guidance to the individual departments in formulating the overall data base.

   c) Eliminate feedback of information within the individual departments.

   d) Assign responsibility to a new high-level business information staff.

5. Computer methods handle the accounting function with a capability that is a considerable extension of manual methods. From our brief discussion in Section 14.2.1.1, what do you judge are two main advantages of financial control with computer methods?

6. After being confronted with dozens of queries on stock levels, the keepers of even small stores finally resign to maintain a list of quantities on hand. This list along with unit price values may be called an inventory record and provide useful information for preparing tax reports. This expediency may stop the original queries but others continue. Name at least five useful purposes of an inventory control system. Consider an inventory that is large enough to justify computer methods.

7. Manufacturing organizations can use computer methods for production control on the shop floor. What are three criteria that define a computer controlled factory? Make an estimate of the percentage of U.S. factories that are now operated by computer control. Give reasons for your estimate.

8. Do numerical control machines and the mechanisms in an automated factory fit your definition of computer control? Explain.

9. Suppose you have interest in applying computer methods to save costs in a large ongoing manufacturing operation. Give three examples of improvements you might study for feasibility and expect consideration from management.

10. What are typical computer applications in a business organization that is responsible for planning shop operations? What applications exist in organizations doing market research? Would you expect typical businesses to have a decision making department? Explain.

CHAPTER 15

1. Suppose computer methods are used to analyze the tape recorded data from an engineering experiment. What computer language would you recommend?
   - a) FORTRAN with a COBOL DATA DIVISION.
   - b) COBOL.
   - c) FORTRAN.
   - d) An analog computer language.

2. Consider a simple chemical process in an industrial application. In normal situations, the instruments monitoring the process show a stable reading. Analytical techniques must be used to identify the cause of process instabilities and to calculate the magnitude of corrective action. We'll assume there are 15 monitored parameters, 8 calculated indicators of instabilities, 4 control parameters, and a short historical log of previously monitored or controlled parameters. Using floating-point and fixed-point FORTRAN variables and arrays, assign data names and data formats for this application.

3. The FORTRAN compiler converts the statement $X = Y + 1.8$ into a sequence of machine codes which assigns $Y + 1.8$ to the memory address allocated to X. The Y parameter in the sum is stored in the address allocated to Y and the decimal number 1.8 is
   - a) stored in a memory address allocated to the constant 1.8.
   - b) stored in an internal register that is set aside for constant values.
   - c) stored in the constant section of internal memory.
   - d) converted to binary by an encoder and then added to Y.

4. The assignment statements in a FORTRAN program are
   - a) all statements in the source deck that begin in column 7 on a punch card.
   - b) all statements with an assigned statement number.
   - c) statements that assign a binary number to the memory address allocated for the data name on the left hand side of the equal sign.
   - d) all statements in the program except comment statements.

5. Consider the following sequences of FORTRAN statements, each having three errors. Identify and correct the errors.
   - a) $A = 2$
     $B = 1.6$
     $A * (B + C) = A * B + A * C$
   - b) $X = 4.0$
     $I = 2$
     $XI = X/I$
     $IX = I/X$
     $JX = J/X$
   - c) $A = 8.1$
     $B = 16.2$
     $B/A = 2.0$
     $C = B(A + B)/((1 + B/A) * B/A)$
     $CB = B/(A^2 - C)$
     $D = A + B(6)$

Index